D0562029

# THE LAST
# CONTINENT

DISCOVE

*I dedicate this book to*
*Neil and Mary Jephcott, whose generosity,*
*through the Jephcott Charitable Trust,*
*made our research possible*

# THE LAST CONTINENT
## DISCOVERING ANTARCTICA

**Bernard Stonehouse**

SCP
BOOKS

Shuttlewood Collinson Publishers

First published in Great Britain 2000 by
SCP Books Ltd
Westdene House
Burgh Castle
Norfolk NR31 9QF
Tel.: 44 (0)1493 781695    E-mail: scp@paston.co.uk    Internet: www.paston.co.uk/scp

Published in the USA by Odyssey Publishing Ltd, in association with SCP Books Ltd

*British Library Cataloguing-in-Publication Data*
A catalogue record for this book is available from the British Library

ISBN 0 9537907 0 3

**Distribution in the United States by W. W. Norton & Company, Inc., New York**

Designed, edited and typeset in 10/12 Monotype Galliard by Originator, Gorleston, Norfolk
Printed in the UK

Title page photograph courtesy of Tony Stone Images, New York
Maps produced by BJ Chemtech, Gorleston, Norfolk

# Contents

# Preface

Antarctica offers a bewildering panorama of spectacular scenery, flourishing wildlife and a lot of ice. It is probably the most beautiful and at the same time the most awesome place any of us are likely to see in a lifetime of travel and exploration. But to enjoy it to the full you need the companionship of a guide who knows the landscape and the penguins and the seals and the complexities of ice and polar seas. Fortunately for all of us the right man offers his highly competent services in this book.

Bernard Stonehouse is a man who has straddled the twin worlds of science and tourism in the deep south. In earlier days he flew over Antarctica, and led journeys of exploration with dog teams. More recently he has led more than a dozen scientific expeditions to both sides of the continent, and he is a gifted lecturer on today's expedition ships. He is the sort of man you pray for as expedition leader. Sadly we can no longer sign on to sail with Shackleton, but here in Stonehouse we are in company with the twenty-first century version. He knows where and when to go, but, above all, he breathes the life of the place with irrepressible good humour and academic enthusiasm.

I have had the great good fortune to sail polar waters with Bernard, the proverbial fount of all knowledge, the best of companions. Sail with him if you get half a chance, but read his book to savour the majesty and the sheer enjoyment of discovering the last great wilderness and its abundant wildlife.

Tony Soper, *ornithologist, expedition leader, TV correspondent*

# Introduction

Thirty years ago there would have been little point in writing this book. In the mid-1960s Antarctica and the Antarctic region were almost exclusively the haunt of scientists and their technical support staff. Immersed in their immediate problems, neither the scientists nor the supporters—seamen, aviators, radio operators, mechanics, cooks, storesmen and administrators—would have had time or inclination to read a guidebook on Antarctica.

By that time Antarctic tourism had started, but was relatively undeveloped. Only one or two ships plied south, costs were high, and very few travellers had yet had opportunities to visit for recreation, fun, or simply to satisfy their curiosity. For most travellers Antarctica was too cold, too far away, too little known, and too expensive to attract any but the wealthier connoisseurs of up-market adventure travel.

Now things are different. Though the Antarctic region is just as cold and remote as it ever was, it has become known to millions through television and travel writing. Travel in general has become relatively cheap and fast-growing, and adventure travel—which includes the penguin trail to Antarctica—is the fastest-growing sector of all. Today tour companies compete to bring travellers to Antarctica. More people are thinking about visiting the region, mulling over brochures, and starting to compare ships, itineraries and costs.

Thirty years ago about a thousand tourists per year visited Antarctica. Today there are ten times as many. Within the past decade numbers visiting per year have doubled and redoubled. Advertising has increased, glossy brochures proliferate, and Sunday travel supplements feature Antarctic cruises. Each year new sections of the market are tapped, and new categories of travellers are drawn to Antarctica. Those who are studying the industry see every reason to think it is growing. Numbers may well double again within the next decade.

What attracts travellers to Antarctica? In surveys that ask tourists to give first, second and third reasons for wanting to visit, wildlife most often heads the list. Word has gone out that Antarctic birds and mammals especially are worth seeing. Botanists want to see the plant life, however meagre. Birdwatchers from the northern hemisphere seek to add southern-hemisphere species to their life lists. Seabird enthusiasts want to revel in the wide variety of Southern Ocean birds. Everyone wants to visit penguins, seals and whales on their home ground.

The second most often-quoted reason for visiting is the lure of the last continent. Those who have visited several continents seek Antarctica as a new one: those who have visited every other continent want to visit Antarctica too. A wish to collect continents may seem a trivial aim. A more charitable explanation, and I think a more correct one, is that recreational travellers know that they gain immensely from their travels, and now want to learn from Antarctica too.

The few who seek Antarctica as a collector's item usually want to add countries, not merely continents, to their list. Some have visited over two hundred and something countries—almost as many as may be said to exist. Like avid bird spotters, they now seek to add the last few to their life list. Their questions are simple: How many countries make up Antarctica, how many will we visit on this trip, and can we please visit more? The answers are politically complex—usually too complicated to sustain their interest (Chapter 11). So they settle, though not without grumbling, for a single continent.

Scenery, ice, adventure and historic interest follow closely as first choices. Most Antarctic tourists in their sixties to eighties grew up during or soon after the 'heroic age' of exploration, the first few decades of the 20th century. Britons of these times were brought up on stories of Robert Scott, Ernest Shackleton, Roald Amundsen and Douglas Mawson: just a few of the older ones remember meeting them, or being stirred by newspaper accounts of their exploits.

Far more Americans carry personal memories of Richard Byrd, who used to the full the newly developed media of newsreels and broadcasts, and lectured to audiences all over the USA. Between expeditions Byrd clearly spent much of his time patting small boys on the head and saying 'Son, one day you must go to Antarctica'. In 10 years of travelling with American tourists I have met dozens of those small boys, now more or less grown up, at last fulfilling the pledge made long ago to a real-life childhood hero.

The areas that are most easily available for tourists, in the South American sector, are sadly not those where the 'heroic' explorers made their names. Scott, Amundsen, Mawson and Byrd worked mainly on the other side of the continent; only Shackleton spanned both. However, no visitor to South Georgia misses Shackleton's grave, and those who visit Antarctic Peninsula follow other explorers—Weddell, Biscoe, Bransfield, Dallmann, Nordenskiöld, Bruce, de Gerlache, Charcot, and dozens of nameless sealers and whalers—whose explorations were no less valid, and whose feats were certainly no less heroic.

There are many other reasons why people visit Antarctica. Some saw the Arctic last year and became hooked on ice and snow. One couple I met usually took their summer vacations in the Arctic, but wanted to try Antarctica as somewhere warmer. Some go because it is there, because their friends went, because their spouses booked and expected them to trail along. Some, for all I know, may just want to impress their neighbours. Whatever their motivation, surprisingly many travellers, even well-seasoned ones, admit to approaching Antarctica with a sense of awe and mystery that they bring to nowhere else on earth. Even more surprisingly, they do not leave disappointed. The reality they experience may not be what they had imagined, but it is seldom less, and does not diminish their awe. *The Last Continent: Discovering Antarctica* was written particularly with tourists in mind. I have had the good fortune to travel on many cruise ships and come to know many tourists. I have been quizzed by them on all kinds of issues, and prodded cheerfully into finding answers. This book is written in gratitude for my fellow-travellers' questions. I hope that other tourists on other ships will read it, and find more questions to ask.

However, *The Last Continent: Discovering Antarctica* is also for non-tourist visitors, who may want to know more of the curious place in which they find themselves. Perhaps even more it is written for armchair travellers—the majority who have never been to Antarctica, may never go, but still hope to share what they can of its wonders. Much of the text was drafted and some of it was written on cruise ships. The rest has been written at my home near Cambridge, and at the Scott Polar Research Institute, University of Cambridge, where for the last few years I have led a group of postgraduate students in research on the management of polar tourism. I am grateful to many students and colleagues for help in writing this book. Views expressed are my own—not those of my colleagues at the Institute, nor, so far as I know, those of the Chancellor, Masters and Scholars of the University.

Royalties from *The Last Continent: Discovering Antarctica* are dedicated to an Antarctic research fund which helps young researchers to work in Antarctica and contributes to the library fund of the Scott Polar Research Institute.

*Bernard Stonehouse*
Swaffham Bulbeck, Cambridge

*This well-briefed and caring photographer keeps far enough from the procession of chinstrap penguins, neither stopping nor diverting their progress to and from inland nests. Baily Head, Deception Island, South Shetland Islands.*

# Chapter One

# The southern region

## Introduction: Arctic and Antarctic

The two polar regions are geographically as different as possible. The Arctic is an ocean almost completely ringed by land. The Antarctic is a continent entirely surrounded by ocean (see inside back and front covers). At the north pole you stand close to sea level in a featureless ocean basin, on ice floes that are drifting slowly in the direction of Svalbard and northern Europe. At the south pole you stand 2835 m (9300 ft) above sea level, on an equally featureless ice cap of about the same thickness, moving even more slowly towards India.

Tourists these days can visit either pole. I know several otherwise quite ordinary people who have visited both. However, visiting the poles is a time-consuming and very expensive hobby. Indeed I have turned down offers to visit both—though don't let that put you off—because so far as I can judge, there is not a lot to see or experience when you get there. A Russian nuclear icebreaker will take you to the North Pole, in a scheduled voyage of about 2 weeks from Murmansk: there are several such voyages each summer. You see and break through a lot of pack-ice on the way. There is a lot more ice to see when you get there. You have a barbecue on the ice and a swim if you feel like it, and there is a lot more ice to see on the way back. But you have been to the North Pole. If that is what you want, book well ahead, because these are very popular cruises.

The South Pole is more difficult, but there is a Canadian airline (yes, Canadian: it's a crazy world) that will fly you there from South America (Chapter 3). Again you see a lot of ice—this time land ice—possibly more ice and snow than you imagined existed. This time too there is something to see at the Pole itself—a barber's pole, ringed by 40-gallon drums and a row of flagstaffs flying the flags of the Antarctic Treaty nations. Nearby stands a geodetic dome housing a group of US scientists and technicians. They are busy people, so do not expect them to be welcoming. It will be very cold. You can warm yourself by running around the world in 5 seconds, but don't do it too often; the atmosphere is thin and you will soon find yourself out of breath. Then it's time to go home. But you will have been to the South Pole, and that's something to tell the neighbours.

## The Antarctic region

Fortunately, there is a lot more to polar regions than the poles themselves. The core of the Antarctic region is the Antarctic continent. Beyond continental shores the region extends far into the surrounding ocean, that by a quirk of history is called the Southern Ocean, not the Antarctic Ocean (p. 16). Where does the Antarctic region end? Well, there is a series of boundaries—ecological, geographical and legal—that geographers, lawyers, politicians, ecologists and oceanographers all define differently for their own purposes. Here, we use mainly natural boundaries—the northern limits of pack ice, the Antarctic Convergence, or limit of Antarctic surface waters (which defines the Southern Ocean), and others, relating to pack-ice distribution, that lie beyond (Map 1, see also Map 2 on p. 65). Ecologists in fact divide this whole oceanic region into concentric climatic zones, which help them to make sense of the ecology and distribution of flora and fauna.

The region can also be divided into longitudinal sectors; for example, the South American, New Zealand, Norwegian or French sectors. These names arise from their closeness to other continents or oceans, or to claims of ownership that, despite the Antarctic Treaty, are still in force (Chapter 11). We use these too because, although sectors have very little current political or geographical significance, they are useful in helping travellers to discover how to get to different parts of the Antarctic region.

## Antarctica: A continent apart

Antarctica, the world's fifth-largest continent, has an area of 13.9 million km$^2$ (5.9 million sq. miles), almost twice that of Australia or Europe, three-quarters that of South America. The ocean basin surrounding the continent has a mean depth of 4000 m (13 100 ft), and is over twice as deep close to the South Sandwich Islands.

Antarctica is best described with the Greenwich Meridian central, and the Antarctic Circle drawn in Map 1. From this viewpoint the continent is roughly comma-shaped, humped toward Africa, India and Australia, with a tail pointing to South America. The comma body, lying east of the prime meridian, is the province of East Antarctica. The tail and its root, lying west of the meridian, together make up West Antarctica. Geologically East and West Antarctica are entirely different (p. 12). They may well be separated physically by deep channels under the thick ice that links the Weddell and Ross Sea basins.

The continent fits asymmetrically into the polar circle, a line drawn 23° 27' or 2589 km (1618 miles) distant from the South Geographical Pole. In the Australian sector of East Antarctica the continental coast lies on or close to the circle. In the Norwegian sector, and in the Pacific sector of West Antarctica, the coast falls away to the south, dipping furthest to 78°S in the Ross and Weddell Seas.

The circle cuts through the base of Antarctic Peninsula, leaving the South Shetland Islands and northern end of the peninsula far to the north. This often comes as a surprise to visitors travelling by sea to the peninsular sector of Antarctica. After several days sailing south across Drake Passage and Bransfield Strait, finding themselves surrounded by glaciers and clearly in a polar environment, they still have many miles to go to reach the Antarctic Circle.

# The ice sheet

Like every other continent Antarctica has mountains, hills, plains, valleys and a shoreline (Box 1.1). Unlike any other, over 98% of its area, including 96% of its true shoreline, is hidden under an immense layer of ice. With a mean surface elevation of over 2000 m, the ice cap makes Antarctica by far the highest continent. Asia, the next highest, is less than half as high, with a mean elevation of 960 m.

Antarctica's ice is formed from snow and hoar frost that has fallen, accumulated and consolidated under pressure. The flakes of snow and frost turn first to granular, air-filled névé, which at depths of 50 to 60 m (160 to 200 ft) compresses to solid, blue-grey ice cloudy with air bubbles. Lower still it forms clear blue ice from which all the bubbles have disappeared. This is a continuous process: ice is constantly added to the ice sheet, and constantly lost by evaporation, melting and calving into icebergs. Chemical analyses of cores taken from the ice sheet show that much of the thick inland ice is very old, and accumulating slowly from light falls of snow and ice crystals. Much of the coastal ice is by contrast relatively new, forming from heavy local snow that fell tens or hundreds of years ago, rather than thousands. A station built at the South Pole remains at or close to the surface indefinitely. One built in an area of heavy coastal snow is blocked up in a year, disappears under the surface in 2 to 3 years, and within a decade lies several metres deep.

Renewed constantly by snowfall, the ice sheet slumps outward under its own weight, filling valleys, overflowing and eroding mountain chains. Though much of the Antarctic ice sheet is relatively static, it contains within it huge rivers of ice, including both glaciers that flow between rock walls, and ice streams that flow between walls of stationary ice. Moving ice has enormous capacity for carving the underlying bedrock and carrying millions of tons of boulders, rubble and finely ground rock flour toward the sea.

The ice sheet overspreads the shore of the continent to create a coastline of spectacular ice cliffs. Grounded ice sheets make up about one-third of the coastline, slow-surging ice shelves almost half, and active ice streams and glaciers some 13–14%. As ice is less dense than water, the seaward edges of the ice sheet float, breaking off periodically to form ice islands and bergs that drift out to sea (p. 21).

# Antarctic climates

Height and latitude combine to make Antarctica by far the coldest continent. Winter and summer alike, the central Antarctica Plateau is the world's coldest region. Vostok, a permanent Russian research station 3488 m (11 443 ft) high on the icy plateau of East Antarctica, regularly logs minimum winter surface temperatures well below −80°C, usually in late August. Amundsen-Scott, the permanent United States research station at the South Pole, is 653 m (2142 ft) lower in altitude and correspondingly warmer. Mean midwinter temperatures at Vostok range around −68°C and at Amundsen-Scott around −59°C. Summer means they shoot up respectively to −32°C and −28°C. (Box 1.2). Low temperatures on the plateau are often accompanied by light winds, and in

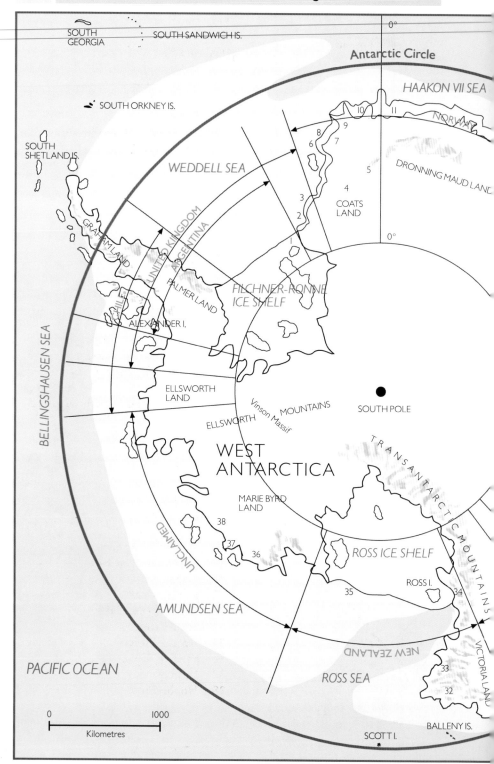

SOUTH GEORGIA

SOUTH SANDWICH IS.

0°

Antarctic Circle

HAAKON VII SEA

SOUTH ORKNEY IS.

NORWAY

10

11

9

8

7

6

5

DRONNING MAUD LAND

SOUTH SHETLAND IS.

WEDDELL SEA

4

COATS LAND

3

2

0°

GRAHAM LAND

CHILE

UNITED KINGDOM

ARGENTINA

PALMER LAND

FILCHNER-RONNE ICE SHELF

BELLINGSHAUSEN SEA

ALEXANDER I.

ELLSWORTH LAND

ELLSWORTH

Vinson Massif

MOUNTAINS

SOUTH POLE

TRANSANTARCTIC MOUNTAINS

WEST ANTARCTICA

MARIE BYRD LAND

38

UNCLAIMED

37

36

35

ROSS ICE SHELF

ROSS I.

34

AMUNDSEN SEA

33

NEW ZEALAND

ROSS SEA

32

VICTORIA LAND

PACIFIC OCEAN

0　　　　1000

Kilometres

BALLENY IS.

SCOTT I.

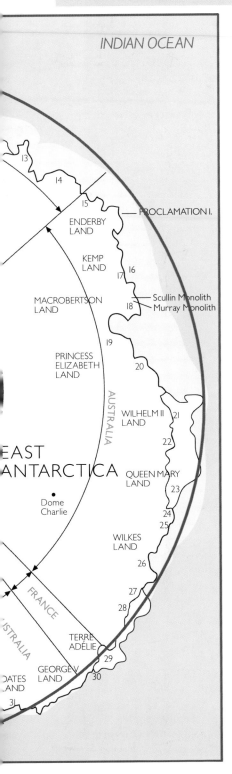

**Map 1**

Political boundaries in red

1 General Belgrano II
2 Luitpold Coast
3 Halley
4 Stancomb-Wills Ice Stream
5 Heimefront Fjella
6 Drescher Inlet
7 Riiser-Larsenisen
8 Kapp Norvegia
9 Kronprinsesse Märtha Kyst
10 Sanae
11 Prinsesse Astrid Kyst
12 Prinsesse Ragnhild Kyst
13 Prins Harald Kyst
14 Syowa
15 Molodezhnaya
16 Mawson Coast
17 Mawson
18 Lars Christensen Coast
19 Ingrid Christensen Coast
20 Davis
21 King Leopold and Queen Astrid
　　Coast
22 Gaussberg
23 Knox Coast
24 Casey
25 Budd Coast
26 Sabrina Coast
27 Banzare Coast
28 Wilkes Coast
29 Dumont d'Urville
30 Commonwealth Bay
31 Leningradskaya
32 Pennell Coast
33 Borchgrevink Coast
34 Scott Coast
35 Bay of Whales
36 Ruppert Coast
37 Russkaya
38 Hobbs Coast

## Box 1.1   *Antarctica and its ice*

Isolated at the centre of the southern hemisphere, Antarctica lies 1000 km (625 miles) from the tip of South America, 2200 km (1375 miles) from southern New Zealand, 2250 km (1406 miles) from southern Tasmania, and 3600 km (2250 miles) from South Africa.

East Antarctica is 4500 km (2800 miles) across at its widest, with an area of about 10.40 million km² (4.05 million sq. miles). West Antarctica minus Antarctic Peninsula is less than half as wide, with an area of about 2 million km² (77 000 sq. miles). The Peninsula is 1200 km (750 miles) long, with an area of 520 000 km² (203 000 sq. miles).

Antarctica is covered in ice of mean thickness 1800 m (5900 ft). The highest point of the ice sheet, Dome Argus in East Antarctica, rises a little above 4000 m (13 000 ft). The highest point of the West Antarctica ice sheet is 2400 m (7870 ft). Overall, Antarctica carries approximately 30 million km³ (7.3 cubic miles) of ice, about 90% of all the ice currently in the world.

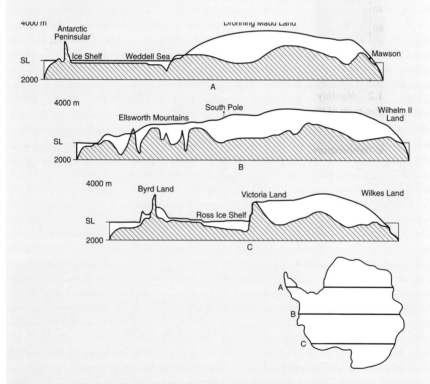

**Figure 1.1** *Ice overlies Antarctica like icing on a crazy wedding cake. Ice thickness has been measured mainly by radar from overflying aircraft.*

In a coastline of estimated total length 31 900 km (19 940 miles), 17 800 km (11 125 miles) are made up of floating ice shelves and 12 800 km (8000 miles) of grounded ice. Only some 1300 km—about 4% of the total length—are exposed rock.

## Box 1.2   *Summer and winter temperatures*

*This graph shows the month-by-month sequence of temperatures at Antarctic plateau and coastal stations, and coastal stations on southern oceanic islands. Plateau stations (Vostok, Amundsen-Scott) have typical 'continental' temperature regimes, with wide summer–winter differences. Oceanic stations (Orcadas in the South Orkney Islands, Grytviken on South Georgia), have typical 'maritime' temperature regimes, with small summer–winter differences, and coastal stations (McMurdo, Mawson) lie somewhere between.*

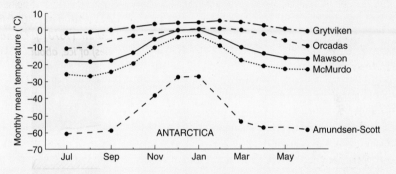

**Figure 1.2**  *Monthly mean temperatures (°C) throughout the year at five Antarctic stations. Positions of the stations are shown below.*

Winter temperatures on the continent depend on latitude and altitude. Along the coast, summers are cold where sea ice is present, much warmer where ice-free. Anywhere in these regions summer weather can shift quickly from sunny, calm and warm to cloudy with gales and rain, sleet or snow.

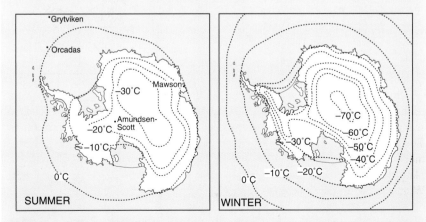

**Figure 1.3**  *Mean temperatures (°C) for January (summer) and July (winter). Many coastal stations in summer have temperatures close to freezing point (0°C), or a little below.*

summer by continuous round-the-clock sunshine. Scientists who have worked there find conditions tolerable down to −40°C, difficult to about −50°C, and dangerous at −60°C and below.

Summer or winter, very few Antarctic travellers reach the polar plateau, unless they have arranged special journeys to do so. Most of them travel by cruise ship, only to coastal regions and only in summer, when conditions, though seldom benign by tropical standards, are very much milder. Low-pressure systems alternate with anticyclones, much as they do in Britain and other north temperate regions, bringing thick cloud, strong winds, and rain, sleet and snow, punctuated by spells of clear skies and warm sunshine. However, mean coastal temperatures in summer seldom depart far from freezing point. Summers at sea level over much of the Antarctic region are comparable with winters in maritime Europe and North America, and far warmer than winters in, for example, central USA and Canada.

Passengers booking cruise ships are quite rightly warned to bring warm clothing. Having read their Scott, Amundsen and Byrd, many bring densely padded and helmeted gear—often hugely expensive—that would be fine for a 2-month march to the Pole. Some feel cheated when they reach Antarctica to find the sun shining, the air warm, and not a blizzard in sight. They wonder what all the fuss is about: their old parka would have done just as well. It is good to be well clothed when the sun disappears and the blizzards start: but a sound parka, both windproof and waterproof, with woolly jumpers, warm underwear and a woolly hat, is enough for most people.

Changes in Antarctic weather can be rapid and dramatic: fine sunny conditions may shift in minutes to storms with biting winds and snow flurries. Wise travellers in Antarctica do exactly what they would do in winter back home. They dress for the moment, but never fail to carry an extra sweater and foul-weather gear in the backpack.

## Geology

A continent that is over 98% covered with ice is grand fun for glaciologists but tantalizing for geologists, who see only glimpses of the underlying rocks and their structural relations. However, studies of the available exposures, together with soundings through the ice, reveal East Antarctica to be a stable platform of ancient sedimentary rocks, heavily metamorphosed and overlain with younger sediments. The Transantarctic Mountains of Victoria Land, an exposed range some 65 km (40 miles) wide and 2000 km (1250 miles) long, show spectacular sections of both platform and overlying sediments from Cape Adare, northern Victoria Land to the Wisconsin Mountains and beyond.

West Antarctica by contrast is a complex of folded and metamorphosed sediments, mostly of volcanic origin. Its structure appears most clearly in the mountains of Antarctic Peninsula. East and West Antarctica evolved in different ways, coming together only relatively recently in the geological history of the world.

**Figure 1.4** *Waterboat Point, in Paradise Harbour, Danco Coast. Little remains of the original waterboat, a relic of whaling days, in which two men overwintered (p. 166). The red huts form part of the Chilean station González Videla. At low tide the island becomes part of mainland Antarctica.*

Antarctica's highest mountain, Vinson Massif (5140 m, 16 859 ft) stands with a cluster of other high peaks in the Eternity Range, clear above the ice cap of Western Antarctica. Travellers wanting to climb these peaks can arrange to fly in via Chile and the South Shetland Islands. Many lesser ranges lie hidden under the ice, where there are also extensive plains and deep ice-filled channels, some dropping more than 1000 m (3280 ft) below current sea level. The weight of overlying ice depresses the underlying continent more than 300 m (1000 ft) lower than other continents. Should the ice cap melt, experts tell me that Antarctica would rise to become the world's second-highest continent, with mean bed-rock elevation of about 860 m.

Cruises to Antarctica Peninsula offer scope for geologically minded travellers to see and touch the rocks of Antarctica, far more so than cruises to the Weddell Sea or other sectors of the continent where ice cliffs predominate. There is scope too at several points for travellers to 'stand on the continent' (Figure 1.4). Some travel brochures advertise this as a stated objective of their cruises. A moment's thought should make it clear that this far corner of West Antarctica is remote from the main continental mass of East Antarctica, and may or may not be joined physically to it. Is it therefore part of the continent? And if not, does anyone really care?

In my experience about half the passengers on any cruise care deeply. 'Landing on the continent' becomes a surprisingly sensitive issue, which cruise leaders have to take seriously. The best they can do is arrange landings in good faith at Hope Bay, Cape Legoupil, Neko Harbour, Waterboat Point (which becomes part of the mainland at low tide) or any of a dozen other points along the mainland Peninsula.

This satisfies many good people who have travelled far and paid much for the privilege of standing on the seventh and last continent.

## Coastal landings

Much of Antarctica's true coastline lies buried deep under the edges of the ice sheet. Most of the coast that presents itself to passing ships (in fact some 96%: see Box 1.1, p. 10) is made up of ice cliffs, beautiful to see but virtually unscalable by cruise-ship passengers (Figure 1.5). Few cruise ships carry helicopters to land people on the ice shelves, and there is not much to see or do up there when they succeed. Cruise operators concentrate instead on making their landings along Antarctica's few thousand kilometres of rocky shore, and on the Antarctic and Southern Ocean islands.

In this they are not alone. Almost everyone else who has used Antarctica over the last two centuries has concentrated on the bare rocky areas. Sealers may have hunted over them for furs and oil, though most of their efforts were concentrated on islands to the north. Overwintering explorers built huts on them: so, in rapidly increasing numbers from the 1940s onward, did operators of scientific research stations and support facilities, many of which were installed for political reasons (Chapter 11). However, the first to show preference for rocky shores were Antarctica's aboriginal inhabitants—some of its breeding seals, most of its seabirds and virtually all of its vegetation.

**Figure 1.5** *Ice coast. The shelf of continental ice, with its 30 m (100 ft) cliffs, advancing from the right, has shed tabular bergs, now immobilized by sea ice. Open water of the Weddell Sea is a few miles away (top). Brown streaks across the sea ice mark the track of a mobile emperor-penguin colony.*

**Figure 1.6** *Steep rocky coast typical of southern Antarctic Peninsula, lined with ice cliffs, punctuated by occasional headlands and beaches. Mountains make up only a small proportion of Antarctic coasts, mainly along the Peninsula and in Victoria Land.*

So many demands on so small an acreage have left their marks, of which only the most recent are strongly apparent. Though sealers may have destroyed fur seals, elephant seals and penguins on parts of Antarctic Peninsula, stocks have largely recovered and there is little left to show where they hunted. Early explorers took small numbers of seals and penguins for food, but again stocks quickly recovered, and the artefacts of this period—cairns, huts and graves—are now historic relics.

By contrast conflicts between wildlife and more recent research facilities have been obvious for many years, especially along Antarctic Peninsula and on the South Shetland Islands where much of the scientific and political effort has been concentrated. Research stations have been sited in areas that answered immediate logistic needs, without much reference to the presence of wildlife (Figure 1.7). In consequence colonies of penguins and petrels have disappeared or been greatly reduced, vegetation destroyed and scenic beauty marred. Oil tanks have been built on botanically sensitive sites. Rubbish has been allowed to accumulate at stations, buildings have been abandoned and left to rot, sometimes to the detriment of wildlife, always at the expense of Antarctica's natural beauty.

Impacts on wildlife tend to be transient, and time will heal many of the physical scars inflicted by these human activities. A growing sense of responsibility on the part of those who operate national scientific programmes is speeding the healing and reducing future damage.

Now the growth of tourism—an industry that is proliferating as rapidly as research stations once proliferated—brings possibility of further conflicts and impacts. After sealers, explorers and scientists, tourists in their turn are making

**Figure 1.7** *Conflict or cooperation? Scientists and wildlife sometimes compete for limited beach space. This refuge hut, built in the 1950s on a gentoo-penguin colony on Petermann Island, and now almost derelict, provides both a wind scoop and shelter for the nesting penguins in early spring.*

use of the ice-free areas of Antarctica. Will their impacts be equally traumatic? That is a question to be answered towards the end of this book (Chapter 11) when we have discussed the responsibilities of tour operators working in Antarctica, and the effects of visitors visiting.

## The Southern Ocean

The ocean surrounding the North Pole is the Arctic Ocean. That surrounding the South Pole should be the Antarctic Ocean, but is more generally called the Southern Ocean. The name was given by Captain James Cook, who first identified the ocean as distinct from the southern Atlantic, Indian and Pacific Oceans, and named it before he had shown it to be part of an Antarctic region. Whatever its name, this is the fourth-largest ocean, with an area of 35 million km$^2$ (13.7 million sq. miles), extending from continental Antarctica to a northern limit at the Antarctic Convergence. Its southernmost reaches adjacent to Antarctica are designated separately as four great and seven lesser seas (Map 1, see also Map 2, p. 65).

In winter more than half the ocean surface freezes to a depth of a metre or more, forming fast ice and pack ice (p. 18). More ice enters the ocean as snow, and more again as icebergs and ice islands which break off from the continental ice cliffs. Visitors who make the acquaintance of this ocean in summer, when only about one-fifth of its ice cover remains, find it hard to imagine conditions in winter, when waves are stilled, land and sea merge, and ice extends in all directions to the horizon.

The Southern Ocean, like all other oceans, is made up of separate water masses or layers. Each has a distinctive combination of salinity, temperature and density: each flows in a different direction under the influence of winds and geostrophic (earth-generated) forces. At the surface are two strong currents, pushed in opposite directions by strong prevailing winds. Beneath at various depths run counter-currents generated by gravity and Earth's rotation, which carry cold Antarctic waters northward and bring warm subtropical waters southward to replace them.

Surface currents are driven mainly by winds. Between latitudes 50° and 60°S successive cyclonic storms produce strong northwesterly to southwesterly winds that drive a broad river of surface waters, the West Wind Drift, eastward around the continent at a mean rate of 1 m per second (2.2 miles per hour). The northern flank of this cold surface current tends to spread northward, where it converges on warmer, saltier waters from temperate latitudes. The cold water, being denser, disappears beneath the warmer. The zone of meeting between these water masses, called the Antarctic Convergence or Polar Front, is now generally accepted as the northern boundary both of the Southern Ocean and of the Antarctic region.

The Convergence, which winds around the world between 40° and 50°S, lies further north in the Atlantic than in the Pacific sector. It can usually be identified as a sudden change in sea surface temperature, which most ships record automatically from their engine-room intake of cooling water. A ship moving southward in summer may record a fall in temperature from 5° to 2°C within 2 or 3 hours. Though its mean position can be drawn on charts, the actual position of the Convergence shifts slightly from day to day and month to month. Aboard cruise ships, crossing the Convergence on the southward run is usually a matter for mild celebration. There may even be a sweepstake on the exact time of crossing—a benevolent fiddle, because even the Captain cannot determine the crossing to the nearest minute.

Some 10° further north lies the Subtropical Convergence or Front, a less well-defined boundary where subantarctic waters sink below still-warmer subtropical waters. The convergences create latitudinal zones of ocean, within which small islands tend to take their mean monthly and annual temperatures from the surrounding waters. Hence islands south of the Antarctic Convergence are consistently colder than those between the convergences, which in turn are colder than those north of the subtropical convergence. The differences in temperature, though seldom more than a few °C, make for profound differences in the ecology of the islands (Chapters 5 and 10).

Closer to Antarctica, southerly winds blowing off the continent are diverted by Earth's rotation to produce prevailing easterlies. These drive the East Wind Drift, a relatively narrow belt of surface waters, which flows westward around the continent at one-tenth the speed of the West Wind Drift. Between the West Wind and the East Wind drifts lies a narrow circumpolar zone, the Antarctic Divergence, in which subsurface waters, rich in nutrients, are drawn upward and spread over the surface, to the delight and well-being of krill, fish, seabirds, seals and whales.

More immediately interesting to most travellers is the turbulence of the Southern Ocean. The Roaring Forties, the Howling Fifties, the Shrieking Sixties—this is an area renowned for stormy seas. Persistent westerly winds generate strong swells, particularly in the Indian Ocean sector, which ships plying north and south tend to encounter sideways-on. Hence the rolling that makes memorable so many Antarctic voyages. Ships heading east and west, for example between Ushuaia and South Georgia, take swells from the bow or stern, which produce pitching instead of rolling. Those travelling obliquely across the swell, for example from South Georgia to Antarctic Peninsula, exhibit interesting combinations of both.

A few passengers claim to enjoy stormy seas and some may actually do so. However, most do not. If you really cannot cope with violent movement at sea, think twice before booking an Antarctic cruise: there are much cheaper ways of making yourself miserable. While there are plenty of quick and effective remedies for seasickness, there are fewer for broken bones and dislocated joints, which can spoil your holiday too.

## Sea ice

For much of the year the southern half of the Southern Ocean develops a skin of sea ice, surrounding and investing continental Antarctica and the southernmost islands. This may be *fast ice*, which grows out from the land and forms continuous sheets, or *pack ice* which is made up of floes, the broken remnants of ice sheets. Sea ice usually starts to form when air temperatures fall in March or April. Though fragmented by swell and drifted by wind, it continues to grow and thicken throughout winter, acquiring a burden of fallen and drifted snow that weighs it down in the water and adds to its bulk.

By August or September, Antarctic Peninsula and the rest of the continent are surrounded by semi-continuous sheets of fast ice ringed by a wide band of pack ice, in places over a metre (3 ft) thick and extending many kilometres from the coast (Figures 1.8–1.10). At its greatest winter extent sea ice covers about 20 million km$^2$ (7.8 million sq. miles), almost one and a half times the area of the continent. It chills the hemisphere by reflecting back sunshine that would otherwise warm the sea, and prevents the sea surface from exchanging gases with the atmosphere.

Sea ice seldom remains smooth and unbroken. Winds and currents set up tensions which open channels in the ice sheets, and pressures which push one part of an ice field against another, causing buckling and rafting. These forces may double and redouble the thickness of the ice sheet. Cracks and openings are important to animals, allowing whales to breathe and seals and penguins to use the ice as a floating winter home.

In the early spring, sea ice starts to disintegrate, melting and eroding under the warming influences of the returning sun. The ice edge retreats, the sea once again absorbs sunlight, and the minute plants of the ocean surface start their annual cycle of proliferation (Chapter 2). Some that have spent the winter under thin, translucent ice floes may already have started summer growth.

Not all the annual sea ice disappears completely. In much of the Weddell Sea,

**Figure 1.8** *Sea-ice formation. With air temperature several degrees below freezing point, a flat-calm sea quickly develops a thin film of ice crystals—actually a layer like thin gruel, which may disperse under wind stirring, or thicken to form pancake ice (Figure 1.9).*

**Figure 1.9** *Pancake ice: the second stage of sea-ice formation. If the cold persists, the film of gruel-like crystals (Figure 1.8) consolidates into irregular discs which, through rubbing together, acquire raised edges and resemble pancakes. These may be only a few centimetres across, or up to several metres.*

**Figure 1.10**   *Sea ice may reach up to 2 m (6.5 ft) thick in a single winter. It seldom remains intact, usually breaking through swell and wind into floes. Large floes over 1-m thick are strong enough to support tractors, heavily loaded sledges and even helicopters.*

parts of the Ross Sea, and at several other points around the continent, sea ice tends to accumulate in local gyres from year to year, forming thick and heavy barriers that few ships can penetrate. Here and elsewhere some 3 million km$^2$ (1.17 million sq. miles) remain each summer.

Winds and currents may part the ice, creating polynyas—stretches of open water within ice fields—that allow safe passage of ships. Polynyas constantly open and close: it makes sense to enter them only in ships that are ice-protected or have some capacity for ice breaking. Coastal polynyas caused by offshore winds allow ships to penetrate far south into the formidable ice of the eastern Weddell Sea in summer. Similarly the Ross-Sea polynya allows summer passage to ships down to McMurdo Sound, in 78°S.

The presence of sea ice in surrounding waters profoundly affects the ecology of Antarctic islands and coasts. Islands that lie north of the northern limit of pack ice, warmed by the open sea, remain much milder in winter than those lying to the south. South Georgia, for example, has much milder winters than the South Shetland Islands, a quality reflected in its richer terrestrial flora and fauna.

Ships visiting Antarctic Peninsula in early summer may see rotting remnants of ice floes, and indeed be held up by them. Narrow channels (e.g. the Neumeyer and Lemaire channels), and such enclosed harbours as Deception Island, Port Lockroy and Yankee Harbour, may hold their winter ice as late as November or early December. However, wind and currents keep floes constantly on the move. A barrier that is impenetrable in the morning may have opened up and dispersed by the afternoon, only to close again by the evening.

## Icebergs

Icebergs—huge blocks of ice afloat in the sea—are derived from the cliffs of Antarctica's ice coastline (Figures 1.5, 1.11, 1.12). The largest, called ice islands, are massive sections of ice shelf several hundred kilometres long and broad, that occasionally break away from the mainland ice for reasons unknown. Some are as extensive as the smaller states of the USA, big enough to be seen and kept under surveillance by satellites. Smaller tabular bergs, flat-topped, square-cut, and usually just a few kilometres long, break constantly from the ice cliffs all around Antarctica. These too may be seen by satellites and their drifting monitored. Lesser bergs, called bergy bits, growlers and brash ice, irregular in shape, break away from the glacier streams that pour slowly between the mountains.

Though fashioned originally from layers of snow, icebergs sometimes incorporate boulders and fragments of rock that they have picked up on their journey over the continent. Though superficially white, they are often intensely blue or green, sometimes in layers. Whiteness usually denotes the presence of air, blueness the solidity of hard, compact ice. Between one-quarter and one-seventh of an iceberg's bulk appears above the water, depending on the age of the ice and the amount of air it contains. Tabular bergs from areas of high snowfall, containing a high proportion of relatively unconsolidated ice, ride high in the water. Glaciers that have flowed far downhill from the interior of the continent provide older and more solid ice, that sinks deeper into the water.

**Figure 1.11** *Icebergs break away from ice cliffs and glaciers and float off to sea. Smooth ice shelves yield tabular bergs (Figure 1.6), glaciers and ice streams more irregular bergs. Both gradually disintegrate into fragments of decreasing size, 'growlers', 'bergy bits' and 'brash'.*

**Figure 1.12**  *Rugged, heavily weathered tabular berg. Only about one-sixth of the mass of ice is visible: the rest lies below the water. Icebergs drift for many years, gradually melting, decaying, turning over and falling apart.*

Whatever their origins or original size, icebergs disintegrate slowly from their moment of launch. Warm air, sunshine and sea at temperatures above 0°C cause melting. Dry moving air stimulates surface erosion and evaporation. On warm days freshwater pours from their flanks: when the sun is warm and the air cold, they sprout immense icicles up to several metres long. Currents and winds conspire to drive them: there is more below the surface, so currents usually win. Waves erode their surface, particularly at the waterline: currents eat them away beneath, where they acquire a smooth, dimpled or hammered-pewter finish. Waves and swell generate strong mechanical stresses that cause them to flex like large ships, and eventually break into smaller pieces—bergy bits, growlers and brash ice.

In the process of disintegration bergs shed weight unevenly and shift their point of balance, causing old tide marks to tilt, and revealing smooth areas that were previously under water. They become top-heavy, rolling over like immense whales to expose water-worn underbellies. Large tabular bergs are sometimes hollowed by deep, intensely blue caverns (Figure 1.13). These are not (as some would have you believe) whale hangars. They probably originated as water channels and suffered further erosion from waves during their travels.

Wave and current action are responsible for much of the sculpting you see in fragments of old bergs, especially in shallow water where they run aground and offer resistance to waves. A tour by Zodiac (inflatable boat) among well-worn bergs is like driving round a sculpture park, with works of extraordinary freedom, imagination and talent on view (Figure 1.14). They photograph well and in any light, and penguins, terns and snow petrels especially seem to enjoy them as perches.

**Figure 1.13**  *Formed initially on land from layered, heavily compressed snow, icebergs weather into fantastic shapes, reflecting their internal structure. This one, made up of alternating soft and hard layers, has weathered into columns resembling pillars.*

**Figure 1.14**  *Well-weathered icebergs have surfaces that have been smoothed by melting under the sea, later exposed by overturning and subjected to weathering in air. They provide floating platforms far from land for penguins, other seabirds and seals.*

## Southern Oceanic islands

The Southern Ocean and neighbouring warmer waters have many groups of islands, ranging in climate and ecology from warm-temperate to truly Antarctic. Each island or group has its own blend of history and biology, and all are uniquely interesting. Though not all are strictly Antarctic, several that lie north of the Convergence are included in itineraries of cruises to Antarctica, and so are included in this book. The Falkland Islands and South Georgia are covered in Chapter 5, the remainder appear in Chapter 10.

## Further reading

Hosking, E. and Sage, B. 1982, *Antarctic Wildlife*. London, Croom Helm.
Naveen, R., Monteath, C., de Roi, T. and Jones, M. 1990. *Wild Ice*. New York, Smithsonian Institution.
Stonehouse, B. 1990. *North Pole South Pole: A Guide to the Ecology and Resources of the Arctic and Antarctic*. London, Prion.

# Chapter Two

# Vegetation and wildlife

## Introduction

Though different travellers choose to visit the Antarctic region for different reasons, high in priority for most visitors is the wildlife. Penguins, albatrosses, seals and whales are all major attractions: so to some people are the lesser seabirds, the few hardy species of land birds, and the meagre but unusual vegetation.

What you see as a visitor to the far south depends very much on where you go and at what time of year. Vegetation and wildlife are richest on the cold temperate islands and periantarctic islands (Chapter 10). Not surprisingly, they are thinner in variety and numbers of species but more specialized on the much colder Antarctic islands, Antarctic Peninsula and continent. There is generally less to see in early-season October, when winter snow still lies thick on the ground and the birds are only just starting to think of breeding. By late-season March much of the action is over, winter is drawing on, and it is time for birds, seals and human travellers to leave. From late November to late February is the most popular time, and in many ways the best, for visiting the region.

Dedicated birdwatchers are usually happiest on cruises that involve the longest possible time at sea. Twitchers whose sole ambition is to add new species to their life lists do not bother with Antarctica at all: there are far more species per dollar in Amazon jungle or African bush. Those who come south seem rather to be seeking unusual species, or simply enjoying the birds—predominantly seabirds—which Antarctica has to offer. They organize themselves into round-the-clock watches, spend hours on the bridge or spotting top, and each evening compare notes happily, adding both to their life lists and to their stock of bird-lore.

Dedicated mammal watchers join the bird spotters for the chance of spotting whales, dolphins and porpoises. Stocks of many species of whales in Antarctica are currently depleted, following successful hunting over half a century and more. However, organized watches on voyages between South America and Antarctica usually yield daily tallies of dolphins and whales: the more eyes watching, the more seen. Each year seems to bring increasing numbers of whales to their traditional feeding grounds in the channels of Antarctic Peninsula.

All-round naturalists and ordinary folk are usually happier ashore, savouring the liveliness of penguins, the lethargy of seals, the hardihood of mosses and lichens, and marvelling that Antarctic wildlife does not in general run away. Nature photographers are in paradise: seals yawn to order, adult penguins pose smugly for their portraits, chicks cluster round to have their photographs taken, and colour film burns at prodigious rates.

## Soils and vegetation

The Antarctic region is not noted for its vegetation: if you have seen the Arctic tundra in full bloom, do not expect the same from the Antarctic. Latitude for latitude it has nowhere near the variety of species that are found in the north. Why not? First, because the Arctic has been able to recruit plants from three neighbouring continents, while Antarctica lies isolated from other landmasses and sources of vegetation. The nearest point of contact is the southern tip of South America, and there is not much on offer in southern Patagonia or Tierra del Fuego. Second, there is less land ice and more ice-free ground in the Arctic: that means there is more ground where vegetation can gain a foothold and flourish. Third, parts at least of the Arctic have had longer to acquire their flora. Much of the Antarctic emerged, relatively speaking, only yesterday from under the icesheet. There has been less time for it to acquire soils and plants, and get its show on the road. Fourth, much of the Antarctic region is a dry desert for much of the time, either for lack of water, or because the water is frozen. Much of the Arctic tundra by contrast has plenty of water in summer.

In these difficult circumstances it is interesting to see what kinds of vegetation have managed to make it to these cold, dry and forbidding environments. Most of the southern oceanic islands have emerged relatively recently as volcanoes from the sea floor. Never directly connected to neighbouring continents, each has acquired a flora from seeds or propagules (living fragments) that have been washed up by the sea, blown in on the wind (mostly from South America), or carried on the feet and in the feathers of birds. Some have fared quite well, acquiring a dense green mantle of vegetation, growing from dark, loamy soils. Greening denotes cover in depth, but not necessarily a wide variety of plants: not many species have been able to settle and colonize, but what is there faces little competition and grows well.

The periantarctic and Antarctic islands are more thinly covered, again with few species—far fewer than in equivalent northern latitudes. The British Isles in 54°N support several thousand species of native flowering plants; South Georgia in 54°S has but 15 species. Even Svalbard in 80°N has a far wider selection of flowering plants than South Georgia, with thousands of hectares of tundra flowers that burst into brilliant colour each spring.

As if to show that only opportunity is lacking, plants that are introduced by man often do well on the southern islands. Weeds from the northern hemisphere, carried ashore in fleeces of introduced sheep or imported with packing materials, take root and survive for several seasons; a few become naturalized. By far the brightest flowers on South Georgia are good, familiar northern dandelions, that flourish, for example, in a small area around the graveyard of Norwegian whalers at Grytviken (Chapter 5). They were probably introduced with soil: it is a Norwegian custom to sprinkle soil from the homeland on graves overseas, and soil usually includes a few all-pervading weeds. The dandelions have survived for many years, but only in a restricted area downwind of the graveyard. Over a dozen other, less spectacular northern imports can be found around the whaling stations and scientific bases.

The Antarctic islands and the continent itself have only recently emerged from even heavier glaciation than at present. They have recruited their flora in much the same way as the northern islands, but provide a far harsher environment and have gained a more limited flora. In the whole area south of the northern limit of pack ice there are only two species of flowering plants. On the continent they grow solely in the relatively mild conditions of Antarctic Peninsula. There are no true soils of a kind that a gardener would recognize. There is abundant scree, gravel and fine rock dust, wind-blown, salt-impregnated and relatively sterile, but very little organic material. There are no plant roots to form humus, nor earthworms to till the ground, and an acute shortage of moisture for most of the year makes ice-free areas of Antarctica the equivalent of a very dry desert.

Throughout this colder southern region the most characteristic plants are algae, mosses and lichens, which grow in scattered communities wherever they can find a foothold.

## Algae

Algae (Figure 2.1) require moisture: some grow in shallow pools, others on wet soils, forming green mats up to 1 cm deep. Some fare best on the edges of penguin colonies where droppings have enriched the soil, raising levels of nitrates and phosphates to a point where other plants cannot survive. On the South Shetland Islands an appearance of greenness close to sea level is often due to *Prasiola*, an alga that proliferates quickly in spring on sandy soils, forming a thin but widespread green carpet. Under late spring sunshine it dries out and blows away, to reappear next spring as soon as the ground clears of snow.

**Figure 2.1** Prasiola crispa, *a lettuce-like alga that grows in a green mat between groups of penguin nests within a colony. The alga is killed by concentrated guano (droppings) close to the nests, but draws nutrients from damp soil enriched by diluted droppings on the approaches.*

**Figure 2.2**　*Consolidated snow impregnated with snow algae. These are minute plant cells that live on the frozen surface, proliferating in thaw water in spring, when they stain the surface red, yellow or green. Petermann Island, Graham Coast.*

Some of the most spectacular displays of vegetation are due to minute forms of single-celled algae that flourish on the surface of snow, staining it bright red or green. They are sometimes present in October or November after the last of the winter snow, but usually become more apparent in late summer, when they have had time to proliferate (Figure 2.2). The most colourful displays occur later in summer along the Peninsula, toward the Lemaire Channel and Petermann Island, where snowfields covering whole islands develop improbably vivid pyjama-stripes of red and green.

## Mosses

Mosses (Figure 2.3) form compact clusters wherever there is moisture—on compacted mud, sand and fine gravel, in crevices, in rocky channels that carry meltwater for a few days or weeks each spring. At their best they form turfs and carpets of dense growth up to several metres across, that cover the ground completely, absorb warmth from the sunshine, and keep out cold winds, providing within themselves a microclimate of near-ideal growing conditions. Dense moss turf often overlies several inches—occasionally several feet—of dry peaty material, representing continuous growth over many years. Elsewhere mosses grow in clumps, cushions and clusters, interspersed with lichens and other plants. Their tightly packed stems provide miniature forests where insects, mites and other tiny animals make themselves at home.

**Figure 2.3** *Moss beds at Hannah Point, Livingston Island, South Shetland Islands. Several species of moss form consolidated carpets on a substrate of damp, wind-blown sand. Though disturbed each spring by breeding elephant seals, the carpets quickly regenerate in summer.*

## Lichens

Lichens are a curious blend of fungi and algae that take their moisture from the air. They grow in a variety of forms and in many unlikely situations—particularly on bare rock faces and scree slopes. Some are black, others green or grey, others again bright orange-red. Coastal rocks of the South Shetland and South Orkney islands often bear thin mats of crustose (low-growing, encrusting) orange lichens (Figure 2.4), which probably gain nutrients from salt spray. On higher slopes, where the air is damper, grow miniature forests of foliose (leafy) or dendritic (branched) lichens (Figure 2.5). Very tiny forms of lichens insinuate themselves into rocks, where they grow under individual crystals in greenhouse conditions that are far warmer than outside.

Antarctica and the southernmost islands support only two species of flowering plants, both small and relatively hard to find. One is a grass—Antarctic hair-grass—and the other a pearlwort related to the pinks; you find them only on the Peninsula and islands, not on East Antarctica (Figures 2.6, 2.7).

## Insects and other beasties

South of the Antarctic Convergence, soils are frozen in depth for most of the year: only a thin surface layer thaws out briefly in summer. Not surprisingly there are few

**Figure 2.4** *Crustose lichens, orange, grey and black, form a dense, patchy covering on rocks close to the sea. They flourish where the air is damp and sea spray provides surface nutrients. Half Moon Island, South Shetland Islands.*

**Figure 2.5** *Dendritic (branched) lichens form a miniature forest just a few centimetres high. The lichens trap sandy particles and moisture, providing bed and shelter for mosses and other small plants. Half Moon Island, South Shetland Islands.*

**Figure 2.6** *Hair grass* (Deschampsia antarctica) *(left) and pearlwort* (Colobanthus crassula) *(right). Antarctica's only flowering plants. Here they grow in a soil enriched by decaying limpet shells: the shells are provided by gulls that catch the limpets along the shore and disgorge the shells inland.*

**Figure 2.7** *A colourful natural garden, formed in a damp, sunny corner. The plants include algae, mosses, fungi, orange, grey and black crustose lichens, and hairgrass. Among them will be found small communities of springtails (insects) and mites. Livingston Island, South Shetland Islands.*

soil animals. A microscope will reveal such minute forms as protozoans, nematode worms, rotifers and tardigrades. A keen naked eye or hand lens may show tiny red or black mites and grey springtails (simple insects, also called collembolae) 1–2 mm long, living among the mosses and lichens. Warm spring days bring out springtails in their thousands, forming pale grey rafts several centimetres across on the surface of snow-melt pools.

Springtails are mostly vegetarian, living on fungi and plant debris at the soil surface; mites are carnivorous, living mainly on the springtails. Two species of wingless midges breed in brackish pools above the high-tide mark, where their larvae feed on microscopic algae. Such advanced forms as earthworms, snails, spiders and beetles are found only on the warmer islands, for example South Georgia.

## Inshore flora and fauna

There is not a lot to be seen in the rocky shore intertidal zone: remember that many of the pools that you see ice-free in summer are in winter filled with ice, and possibly under thick snow for several months. In the zone of fast winter ice, shifting floes scour the rocks in spring. However, in many pools are found pink or white encrusting algae, red jelly-like anemones tucked away in corners, cushion stars, long-limbed brittle stars, and even small fish. In the Scotia Arc and along the northern half of Antarctic Peninsula, rock pools in the splash zone above high-water mark that are rich in algal soup may contain the larvae of wingless mosquitoes. On the surface of the same pools you may see the small adult insects themselves. These, for what it is worth, are said to be Antarctica's largest land-living animals.

The seaward side of the rocks often bear a scattering of limpets just at the waterline. Gulls pick them off with their hooked bills and swallow them. They digest the meat and throw up the shells, sometimes in small, neat heaps on the ground, sometimes raining them down from mid-air. Hence the piles and pavements of limpet shells that you find all over the maritime Antarctic (Figure 2.6), as far inland as the gulls are found, and up to tens or hundreds of metres above sea level.

A green seaweed ( *Ulva*) is plentiful in late summer on South Georgia, growing like tufts of fresh green lettuce between the high and low-tide marks. Sheathbills—white, pigeon-like scavenging birds—feed on and around it, perhaps benefitting more from the tiny animals that live on it, rather than from the weed itself. In clear water below the low-tide mark you may see several different kinds of red and brown seaweeds. Their fronds are frequently broken in storms and washed up onto the strand, where more than a dozen different patterns of frond may be identified. Much larger brown seaweeds called 'kelp', with fronds 10 to 20 m long, grow like forests around the shores of South Georgia, the Falkland Islands and other islands north of the limit of pack ice.

On Zodiac tours in the far south, admire the scenery, the icebergs and wildlife—but look down if you can into clear water below, where there is a surprising amount to be seen. Surrounding the barest stretches of coast, the shallows beneath the low-tide mark may be full of life. Rocks and pebbles of the seabed are scattered with sponges, cushion stars, brittle stars, spiny sea urchins, spiral-shelled whelks, crustaceans and bootlace-worms (nemertines), with small fish of several species dodging among them. This is best seen in early spring and summer when the water is clearest: later in the season algae and fine rock-flour from glacial streams make the water cloudy. Port Lockroy, Paradise Harbour and Waterboat Point, for example, have splendid underwater zoological gardens that are easily scanned during Zodiac tours.

## Plankton

Much of the nourishment for these submarine zoos comes initially from surface waters, which in summer fill with minute floating plant cells (collectively called phytoplankton) and similar-sized or larger animals (zooplankton) which feed on them. The business of phytoplankton is to absorb energy from sunlight and nutrients from the water, and for individual cells to grow, divide and grow again ad infinitum. The business of zooplankton is to browse and fatten on these cells, and indeed for some of the larger animals to feed on each other. From this hive of activity in surface waters comes a constant rain of nutrient debris to the seafloor beneath.

How can we see these tiny cells on which so much depends? The most convincing way is to tow a fine net—like the finest nylon stocking—through surface waters for anything from 10 minutes to an hour, and tip the resulting contents into a dish. With luck we see a cloudy mass representing several million cells. Through a hand-lens we may just make out individual cells, but only through a microscope do they become clearly visible, as tiny pill-boxes or strands of transparent shell, often beautifully sculptured, with a living content of green or yellow foam. These are likely to be diatoms, which form the bulk of the phytoplankton. They may not be the most important component: possibly more significant are thousands of very much tinier micro-algal cells, that slipped through the fine nylon mesh and got away. Those we would have had no hope of seeing without a powerful microscope.

There is another way of seeing phytoplankton in bulk, for the diatoms and other cells settle on the underside and lowest layers of sea ice in dense concentrations, staining it yellow, green or brown. Moving through fields of loose pack ice, turning some of the smaller floes over, we see plenty of this staining from late spring onward, sometimes enough to discolour the sea between the floes as well. As the ice melts, the cells are released back into the water, where they continue to multiply.

Often we see tiny shrimp-like creatures on the undersides of the floes, or in the water between. These are some of the zooplankton that live under the floes, penetrating between the ice crystals like mites in cheese, and browsing on the plant cells. After the ice has gone both plant and animal plankton live in the open water, sometimes forming huge shoals that cover many hectares.

Phytoplankton provides a rich table on which tiny animals of many different kinds come to feed. The shrimp-like creatures are crustaceans (animals with

**Figure 2.8**  *Up to 7 cm (2.5 in) long, shrimps of the genus* Euphausia *swarm under ice and in open water, feeding on algae. Krill (the whalers' name for* E. superba*) forms the main food of many fish, birds, seals and whales, and is caught by commercial fishermen. Drawn by the author.*

many-jointed limbs), and probably euphausiids (Figure 2.8), of which there are several species. Other forms of crustaceans are there, together with arrow-worms, pteropod molluscs, polychaet worms, and the larval or young forms of many fish and bottom-living creatures, all feeding on the plant cells and on each other. They in turn are browsed by fish, seabirds, seals and whales. In calm weather zooplankton is often dense enough to be visible as patches of pink sea. A ship travelling through such a shoal may pick up some of the zooplankton—often euphausiids of one species or another—in its water intake (the pipe through which it draws in sea water to cool the engines). Kindly engineer officers may be prevailed upon to bring up samples of still-lively plankton from the filters. The animals are temperature-sensitive, and quickly die if their water is allowed to warm.

Shallow waters too are occasionally filled with shoals of zooplankton. Gulls, terns and small petrels feeding close inshore are often the give-away. Shoals that drift into the crater of Deception Island (Chapter 6) at low tide encounter the hot springs and die, accumulating along the strand and providing a welcome feast of ready-cooked shrimps for the birds. I have seen passengers standing ankle-deep in the lukewarm water, surrounded by dozens of pintado petrels that peck away happily at the plankton within inches of their boots.

Harbours in the South Shetland Islands occasionally swarm with pink medusae (jellyfish), plum-sized comb-jellies or sea-gooseberries with rippling, iridescent bands, and siphonophores—complex, many-stranded jellyfish like Venetian candelabras, that drift and pulsate through the water entrapping small animals. Salps are similar trains of semi-transparent pink cells, each containing a dark red sphere, that drift around filtering off the phytoplankton. After storms, beaches may be littered with shells, sponges and fragments of many other kinds of invertebrate animals—reminders of the wealth of life to be found on the Antarctic sea floor.

## Fish and fisheries

There are no freshwater fish south of the Antarctic Convergence, but marine fish are plentiful in all latitudes of the Southern Ocean. Since the early 1960s major fisheries for fin fish have developed off the Falkland Islands, South Georgia, Iles Kerguelen and Crozet and other southern islands, where the stocks are richest. Krill too has been trawled, and most recently, squid. Indeed the Convention on the Conservation of Antarctic Marine Living Resources (CCAMLR: Chapter 11), an instrument of the Antarctic Treaty, has been drawn up to control fisheries of all kinds throughout southern waters. Tour ships en route to Antarctica from Tierra del Fuego and the Falkland Islands often pass the rusty, weather-beaten trawlers and freezer ships, flying tattered remnants of Russian, Japanese or Argentine flags, that make up the Antarctic fishing fleets.

Over 150 species of Antarctic marine fish are known, two-thirds of which live and feed on the seabed, the rest in surface waters. Of these a high proportion belong to the single sub-order Notothenioidei, a group restricted to cold waters of the southern hemisphere, and only distantly related to any of the familiar northern-hemisphere food fish.

Dangling a baited fishing line for a couple of hours inshore in the Antarctic Peninsula region, you would be likely to catch up to a dozen species of fish, seldom measuring more than 30 cm (1 ft) and on the whole unremarkable except for a tendency toward large heads and small bodies (Figure 2.9). Those that live on the bottom have protective coloration of brown or green: those caught immediately under the ice tend to be pale or silvery. Some, called ice-fish and belonging to the family Chaenichthyidae, lack the red oxygen-concentrating pigment haemoglobin, and are curiously translucent, with transparent skin and colourless gills.

While all Antarctic fishes seem well adjusted to living in cold water, the species that live in the coldest water tend to be restricted to high-latitude coasts, where temperatures (close to $-1.8°C$) remain constant all the year round. Different

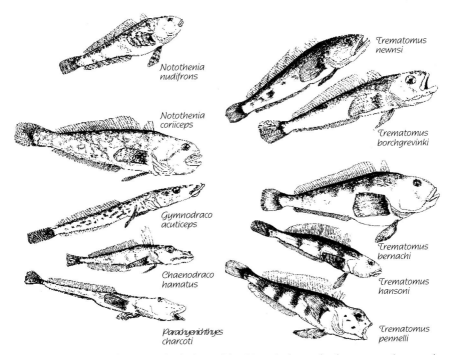

**Figure 2.9** *Typical Antarctic inshore fish. Most feed on the bottom, a few at the surface. Several are the young of larger forms that live in deep waters offshore and are caught commercially. Drawn by the author.*

species occur off the Peninsula and Scotia Arc, where slightly warmer temperatures are experienced in summer. Bottom-living species seem to be in no danger of freezing whatever the temperature. Surface-living species that browse among ice crystals are in more danger of freezing by contact. Their remedy is to develop anti-freeze chemicals in their blood, that lower their freezing point and prevent ice crystals from forming in their tissues.

Since whaling ended and commercial fishing began, many thousands of tonnes of fish have been taken in Antarctic waters, mostly by deep-water or pelagic (shallow) trawling over the shelves surrounding the oceanic islands. Some of the catch becomes human food, but much of it goes for lower-priced protein meal, which is only marginally worth taking. Though stocks in all the major fishing areas have been depleted, there is little evidence that this kind of fishing has adversely affected numbers of whales, seals or penguins.

Sadly, line-fishing in warmer waters beyond the Antarctic Convergence may be harming stocks of great or lesser albatrosses and mollymawks that breed on Southern Ocean islands. Hunting over a wide range of ocean, and attracted by scraps to the fishing boats, the birds take the baits, become entangled in the lines and are drowned. This is thought to account for serious depletion of stocks of these spectacular birds, particularly in the Indian-Ocean sector.

Thousands of tonnes of euphausiid shrimps too have been trawled from the Southern Ocean. Though available in huge quantities, they are individually much smaller than true shrimps or prawns, with less meat in proportion to their shells. Again a few are processed for human food, producing a rather crunchy and none-too-palatable shrimp paste. There is as yet little market for crunchy shrimp paste, and the bulk of the catch becomes low-value meal and oil. At present the annual catch is but a tiny fraction of the estimated annual production of krill. Should food technologists find ways of making krill more palatable to man, catches will no doubt increase, and the many kinds of birds, seals and whales that feed on krill may begin to feel the competition.

The most recently developed Southern Oceanic fishery is for squid, caught in offshore waters by specially equipped jigger ships in fishing grounds south of the Falkland Islands. Here there already seems to be a serious possibility of direct competition, for colonies of rockhopper penguins on the Falkland Islands, for example on New Island and Beauchêne Island, have declined seriously since the fishery started, and some observers blame the one event on the other. Should squid fishing in southern waters expand to other areas, this possibility will need to be closely monitored.

## Birds

Seabirds make themselves known to Antarctic voyagers as soon as the ship leaves the port of departure. Some 45 species (Box 2.1) breed south of the Antarctic Convergence. Some of these breed also in the temperate regions, and many have flying ranges that extend well north of the Antarctic boundary. Southern waters are also rich enough to support birds of warmer latitudes that become summer visitors.

## Box 2.1  Antarctic breeding birds: a key

*(see also Figure 2.22, p. 46)*

## Flightless
### Penguins

| Large penguins | Brush-tailed penguins | Crested penguins |
|---|---|---|
| *Emperor penguin* | *Adelie penguin* | *Macaroni penguin* |
| *King penguin* | *Gentoo penguin* | *Rockhopper penguin* |
| | *Chinstrap penguin* | |

## Flying
### Oceanic or inshore

| Gull-like birds | Sheathbills | Cormorants |
|---|---|---|
| *Dominican gull* | *Lesser sheathbill* | *Blue-eyed shag* |
| *McCormick's skua* | *Snowy sheathbill* | |
| *Brown skua* | | Land birds |
| | | *South Georgia pintail* |
| | | *South Georgia pipit* |

### Oceanic

| Small (wing span <1 m) | Medium (wing span 1–3 m) | Big (wing span >3 m) |
|---|---|---|
| Lesser petrels | Lesser albatrosses | Great albatrosses |
| *Southern fulmar* | *Light-mantled sooty albatross* | *Royal albatross* |
| *Antarctic petrel* | *Grey-headed albatross* | *Wandering albatross* |
| *Cape petrel* | *Black-browed albatross* | |
| *Snow petrel* | | |
| *Kerguelen petrel* | Giant petrels | |
| *Great-winged petrel* | *Northern giant petrel* | |
| *Mottled petrel* | *Southern giant petrel* | |
| *Soft-plumaged petrel* | | |
| *Grey petrel* | | |
| *White-chinned petrel* | | |
| *Blue petrel* | | |
| *Greater shearwater* | | |
| *Little shearwater* | | |
| Prions | | |
| *Antarctic prion* | | |
| *Thin-billed prion* | | |
| *Fairy prion* | | |
| Storm petrels | | |
| *Wilson's storm petrel* | | |
| *Grey-backed storm petrel* | | |
| *Black-bellied storm petrel* | | |
| Diving petrels | | |
| *South Georgia diving petrel* | | |
| *Common diving petrel* | | |

Thus a voyage south can provide spotters with well over 50 species of birds on the wing and in the water.

Nearly all of the region's breeding species are seabirds, feeding exclusively at sea. Exceptions are the species of pipit and two species of ducks that live in South Georgia, feeding along the shore, in the tussock grass and in lakes and streams. Exceptional also are sheathbills, that live all over the South-American sector to about 64°S, feeding along the shore and scavenging on penguin colonies.

Box 2.1 'Antarctic breeding birds' provides a simple key. The penguins (Box 2.2) are unmistakable: they have flippers instead of wings and do not fly. King and emperor penguins have bright orange patches on their neck: kings are exclusively subantarctic, breeding for example on South Georgia and Iles Kerguelen, emperors breed exclusively in the high Antarctic, along the continental coast (Figures 2.10, 2.11). Among the smaller species, the brush-tailed penguins are black and white, gentoos have bright orange bills, chinstraps a black line under the white chin, adelies a white ring around the eyes (Figures 2.12–2.14). These are the species most likely to be seen by 90% of Antarctic travellers. Crested penguins have bushy golden eyebrow crests, which are large and sprawling in macaronis, thinner and tufted in rockhoppers (Figures 2.15, 2.16).

The inshore birds you will see mainly on or near islands. Dominican gulls are like most other gulls, but large and with black upper wings: watch out for juveniles, which are mottled grey-brown. Brown skuas are chestnut-brown gulls with

**Figure 2.10** *King penguins: blue-grey penguins with brilliant orange throat patches, that breed in large colonies on South Georgia and many other southern oceanic islands. The second-largest of living penguins, they are unusual in keeping their chicks in the colonies throughout winter.*

## Box 2.2   Penguins

Penguins (Order Sphenisciformes) are flightless seabirds, restricted almost entirely to the southern hemisphere. The 18 living species are divided into six genera, only three of which are represented in the Antarctic region:

| | |
|---|---|
| Aptenodytes: | Kings and Emperors (two species) |
| Pygoscelis: | Brush-tailed penguins (three species) |
| Eudyptes: | Crested penguins (six species) |
| Spheniscus: | Burrowing penguins (four species) |
| Eudyptula: | Little blue penguins (two species) |
| Megadyptes: | Yellow-eyed penguins (one species) |

Penguins differ from all other birds in (1) loss of flight, (2) all-over plumage except for a brood patch, (3) swimming and diving abilities. The smallest (little blues) stand 30–40 cm (1–1.5 ft) high and weigh 1 kg (2 lb). The largest (emperors) stand up to 1 m (3.5 ft) high and weigh up to 40 kg (90 lb).

About 40 other species are known as fossils, some dating back over 30 million years. Most fossil forms were within the size range of modern penguins: one species probably stood over 1.5 m (5 ft) high and weighed 200 kg (450 lb). They evolved, probably from small, gull-like flying birds, in temperate conditions similar to modern New Zealand. As the polar ice caps developed, some found themselves able to live in the cold southern seas, and to breed on cold lands. Others spread north to tropical waters. However, most remained in warm temperate regions, living as they live today.

Six species (emperor, king, gentoo, chinstrap, Adelie, macaroni) at present live south of the Antarctic Convergence. Of these, emperors and Adelies live farthest south, to about 78° S. Kings and macaronis live farthest north, on South Georgia. All the southern Ocean species are circumpolar except chinstraps, which breed only on the Peninsula and Scotia Arc and are seldom found elsewhere.

Emperor penguins breed only close to the continent, in colonies of a few hundred to a few tens of thousands of pairs: nearly all breed in sea ice. They gather in May as soon as the ice forms, lay single eggs in late May–June, incubate (males only, for about 60 days) through June, July and early August, and feed their chicks until January–February. After moulting for a month they are ready to start breeding again.

Adelie penguins nest in colonies of several thousands mainly on the continent and peninsula, building nests in November and laying two eggs. Both parents incubate (35 days) and feed their chicks until February. Then they moult and spend winter on the pack ice. Chinstraps and gentoos follow similar routines in similar latitudes or further north.

Macaroni penguins nest on the fringes of the Antarctic region in colonies of several thousands. Each pair lays two eggs, one bigger than the other, but usually rears only one chick.

King penguins breed on many Southern Oceanic islands, farthest south in South Georgia. They make no nests, carrying the single egg on their feet. Early breeders (usually those that have lost an egg or chick from the previous season) lay in late November and December. Late breeders (those that were still feeding chicks in November and December) lay in January and February. Both parents incubate (54 days) and feed the chicks, which reach about half-size by May. They then feed intermittently through winter, during which the chicks lose weight and many of the late-hatched ones die.

From September feeding increases, the remaining chicks fatten, and the first (those from early laying) leave in late November and December. Thus adults may be early breeders one season, late breeders the next season, and miss breeding altogether in the third season.

**Figure 2.11** *Emperor penguins: largest and most colourful of all living penguins. Emperors breed in large colonies, mostly on sea ice that forms annually close to the ice cliffs of mainland Antarctica. They incubate their eggs during the coldest months of winter.*

**Figure 2.12** *Gentoo penguins, distinguished by their white head-flash, orange bill and feet. Largest of the pygoscelid (brush-tailed) penguins, they breed in colonies of hundreds or thousands over a wide range from cool temperate to polar latitudes.*

**Figure 2.13** *Chinstrap penguins. Distinguished by the narrow black band across the throat, they breed in colonies entirely in the South American sector of Antarctica, on South Georgia, throughout the Scotia Arc, and far south along the west side of Antarctic Peninsula.*

**Figure 2.14** *Adelie penguins. Distinguished by their white eye-ring and corona of feathers at the back of the head (which they raise when alarmed), they breed on rocky outcrops all round continental Antarctica, and on many islands of the southern Scotia Arc.*

**Figure 2.15** *Macaroni penguins. One of six species of crested penguins, with prominent golden crests, they breed mainly on islands in the cold temperate zone and in the Scotia Arc, as far south as the South Shetland Islands. Closely related royal penguins breed on Macquarie Island.*

**Figure 2.16** *Rockhopper penguins. Smallest of the crested penguins, with thin, drooping yellow crests and red eyes, they are confined mainly to the cold temperate and warm temperate zones. This one belongs to a northern subspecies: see also Figure 10.6.*

**Figure 2.17** *Brown skuas. Gull-like brown birds with prominent white wing bars, they feed at sea, scavenge and hunt on penguin colonies, and are fierce predators of small petrels. In winter they migrate away from the breeding colonies, some to temperate northern latitudes.*

prominent white wing bars (Figure 2.17), McCormick's skuas are similar but greyer. The two species are hard to tell apart (and there are hybrid forms to make things even more difficult) but you will see more brown skuas in the north, more McCormick's further south. Antarctic terns are white with grey-pointed wings and delicate-pointed orange bills. Blue-eyed shags are heavily built birds with small, dual-purpose wings (Figure 2.18). You may see them diving around the ship when anchored close inshore, or nesting on rocky points.

The oceanic birds are the ones seen mostly from the ship. Royal albatrosses and wandering albatrosses and the slightly smaller black-browed, grey-headed and light-mantled sooty albatrosses and giant petrels appear singly or in groups of up to a dozen, with graceful, swooping flight (Figure 2.19–2.22). The lesser petrels are often in larger groups, sometimes numbering hundreds. Notice how they all fly over and around the ship, making use of its upcurrents. Keep a special lookout for several species of blue-grey prions, the all-white snow petrels (usually seen when there is ice about) and the tiny diving petrels and storm petrels.

Antarctic birds evolved in the virtual absence of ground predators, and consequently tend to show little fear of man. You may approach incubating penguins, skuas and shags more closely than, say, eiders or nesting geese in the Arctic, without their getting off the nest and running. This is usually true of small surface-nesting petrels (e.g. pintados or Antarctic fulmars) and sometimes but not always true for giant petrels. However, it is never true for terns, Dominican gulls, South Georgia pipits and pintails, skuas and several other species, which are just as

**Figure 2.18**    *Blue-eyed shags. Forming small colonies of a few dozen pairs, they feed by diving in shallow inshore waters, hunting for fish and seabed invertebrates. The eye-rings are blue, the eyes themselves dark brown. For a more brilliantly plumaged relative, see Figure 10.11.*

**Figure 2.19**    *Black-browed albatross. Among the smaller albatrosses or mollymawks, they breed mainly in the temperate zones, but forage farther south, often accompanying ships far into Antarctic waters. They feed exclusively at sea, mainly on fish and squid.*

**Figure 2.20** *Grey-headed albatross, another species of mollymawk, distinguished by its smokey-grey head and dark-sided bill. This species, like the black-browed albatross (Figure 2.19), often accompanies ships in southern waters.*

**Figure 2.21** *Giant petrel. Graceful as a mollymawk in flight, but distinguishable by the heavier bill, this is a major predator of penguins and scavenger of the sea shore. The bill is strong enough to tear meat from seal carcasses.*

**Figure 2.22** *Some Antarctic flying birds. Petrels (including albatrosses and molly-mawks) far outnumber penguins as the characteristic birds of the Southern Ocean. Drawn by Kim Crosbie.*

twitchy in Antarctica as are their counterparts elsewhere in the world. Why? We do not know.

This is not to say that breeding colonies of birds are unaffected by human presence. It has often happened that, when a research station has been set up close to a giant petrel or penguin colony, within a few years the colony has declined in numbers or disappeared. It seems probable that young birds nesting for the first time may be more wary than established breeders, and decide to nest elsewhere if disturbed. Just where the truth lies we are not sure: indeed my colleagues and I are in the middle of a long-term research project to find out more precisely how people and birds, including penguins, can coexist in Antarctica without damage to either.

Meanwhile there are good working guidelines for visitors to follow. Keep right away from the nesting areas of gulls, skuas, terns, and other birds that show fear. Be alert to their presence: back off if you find yourself approaching them, and warn fellow-travellers who may not have seen them. With other species, do not move quickly or suddenly when close to them. Do not attract their attention or try to arrange them for better photographs. Always yield right of way; try not to crowd them or interfere with their movements. Keep at least 5 m (15 ft) from them: if they approach you (as young penguins are very likely to), sit still and let them investigate you, your knapsack or your bootlaces in peace. Good photographs and happy memories will invariably follow.

## Seals

Seals (Pinnipedia) are mammals—four-limbed, warm-blooded and air-breathing like the rest of us. They evolved from land mammals which, perhaps some 30–40 million years ago, decided to make their living at sea. The Antarctic region has six species. Five of them are hair seals (of the family Phocidae, also called true seals) that are closely related to each other and to tropical monk seals. The remaining species is a fur seal, a remote cousin of different family (Otariidae), distinct in origins, appearance and temperament. In southern South America, the Falkland Islands and some of the warmer islands south of New Zealand you may see sea lions, that are closely akin to the fur seals but keep exclusively to warmer waters.

Antarctic seals are usually to be seen lying asleep or, if awake, crawling clumsily in search of a comfortable resting place, a resting mode that creates an impression of sloth and ineptitude. This is entirely misleading. Seals spend much of their lives at sea, where we cannot follow. Once in water the stubby forelimbs become paddles, the tail and hindlimbs a strong propellor. The heavy body becomes weightless, and the sluggard turns into an active, graceful, and very efficient maritime hunter—one that can outswim fish for a living. Their fat keeps them warm in water that we would find paralysing. Their large, soulful eyes allow them to hunt in near-darkness, and when all light has gone, sonar (reflected sound waves) helps them to feed and find their way about.

Largest of the true seals are southern elephant seals (called 'southern' to distinguish them from a closely related northern species that breeds off California and Mexico). As their name implies, these are massive seals

**Figure 2.23** *Sub-adult male elephant seals playing in shallow water. Fully adult males are larger and heavier, and develop larger 'trunks' during September–November, the breeding season. They breed mainly on the southern islands, and feed on fish and squid, which they catch in deep water.*

(Figure 2.23), elephantine grey. Mature males measure up to 6.5 m (21 ft) nose-to-tail and weigh in at 3–4 tonnes. During breeding they develop a pendulous trunk that hangs over the mouth, and allows them to trumpet defiance to rivals. Females measure up to 4 m (13 ft), weigh up to a tonne, and roar more gently. Pups, true to form, are born at 45 kg (100 lb) and treble or quadruple their birth weight in 3 to 4 weeks.

Southern elephant seals breed communally in large groups in southern South America and on many of the cold temperate and Antarctic islands. On the Scotia Arc breeding is over by November when the visitors arrive, though pups are occasionally born as late as December or January. After breeding the mature animals moult, a process that takes 3 to 4 weeks. It involves groups of 20–100 of them lying together on beaches in steaming, grumbling, belching, highly aromatic heaps—a spectacle never to be forgotten (Figure 2.24). Moulting animals appear regularly as far south as Pléneau Island, Antarctic Peninsula, and occasionally along the Antarctic mainland coast. With moulting finished, they play at the water's edge like holiday-makers, the elderly basking, the young mock-fighting, the pups rolling and squealing like piglets. Elephant seals feed mainly on squid, which they hunt at great depths.

Weddell, crabeater and leopard seals form a closely knit group of similar seals that visitors at first find difficult to tell apart. All grow to about 3 m (10 ft) long. Colours vary much between individuals, and even more according to whether their meagre hair is wet (dark) or dry (generally paler). Leopards tend to be lithe and slender, weighing up to 250 kg (550 lb): often they are slim enough to show hips,

**Figure 2.24** *Elephant-seal wallow. While moulting after the breeding season, elephant seals lie close together in mobs. Here is part of a group of over 100. Hannah Point, Livingston Island, South Shetland Islands.*

pelvic girdle and waist, and a distinct neck. Weddells and crabeaters are usually fatter and more rotund. Females, which grow slightly larger than males, weigh up to 350 or even 400 kg (900 lb).

Weddells are coastal seals, most often seen on beaches or inshore ice, close to the coast of Antarctica and the southern Scotia Arc (Figure 2.25). They are grey or tawny brown, with darker, clearly marked blotches overall. Their faces are round—with large eyes and Cheshire-cat smiles. Weddell seals mate under water and give birth in small groups on inshore ice, usually in September or October. A small splinter population of about a dozen females breeds each year in Larsen Harbour, South Georgia—the species' most northerly outpost. Weddell seals feed mainly on fish and squid, often diving deep under the sea ice and hunting by sonar. On a calm day their submarine trills can clearly be heard at the surface.

Crabeaters are predominantly pale, grey or tan, without prominent spots (Figure 2.26). Creatures of the pack ice, they are more likely to be seen on ice floes than beaches. Small eyes set wide apart give them a worried, polar-bear expression. They have much to worry about: nearly all carry deep gashes on their flanks, believed to be due to attacks of killer whales. They feed almost entirely on krill, which they filter from the water through cheek-teeth that are cusped for straining (Figure 2.27). Crabeaters breed far out on the pack ice in early spring, then many of them make their way closer to land. In the South-American sector they rarely appear before Christmas, but are plentiful during January and February. Migratory groups of several hundred are occasionally reported in the Gerlache Strait region.

**Figure 2.25**    *Weddell seal: dappled seals of inshore Antarctic waters. Smaller and more slender than elephant seals, with round, cat-like faces, they are usually solitary: you often find one asleep on a beach or floating ice.*

**Figure 2.26**    *Crabeater seals. Similar in size to Weddells, they are usually silver-grey or fawn, and more likely to be seen on ice floes than on the beaches. Many bear long wounds or scars, probably inflicted by killer whales. Summer migrations of several hundreds occur in Gerlache Strait.*

**Figure 2.27** *Both Weddell and crabeater seals have cusped, interlocking teeth, that help them to filter krill and small fish from the sea. Crabeaters feed almost entirely on krill (Figure 2.8), Weddells also take fish and squid.*

Leopard seals, white or cream with prominent dark brown or black spots, are by contrast loners (Figure 2.28). They seldom appear in company, usually one or two at a time on floating ice. The slim body and flexible neck accentuate the size and proportions of the head, which has huge jaw muscles and appears enormous. The gape too seems larger than in any other seal. Leopard seals breed on the sea ice, and live by hunting fish, penguins and other small prey. Often one or two associate themselves with a particular penguin colony, from which they take a steady toll throughout the season. Curious by nature, they follow slow-moving Zodiacs, occasionally disconcerting passengers by popping up alongside with a wide grin. When they start to test the boat with their teeth, you should smack the water with a paddle and send them away.

Ross seals are the smallest of the southern phocid or true seals, measuring up to 2.3 m (8 ft) and weighing up to 200 kg. They are also the rarest and least likely to be seen by travellers, for they tend to live deep in the pack ice, well away from shipping lanes. If you happen to be travelling by ice-breaker or helicopter far out over the ice, and see a small, solitary dark seal with thick neck and large bulging eyes, you are luckier than most: it is very likely to be a Ross seal. Few naturalists have seen them, and very little is known of the species.

Fur seals (Figure 2.29) belong to a separate and quite distinct family, in ancestry close to bears and dogs. Distinguishing characters are their sleek, shiny fur, pointed face and much longer, flipper limbs, which they tuck under their body. This gives them greater agility than hair seals on land and snow. Formerly scarce due to 19th-century hunting, they have recently recovered and are now breeding in thousands

**Figure 2.28**  *Leopard seal. Slender, lithe, silver-grey, usually solitary, they are often seen in the shallow water off penguin colonies, where they catch and kill birds returning from fishing. They often follow Zodiacs, but have so far not been known to attack.*

**Figure 2.29**  *Southern fur seals. A male (left) guards two females, one with a recently born pup. Note the small external ears. Formerly hunted almost to extinction for their pelts, they are now returning to their traditional breeding grounds along the Antarctic fringe. Photograph: Ann Stonehouse.*

on South Georgia and Scotia Arc islands. Northeastern beaches of South Georgia are virtually closed to visitors from late November onwards, but the massive breeding groups of mature males, mothers and pups can be viewed safely from Zodiacs close inshore. Pups appear from early December onward. Mating follows shortly after, and the breeding groups disperse in late February or March. Young males that are not involved in breeding spread southward along the Peninsula, often loafing in groups of 10 to 20 on sheltered beaches.

Treat fur seals with great respect. They are not malevolent, and are normally peaceable: when resting ashore they just want to sleep. However, they are quick-tempered animals that like to keep space around them. Guides will usually warn you to keep at least 15 m (50 ft) away. If you approach one closer, it may interpret your upright posture as a threat. If so it will rear up and roar in counter-threat, and then move menacingly toward you. Don't stop to argue or take a photograph. You have already transgressed by disturbing it, so just move away.

Take care that, in avoiding one, you do not step into the path of another. Fur seals can run much faster than you over snow, cobbles or rough rocks. When fighting each other, for real or in play, they grab with their teeth and shake hard. Should one grab you and shake, even in error, it will certainly spoil your holiday.

## Whales, porpoises, dolphins

Whales (Cetacea) are found in all the world's oceans. Living species are divided into two suborders: Odontoceti (toothed whales, about 64 species including dolphins, porpoises and larger forms), and Mysticeti (baleen whales, about 10 species). Both groups are well represented in southern waters. During the Antarctic whale-hunting period (1904–65) almost every whale killed was measured and fully recorded and documented. Others were tagged with markers that, on recovery, gave information about their movements. From these records, coupled with later field observations, it has been possible to discover much about the breeding and life-cycles of Antarctic whales, especially of the commercial species.

The largest odontocetes are sperm whales, which grow to 18 m (60 ft) and weigh up to 55 tonnes. Bulls feed in Antarctic waters in summer, usually alone or in small groups, penetrating south to the edge of the pack ice and taking fish and squid, often at great depths. Their cows and calves are restricted to warmer waters. Southern bottlenose whales, measuring up to 7.5 m (25 ft) and weighing up to 4 tonnes, southern beaked whales (10 m or 33 ft, 8 tonnes) and killer whales of similar size, are present in the far south all the year round, some penetrating far into the pack ice. Bottlenose and beaked whales hunt deep for fish and squid: killers take fish, seals and penguins in surface waters.

Dolphins and porpoises are much rarer in cold waters, but you may well see dusky dolphins up to 2 m (6.5 ft) long, 150 kg (330 lb) and smaller Commerson's dolphins 1.4 m (4.5 ft) long, 60 kg (130 lb) close to or south of the Antarctic Convergence.

Baleen whales feed close to the surface on shoals of plankton and small fish. Southern right whales, up to 16 m (56 ft) long and weighing up to 100 tonnes, and

**Figure 2.30**   *A humpback whale over 10 m (33 ft) long swims up to investigate a Zodiac. Even when accompanied by a calf, they have never been known to attack. Watchers in the far boat are breaking a safety rule. Whatever is happening, remain seated: stand one at a time with the driver's permission.*

humpback whales up to 17 m (52 ft) and 35 tonnes penetrate south in summer, often keeping within sight of land. Humpbacks (Figure 2.30), formerly plentiful around the southern islands, were the main prey of whaling operations from South Georgia and the South Shetland Islands. Stocks seem now to be recovering: this is the species you are most likely to see around the Scotia Arc and in the sheltered waters close to Antarctic Peninsula, especially from early January onward.

In the open ocean watch out for four species of rorquals (fast-moving mysticetes with pleated expandable throats). Blue whales, up to 33 m (110 ft) long, 120 tonnes and the largest, are still relatively rare, though one or two are recorded each season by visiting ships. Fin whales, up to 25 m (80 ft), 40 tonnes and sei whales up to 17 m (56 ft), 15 tonnes are more frequently seen, penetrating southward to the ice edge and beyond. Minke whales up to 9 m (30 ft), 9 tonnes, the smallest rorquals, are also the commonest, and the ones most likely to appear in narrow fjords and sounds. Some at least overwinter in Antarctic waters, so you may well see them early in the season.

Most cruise-ship captains are glad to stop for a few minutes when whales are close by, and manoeuvre the ship so that everyone gets a photograph. Expect this as normal in Antarctic waters, though not necessarily on the way out and even less on the way home, when schedules may be tight. The whales themselves do not seem to mind the attention: they sometimes seem attracted toward the ship, and come over to rub against it.

On pleasant days during the second half of the season your guides may be able to predict where the whales will be. If so, and if there is time, they can put down the Zodiacs and wait for them. To have a humpback whale rest its knobbly nose on the side of your Zodiac can be an unforgettable experience (see Figure 7.21, p. 179). From following several species in small boats I gain an impression that humpbacks (which I know best) and minkes have a cow-like curiosity that lasts for a few minutes, then wanes. They are glad to see a ship or Zodiac, interested to explore it, then move on. Killer whales seem smarter, more wary, and less inclined to fraternize with strangers. I feel much the same way toward them.

## Further reading

Bonner, W. N. and Walton, D. W. H. (editors). 1985. *Key Environments: Antarctica.* Oxford, Pergamon Press.
Murphy, R. C. 1936. *Oceanic Birds of South America.* New York, Macmillan.
Stonehouse, B. 1985. *Sea Mammals of the World.* London, Penguin Books.
Stonehouse, B. 1989. *Polar Ecology.* New York, Chapman and Hall.

# Chapter Three

# How do we get there?

## Introduction

Ask in the average high-street tourist agency about a trip to Antarctica and they'll probably look blank: they may even ask 'Where is Antarctica?'. Given time, an average-to-good agency should come up with one or two company brochures, but you would be lucky this way to learn the full range of tours available.

A better way is to approach an agency with positive information—the name, address and telephone or fax number of a tour company, perhaps one recommended by a friend, advertised in a travel magazine or featured in a newspaper article. Better still, approach the company yourself. Best of all, make a point of looking for advertisements and approach several companies directly. They will be glad to send you brochures, and tell you if they deal directly or only through agents. A list of current operators is shown in Box 3.1.

The first choice to be made is: 'Do you want to see Antarctica from the air or from the sea?' Airborne travel includes both the cheapest excursions—overflights without landing, lasting a few hours—and the most expensive—special charters to out-of-the-way places, lasting as long as you want to pay for. Seaborne travel is a more leisurely affair, with cruises lasting 8 days to several weeks, and a wide choice of itineraries and costs.

## Antarctica by air

### Overflights

The cheapest way to see Antarctica is by a 1-day overflight, currently from Sydney, Australia, that takes you over the Southern Ocean and the nearest areas of Antarctic mainland. You are airborne for 11 hours, you do not land, and how much you see depends largely on the weather. It is usually fairly clear over the continent, giving you a map-like panorama of pack ice, a coast, and an extent of inland ice, possibly with mountains. Guides on board tell you about it; videos and other in-flight entertainment ensure that dull moments, if any, are rare.

It is fair to mention that this form of airborne travel resulted some years ago in Antarctica's worst air disaster. On 28 November 1979 an Air New Zealand DC10 aircraft on a sight-seeing overflight crashed into the side of Mount Erebus, McMurdo Sound, killing all 257 passengers and crew. However, there had been many such flights from South America, New Zealand and Australia, and all but this

## Box 3.1   *Antarctic tour operators*

This listing of Antarctic tour operators, kindly provided by IAATO (International Association of Antarctica Tour Operators), includes all current (1999) full and provisional members of the Association; for a listing of associate members see the Association's website. IAATO sets high standards of conduct both for its constituent members and for visitors who travel with them. All operators listed will be glad to supply brochures of forthcoming trips. You usually need to book several months in advance, especially for high-season (December–January) tours.

### Office of the Secretariat

Executive Secretary
Denise Landau
PO Box 2178
Basalt, CO 81621
**UNITED STATES**
TEL     970 704-1047
FAX     970 704 9660
EMAIL   iaato@iaato.org
WEB     www.iaato.org

### Full members

**ABERCROMBIE & KENT/EXPLORER SHIPPING**
1520 Kensington Road, Suite #201
Oak Brook, IL 60523-2141
**UNITED STATES**
TEL     630 954 2944
FAX     630 572 1833
EMAIL   vunderwood@compuserve.com
WEB     www.abercrombickent.com

**ADVENTURE ASSOCIATES**
197 Oxford Street Mall
PO Box 612
Bondi Junction, Sydney, NSW 2022
**AUSTRALIA**
TEL     61 2 9389 7466
FAX     61 2 9369 1853
EMAIL   mail@adventureassociates.com
WEB     www.adventureassociates.com

**AURORA EXPEDITIONS**
Level 1, 37 George Street
Sydney, NSW 2000
**AUSTRALIA**
TEL     61 2 9252 1033
FAX     61 2 9252 1373
EMAIL   auroraex@world.net
WEB     www.auroraexpeditions.com.au

**NEW WORLD SHIP MANAGEMENT COMPANY LLC/CLIPPER CRUISE LINE**
7711 Bonhomme Avenue Suite 300
St Louis, MO 63105
**UNITED STATES**
TEL     314 721 5888
FAX     314 727 5246
EMAIL   smallship@aol.com
WEB     www.clippercruise.com

**HAPAG-LLOYD KREUZFAHRTEN**
Ballindamm 25, D-20095 Hamburg
**GERMANY**
TEL     49 40 3001 4798
FAX     49 40 3001 4761
EMAIL   info@hapag-lloyd.com
WEB     www.hapag-lloyd.com

**HERITAGE EXPEDITIONS**
PO Box 6282, Christchurch
**NEW ZEALAND**
TEL     64 3 3389944
FAX     64 3 3383311
EMAIL   hertexp@ibm.net
WEB     www.heritage-expeditions.com

**LINDBLAD SPECIAL EXPEDITIONS**
720 Fifth Avenue
New York, NY 10019
**UNITED STATES**
TEL     212 765 7740
FAX     212 265 3770
EMAIL   explore@specialexpeditions.com
WEB     www.expeditions.com

**MARINE EXPEDITIONS**
890 Yonge Street, 3rd Floor
Toronto, Ontario
**M4W 3P4 CANADA**
TEL     416 964 5751
FAX     416 964 2366
EMAIL   info@marineex.com
WEB     www.marineex.com

**MOUNTAIN TRAVEL-SOBEK**
6420 Fairmount Avenue
El Cerrito, CA 94530
**UNITED STATES**
TEL     510 527 8105
FAX     510 525 7710
EMAIL   olaf@mtsobek.com
WEB     www.mtsobek.com

**PELAGIC EXPEDITIONS**
92 Satchell Land
Hamble, Hants SO21 4HL
**UNITED KINGDOM**
TEL     44 1703 454120
FAX     44 1703 454120
EMAIL   skipnovak@compuserve.com
WEB     www.pelagic.co.uk

**QUARK EXPEDITIONS**
980 Post Road, Darien, CT 06820
**UNITED STATES**
TEL     203 656 0499
FAX     203 655 6623
EMAIL   quarkexpeditions@compuserve.com
WEB     www.Quark-expeditions.com

**SOCIETY EXPEDITIONS**
2001 Western Avenue, Suite 300
Seattle, WA 98121
**UNITED STATES**
TEL     206 728 9400
FAX     206 728 2301
EMAIL   Societyexp@aol.com
WEB     www.societyexpeditions.com

**WILD WINGS**
International House
Bank Road, Bristol BS15 8LX Avon
**UNITED KINGDOM**
TEL     44 117 9610200
FAX     44 117 9674444
EMAIL   wildinfo@wildwings.co.uk
WEB     www.wildwings.co.uk

**ZEGRAHM EXPEDITIONS**
1414 Dexter Avenue, Suite 327
Seattle, WA 98109
**UNITED STATES**
TEL     206 285 4000
FAX     206 285 5037
EMAIL   zoe@zeco.com
WEB     www.zeco.com

### Provisional members

**EXPEDITIONS INC**
1465 NW Baltimore
Bend, OR 97701
**UNITED STATES**
TEL     541 330 2454
FAX     541 330 2456
EMAIL   expeditions@exp-usa.com
WEB     www.expeditioncruises.com

**OCEANWIDE EXPEDITIONS**
Bellamypark 9, 4381 CG
Vlissingen
**THE NETHERLANDS**
TEL     31 118 410410
FAX     31 118 420417
EMAIL   expeditions@ocnwide.com
WEB     www.ocnwide.com

**PEREGRINE ADVENTURES**
258 Lonsdale Street
Melbourne, Victoria 3000
**AUSTRALIA**
TEL     61 3 9663 8611
FAX     61 3 9663 8616
EMAIL   AndrewP@peregrine.net.au
WEB     www.peregrine.net.au

If you find yourself in Stanley (Falkland Islands) and fancy a cruise to Antarctica, contact the Falkland Islands Company, who will be able to tell you of the next cruise ship coming through, and possibly book you a passage.

one resulted, not in disaster, but in a plane-load of passengers enjoying a splendid experience. Overflights passed quickly out of fashion after the crash, but were reintroduced in 1994 and are again proving very popular.

Would passengers survive a forced landing in Antarctica? It would be reasonable to ask the airline concerned what plans, if any, are made for this contingency. However, it is also reasonable to remember that, elsewhere in the world, hundreds of airline flights are made daily over wide expanses of ocean and inaccessible mountain ranges, and several flights each month pass over icy wastes in both the Arctic and the Antarctic. From none of these would chance of survival be high, but we make them without even taking out extra insurance. Are tourist flights over Antarctica significantly more dangerous?

## Adventure travel

More adventurous airborne travel is provided by Adventure Network, a Canadian company with offices in Seattle and the UK, that will fly you practically anywhere you want in Antarctica, and charge you accordingly. AN flies parties of climbers to the Ellsworth Mountains, birdwatchers and photographers to emperor penguin colonies, skiers and man-hauling sledgers to the South Pole. With a team of experienced pilots and groundcrew, working mainly from the South-American sector, they have maintained an excellent safety record over many years.

## Antarctica by sea

Over 95% of recreational visitors (as tourists seem to be called these days) to the Antarctic region travel by sea. Of these, over 90% voyage by cruise ship from southern ports in South America, visiting the South Shetland and South Orkney Islands, and Antarctic Peninsula. Some extended cruises take in the Falkland Islands and South Georgia, and rather fewer, involving icebreakers, include the South Sandwich Islands and ice-bound Weddell Sea coast. A very few each year start from South America and cruise to the Ross Sea, or circumnavigate the continent completely (Figures 3.1–3.4).

Smaller numbers of cruise ships start also each year from southern ports of Australia or New Zealand, visiting stations in the Ross Sea and along the extensive coast of East Antarctica. These cruises also take in some of the cold temperate and Antarctic islands of the Southern Ocean, including Macquarie Island south of Tasmania and Campbell Island and the Auckland Islands south of New Zealand. Cruise ships heading southward at the start of the Antarctic season and northward at the end sometimes offer interesting 'repositioning cruises' that may include Tristan da Cunha, Gough Island, South Georgia and the Falkland Islands.

Do you want a luxury cruise on a liner, with orchestras, entertainers and casinos? Do you want more of an expedition kind-of-cruise, with excellent cuisine and comfort, but less entertainment and more education? What about a no-frills cruise, in a scientific research ship modified to take passengers in reasonable comfort with one cook, perhaps a very good one, instead of five chefs? A 2-to-3-weeks cruise or longer? An 8-day cruise that spends 2 days getting there, 2 coming back and just

**Figure 3.1** Explorer, *formerly* Lindblad Explorer *and* Society Explorer, *this ice-strengthened ship was built in the 1960s, especially for Antarctic cruising. Known affectionately as 'the little red ship', she carries about 80 passengers.* World Discoverer *(Figure 7.20) is similar but slightly larger.*

**Figure 3.2** Kapitan Khlebnikov, *a Russian icebreaker. Formerly an oceanic research vessel, this powerful ship has been refitted for polar tourism, and can safely penetrate polynyas deep into the pack ice. Equipped with two helicopters, she carries about 120 passengers.*

**Figure 3.3** Professor Molchanov, *named for a Soviet research scientist, is one of several smaller, ice-strengthened cruise ships that were formerly Russian research vessels. Comfortable, handy in shallow coastal waters, she carries about 45 passengers.*

**Figure 3.4** Marco Polo. *A cruise liner with cabarets, casinos and palm-court elegance. Deep-drafted, superficially more suited to tropical cruising, she has nevertheless operated safety as far south as 78°S in McMurdo Sound, and regularly carries 400 or more passengers to the Peninsula.*

4 days in Antarctica? Remember that, however long the cruise, you usually have to add a further 4 days at least for flights.

Apart from commercial cruise ships, research and resupply ships of some of the national expeditions from time to time take paying passengers to parts of Antarctica and some of the southern islands. For example, the French resupply vessel *Marion DuFresne II* makes four voyages yearly from the island of Réunion to Iles Kerguelen, Crozet and Amsterdam in the southern Indian Ocean. Expedition cruises are not widely advertised: the best source of information is the headquarters of the national expedition concerned.

Yet another way of travelling to Antarctica is by private yacht. Of a dozen or more yachts that leave Ushuaia and Punta Arenas each summer, several take individuals or small groups of paying passengers. This mode of travel has particular appeal for TV camera teams, photographers and naturalists who do not want to be constrained by the limited landings and tight itineraries of larger ships. A useful source of information is a book by Sally and Jerome Poncet (1991), who have sailed for many seasons in southern waters, and probably know the South-American sector of Antarctica better than anyone else. It makes good reading even if you never step aboard a yacht.

## To the southern hemisphere

Whether ultimately airborne or seaborne, most Antarctic travellers start from the northern hemisphere. The long flights from the United States, Europe or Japan are usually arranged by the tour companies and included in the overall price. Visitors to the South-American sector may find themselves routed through Miami or Los Angeles, preparatory to flying to Santiago, Chile or Buenos Aires, Argentina.

Early-season cruises occasionally leave from Montevideo, Uruguay or Buenos Aires, in ships that are making their maiden voyage of the season. Most cruises leave from points farther south in Tierra del Fuego, now almost exclusively from Punta Arenas, Chile, or Ushuaia, Argentina, requiring a further 3 to 4 hours' flying. In daytime these can be spectacular flights, the western route over the high peaks of the Andes, the eastern route over Patagonia and the Andean foothills.

A few cruises start or end in Stanley, Falkland Islands. Visitors starting from Britain can fly directly from RAF Brize Norton, on a flight of 12 to 14 hours that stops for refuelling at mid-Atlantic Ascension Island. Passengers starting from the USA or UK may also fly to Stanley via Santiago.

Those visiting the Ross Sea and Australian sectors are routed through Hobart (Tasmania, Australia), or Lyttelton or Bluff (New Zealand). Australians and New Zealanders opting for the South-American sector have to fly to Santiago or Buenos Aires. Their flight may take them in daylight over part of East Antarctica, though at 40 000 ft there is not much to see from the windows.

Flights from Europe, Japan and North America to the port of departure seldom occupy less than 2 days, usually involving at least two changes of aircraft, immigration and customs clearance. Most companies try to arrange flights that get you to the port of departure as quickly and cheaply as possible, though not always as comfortably. The better ones provide their group travellers with airport couriers, club or hotel day-room facilities where there are delays between flights, or if necessary an overnight booking in a good hotel.

You do not have to travel south with the tour operators. Some travellers prefer to make their own arrangements, which may include starting earlier, ending later, and seeing more of the southern hemisphere en route. With the companies sightseeing is likely to be minimal: the most you are likely to get is a coach tour around town or to a national park with local guides—an agreeable and informative diversion between stages of the journey. Making your own arrangements usually costs more but gives you more scope for side-trips. Some tour companies are happy to advise on local agents who will if necessary arrange your further travels.

A few brave souls reach Punta Arenas or Ushuaia by their own means of travel and book for Antarctica on the spot. If lucky, especially early or late in the season, they may find an under-booked ship and secure a cut-rate passage to Antarctica. If not, they explore Tierra del Fuego or move on.

It may be worth noting that all seaborne bookings to Antarctica on commercial cruises are currently round trips. Unless involved in a scientific research programme approved by your government, you cannot generally leave your ship and stay ashore in Antarctica, even for a few days. One or two tour companies are trying to remedy this by providing accommodation ashore for a few days at scientific stations, tidying up or taking part in the scientific work, or camping. More options to stay ashore for purposes other than science will almost certainly come.

## Health, travel insurance

There is a story that in 1914, recruiting for the Imperial Transantarctic Expedition, Sir Ernest Shackleton advertised in the press offering '. . . bitter cold, long months of complete darkness, constant danger, safe return doubtful . . .'. I doubt if the story is true. That is an ad-man's view of Antarctica, not an experienced traveller's; Shackleton would not have wanted anyone aboard who did not expect to return safely. Wear the sentiment on your T-shirt if you like, but take a cooler view when you are thinking about your own Antarctic trip.

Of the thousands of travellers who make it to Antarctica each year, many are elderly and not especially fit. Many, for that matter, are young and not especially fit—you can be overweight, flabby, and not used to exertion as easily at 25 as at 75. Most of these modern travellers return from Antarctica happy, weary, but safe, and without a scratch.

A few—a very few—die on board, usually of heart conditions or other medical problems that they brought with them. They could just as easily have died on a long-distance flight across the USA. A few—again a very few—go home on stretchers or in splints. Of these, some have succumbed to long-standing complaints that have caught up with them on board. Most others have sustained accidents. I mention a few possible accidents in Chapter 4, but people are good at thinking up new ones for themselves.

If you have long-standing medical conditions that may flare up and incapacitate you, remember that Antarctica is a long way from anywhere else. If your condition is likely to create a medical emergency on board, consider if it is worth the risk to yourself and to your fellow passengers. Your ship's medical facilities are likely to be very limited. Should your health create an emergency, the ship may have to break schedule and return you to civilization, and that could spoil other people's vacations as well as your own.

Note particularly that your ship will hold very limited stocks of drugs and medicines. If you have special requirements, bring with you all that you will need, plus 50% extra in case you are held up somewhere. You may be able to stock up at your port of departure, but do not count on it. Carry your medicines with you along the way in case you lose your baggage. If you need to take them every few hours, carry a small supply with you on landings, in case you are stuck ashore for a few hours by bad weather. Keep them in an emergency ready-bag (p. 71), to grab if the ship goes down. Who needs a ready-bag? I'll bet even money that the Captain has one.

Medical insurance? Read the advice that your tour operator offers, and read carefully the small print of your contract with them. Remember that a relatively small accident might result in the need for expensive treatment before you return home. A worst-case emergency could involve treatment on board, hospital treatment in South America, evacuation by air ambulance, more hospital treatment at home, and a long convalescence. Medical insurance does not come cheaply, but neither does this kind of medicine. Several companies specialize in travel insurance for the over-60s.

So it's all too risky and you'll cancel your holiday of a lifetime in Antarctica. Where will you go instead? Miami, New York, London, Paris, Florence? Have you read the newspapers recently? Have you checked last month's statistics on traffic accidents, muggings, gangland murders, crazy guys with bombs, air pollution? So you'll go to the tropics instead. What about insect bites, heat stroke, tropical diseases, floods, warfare, revolutions, killer bees? Wise folk play safe and go to Antarctica. But they make sure they have good medical insurance coverage, and a Band-aid or two in their ready-bag.

## Further reading

Poncet, S. and Poncet, J. 1991. *Southern Ocean Cruising Handbook*. Published privately (available direct from authors, Beaver Island, Falkland Islands).

Travel brochures. Write to travel agents and Antarctic tour operators at their addresses, get their brochures and study them carefully. They are beautifully produced, and make excellent reading for a winter's evening. Apart from everything else, this will show you the wide range of opportunities available, and help you to make a wise choice.

# Chapter Four

# On our way: The South American sector

## Introduction

Most tourists who visit Antarctica do so by sea, and nearly all travel from South America to South Georgia, the South Orkney and South Shetland Islands and Antarctic Peninsula—the so-called South American sector (Map 2). Why is this the favoured route? First, because Tierra del Fuego is relatively easy to reach by scheduled flights from North America (where most of the passengers originate), and second, because the 2-day sea passage from there to a starting point in the

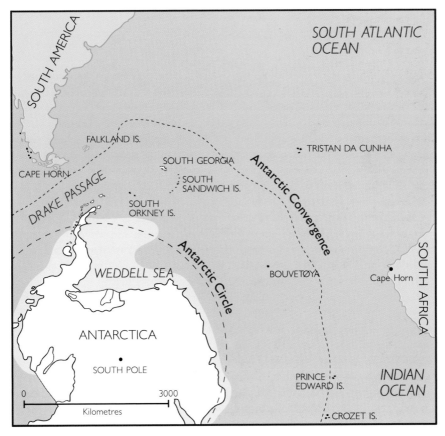

**Map 2**  *South American sector.*

Antarctic region is the shortest possible—less than half that to be endured between Antarctica and any other continent. The shorter the sea journey, the longer passengers can stay in the Antarctic, which is what they are paying for.

A third reason is the area itself. To any but a glaciologist with fascination for ice cliffs, the South American sector is by far the most interesting, most beautiful and most varied of the whole Antarctic region. It lacks only direct associations with the 'heroic' age of exploration, though it compensates amply with many less heroic historical associations, and is in all other respects by far the most interesting sector.

Tierra del Fuego is not over-inhabited, and has few ports that are capable of providing even basic services for passenger ships. As ships bound for Antarctic waters began to appear, three ports in the region became possible contenders for business—Ushuaia in Argentina, and Punta Arenas and Puerto Williams in Chile (Map 3). Stanley, in the Falkland Islands, was an outside runner. There was little competition. Only the three commercial ports could hope to deal with the impending traffic, and Ushuaia, on the Beagle Channel, won handsomely. It expanded to meet the challenge, and has the immense natural asset of being a day's sailing closer to Antarctica than its rivals.

## Ports of departure

### Punta Arenas

A small city of considerable though faded dignity, Punta Arenas is the main port of the historic Strait of Magellan. Founded in 1849 on a sandy point on the western flank of the strait, the settlement replaced Fort Bulnes, a small timber stockade set up 5 years earlier to mark Chile's claim on the Magellanes region. German settlers, later to be joined by immigrants from Britain and the Balkans, farmed the region and developed the port as a coaling and provisioning station for ships passing between the Atlantic and Pacific Oceans. In addition Punta Arenas exported local produce of timber and wool, and became a fishing and naval port.

Planned on a generous scale with a central park and wide roads, the town reached a peak of prosperity in the late 19th and early 20th centuries, the period from which many of its most imposing buildings date. The Panama Canal, opening in 1914, diverted much of its international trade, and Punta Arenas declined to the status of a small port and market town. Fortunes of its current population (about 120 000) have recently revived with the discovery of offshore oil nearby.

The town has an all-timbered cathedral, an unusual concrete Parthenon (close to the dock gates), and pleasant central gardens with labelled local trees and shrubs. A bronze statue of Ferdinand Magellan, surrounded by recumbent Indians, dominates the main square. The highly polished toe of one of the Indians reflects local folklore: kiss the toe, and you are ensured a safe passage on your next sea journey. Many Antarctic tourists have reason to swear by it.

Tourist information is dispensed at a friendly office in Plaza de Armas, and many tourist agencies provide specific information on their own products, from scenic flights to pony trekking. There are several interesting museums within walking distance of the quay. Museo Regional de Magallanes, close to the central Plaza de

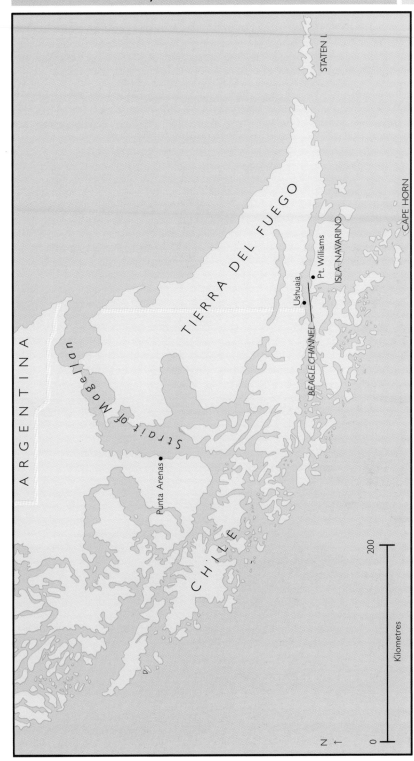

**Map 3** *Tierra del Fuego.*

Armas, is a mansion furnished in the style of a prosperous turn-of-the-century expatriate family. The Instituto de Patagonia shows farming implements and vehicles of the same period, and the museum of Colegio Salesiano displays the natural history of the area and the decline of local Indians under European rule. There are market stalls with local produce and handicrafts, old bookshops and antiques. Punta Arenas is an interesting place for browsing on a sunny day.

For those with more time to spare there are day-long excursions to see Magellanic penguins along the coast, and restored Fort Bulnes, the original settlement, just over an hour's coachride away. Though superficially bleak and uninviting, Tierra del Fuego has extensive forests, mountains, lakes and waterways, with rich native flora and avifauna (see Ushuaia). These can be sampled during longer coach excursions to Puerto Natales and Parque Nacional Torres del Paine, where trekking, camping and climbing are catered for.

## Ushuaia

Known locally (at least in the tourist trade) as the city at the end of the world, Ushuaia stands in a sheltered bay on Isla Grande de Tierra del Fuego, which forms the north shore of Beagle Channel (p. 67), in a picturesque setting of forested mountains close to the Chilean border (Figure 4.1). Originally a Fuegian Indian fishing settlement, with a name meaning 'bay that is open toward the west',

**Figure 4.1** *Cape Horn, southernmost point of an island off the south coast of Tierra del Fuego. In good weather you can see a small Chilean naval station and albatross monument at the eastern end of the ridge. Landing is possible on the north side of the island, but only with prior permission..*

Ushuaia in 1869 became an outpost of the British South American Missionary Society, and a centre for several British estancias (ranches) in the area. On 12 October 1884 the South Atlantic Expeditionary Division of the Argentine Navy founded the township that established Argentine government control over this corner of Tierra del Fuego.

The settlement remained tiny until 1902, when it acquired a federal prison for long-term convicts, who were put to work in the surrounding forests. The town grew as a port and naval base, expanding in the 1940s under a policy of subsidized immigration. The jail closed in 1947, the buildings first becoming part of the naval station, and later reopening as a museum. Ushuaia's current population is about 30 000.

In the 1980s Ushuaia became the administrative capital of the Province of Tierra del Fuego, Antarctica and the South Atlantic Islands. In 1982 it attracted Centro Austral de Investigaciones Científicas (CADIC), a scientific institution that specializes in anthropological and biological research in the Fuegian region. By providing bunkering, water and hotel accommodation, and recently extending its airfield to take large passenger aircraft, the city has effectively captured the rapidly growing Antarctic tourist traffic, which in summer dominates its activities as a seaport. Tax incentives and federal funding are attracting new light industries to the area. Currently the city is adding suburbs and shanty towns that sprawl toward the surrounding hills.

Ushuaia is also an important centre for local tourism. The city information centre (located at San Martin 600), and the Fuegian information centre (Maipu 505) have handouts offering a wide variety of local tourist activities, taking anything from a couple of hours to several days. If you are considering an excursion, be warned that Ushuaia's weather is unreliable and may quickly become atrocious. Even on a calm summer's day be prepared for sudden shifts to gales and rain squalls.

The simplest outing is a self-guided walk around the rectangular grid of the old port, within easy reach of the quay, viewing some of Ushuaia's early houses. A locally formed heritage group has labelled many of them with historical information in Spanish and English. Though building materials were scarce and expensive, early settlers managed to raise small, attractive dwellings clad in flat or corrugated iron, with minimal but very effective timber decorations.

Note in your travels the valiant efforts of the municipal gardener (whose vocation cannot be a rewarding one) to plant the parks and public highways with trees, shrubs and attractive flower beds, in the teeth of Fuegian gales. Take great care on the streets. From fellow-pedestrians and motorists you will receive nothing but consideration. However, something goes seriously wrong with concrete in Ushuaia, and whatever it is badly affects the pavements. Pounding the sidewalks, especially after a light fall of snow, is good training for landing on Antarctic beaches. There is an interesting local museum at Maipu (the shore road) and Rivadavia, and the old prison often mounts a worthwhile art or craft exhibition.

Longer excursions include all-day trekking in nearby Valle de Tierra Mayor, and coach outings to Lapataia in Parque Nacional Tierra del Fuego, on the Chilean border. Tierra del Fuego has about 500 native species of flowering plants including orchids, yellow violets, daisy-flowered senecios, and delicately scented campanillas, many of which can be seen in town close to the roadsides.

There are also some 200 species of breeding birds, augmented by a few species of summer migrants from North America, and both native and introduced mammals. For seabird spotting consider a half-day or full-day excursion by cabin cruiser or catamaran to islands in Beagle Channel (Canal Beagle) where there are also breeding sea lions. Some 10 species of seabirds breed on islands between Ushuaia and Islas Becasses 60 km to the east, including kelp and dolphin gulls, gentoo and Magellanic penguins, imperial and rock cormorants, South American terns, Chilean skuas and both Magellanic and common diving petrels. Some day cruises go as far east as Estancia Harberton, one of the early British farming settlements. Longer overnight cruises take you to westward and north to Punta Arenas.

### Puerto Williams

Isla Navarino forms the southern, Chilean shore of Beagle Channel, and on it stands Puerto Williams, a small settlement that is occasionally used by tours ships for transferring passengers by air to Santiago. Starting as a sawmill (said inevitably to be the world's southernmost) and an outlet port for timber, the township expanded slightly in 1953 to become a naval base. It also acquired an airstrip which, together with the small jetty and a pleasant little hotel for daytime stopovers, is its chief attraction for Antarctic tour operators. While Ushuaia is the world's southernmost city, Puerto Williams is the world's southernmost town.

A quiet, curiously attractive little township in a setting of wooded mountains, Puerto Williams offers only a few tiny shops, some short trails into the forest, and a small but interesting museum displaying Indian relics and local flora and fauna. Some of the few remaining Yahgan Indians live at the east end of the settlement.

However, a walk along the main street reveals one outstanding relic of great interest to Antarctic buffs. There, set in concrete, is the bow of *Yelcho*, the tiny Chilean naval tug that in 1916 rescued Shackleton's party from their stranding on Elephant Island (p. 138). Alongside is a bust of her captain, Piloto Pardo, rightly considered a Chilean naval hero.

### Stanley

See Falkland Islands (Chapter 5).

## Starting off

Ships leaving Punta Arenas in the evening for South Georgia and the Falkland Islands pass eastward through flaring oil rigs to the Atlantic Ocean. Those heading directly for Antarctica head south past Cape Froward (the southernmost point of mainland South America) through Canal Cockburn to the edge of the Pacific Ocean, then immediately double back southeastward into the sheltered waters of Beagle Channel.

These channels form part of a complex of fjords, formerly ice filled but now heavily forested. Their British names are a reminder that the area was charted originally in the 1820s and 1830s by Captain Robert FitzRoy RN, in HMS *Beagle*. On the second voyage (1831–36) *Beagle* carried a young theologian, Charles Darwin—a naturalist on the threshold of his career. Darwin's name is commemorated in the main cordillera, icefield and a peak; Cerro Fitzroy was named for the captain.

The forest extends upwards to open fells and snowfields. There is not a lot of wildlife to see in these southern channels. Watch out for shags, dolphin gulls, condors (usually sailing very high above the peaks): in the water you may be lucky enough to see otters, sea lions and dolphins. Be ready to photograph five spectacular glaciers on the port side. The westernmost is named for the French scientific ship *Romanche*, that explored the area in 1882–83. The next four are named Allemagne, Français, Italie and Polsk from the nationalities of the scientists on board. All these glaciers have retreated considerably during the past few years: only the Romanche now reaches the sea.

Continuing eastward we keep Argentina to port and Chile to starboard. Watch out for Ushuaia on the port side: ships starting from Punta Arenas usually pass it toward the end of the first day, with its spectacular harbour and mountain backdrop lit by late evening sunshine. However, these days most journeys to Antarctica start from Ushuaia, again usually in the evening when the wind has dropped and the sky cleared.

Moving eastward down the channel, note the scattered ranches and tiny settlements cut from the forests along either shore. Some 25 miles along on the Chilean side we see the houses and quay of Puerto Williams. The channel becomes tortuous, dotted with islands, reefs and lighthouses, with an occasional wreck to remind us that even these calm waters hold traps for the unwary. About 6 hours from Ushuaia we feel the ship lifting to a slight surge. This marks the end of the channel, where we drop the pilot. Often he provides a pleasing diversion by leaping into a launch that comes alongside at full speed.

While we are still in sheltered waters it is customary to hold the obligatory ship safety drill. However tired you feel after your journey south, do not be tempted to dodge this. It makes very good sense to know how to wear your life jacket, how to get up to the boat deck, and how you will be expected to enter the lifeboat. Dress warmly: evenings are cold in the Beagle Channel, and could be a whole lot colder should we have to abandon ship in Antarctica. The drill may fire your imagination: what would you need to take with you in emergency, to survive 2 or 3 days in an enclosed lifeboat? Band-aids? Medicines? A good novel? Chocolate? Brandy? Spare gloves? Whatever you decide on, pack it in a ready-bag and keep it handy. Cruise ships have a safety record second to none, but you've embarked on a holiday with an element of danger attached: it makes sense to play as safe as you can.

## Sea sickness: Ship safety

From here onward we emerge from the shelter of the southernmost islands, and the swell increases steadily. If you are liable to seasickness, this is a good point to take your pills. You are entering a part of the world where you may encounter seriously rough seas. While seasickness is seldom fatal, it is an unpleasant, curiously demoralizing illness, for which there is no certain cure.

If you know that you are liable to seasickness, be aware from the start that different ships vary considerably in their degrees of movement. Some are very stable, others less so, depending on the shape, length, depth and other built-in factors. In general terms, the larger the ship, the less violent the movement. Big cruise liners fitted with stabilizers, for example, tend to be very steady in all but the most lively seas. However, big icebreakers with rounded hulls and high superstructure tend to roll and pitch, sometimes more so than smaller research ships for which stability may be a key design factor.

Once aboard and at sea, there are many remedies, mostly in the form of pills that limit your perception of movement, and many of which have side effects that include drowsiness. If you have no previous experience of these remedies, buy a selection and try them until you find the one that suits you. Whatever you take, it is usually best to start early, before you begin to feel the effects of movement. Start with a good sleep: with luck, after 7 or 8 hours in your bunk, you may wake to find yourself a seasoned traveller.

Take plenty of fresh air, and solid meals if you can. Many travellers have their own remedies that do not include pharmaceuticals. Mine is an evening tot of brandy and ginger ale, which I strongly recommend.

Sea sickness is one problem: more serious are the mechanical hazards found around any ship—curious bits of iron and timber sticking out in unlikely places, waiting to catch the unwary. They are bad enough with the ship tied up in port: once we start rolling and pitching they leap into action, and cause the kind of damage that can spoil your holiday. Watch out for slippery decks (especially slick after a light fall of snow) and metal bits to trip over. Hold on to deck rails and bannisters. Watch out for swinging doors: avoid holding on to doorframes, where a door can slam and trap your fingers—a surprisingly common and very painful accident.

When the ship becomes lively, do not trust the chair you are sitting in, unless you are certain that it is anchored down. Be careful crossing open spaces. In a particularly rough sea I have seen a heavyweight passenger fly headlong across the width of a bridge and end up in the corner—despite warnings, he was intent on taking a video shot instead of holding on. With him he took the Captain and Second Officer, who were not pleased and asked him to leave. In bad weather the decks may be declared off-limits: stay indoors. In really bad weather you may be advised to stay in your cabin. Do so: nobody will thank you for wandering at large and breaking your leg.

## Cape Horn

Some ships head immediately south: others move south-westward to arrive off Cape Horn early in the morning. This is often the best time to see the Cape, in early light. It is also likely to be the calmest, if a landing is contemplated.

The Cape, a massif of reddish-brown granite (Figure 4.1), forms the exposed southern flank of a small island, Isla Hornos. Though known earlier to southern navigators, it was first rounded in January 1616 by the Dutch merchantman *Eendracht*, commanded by Willem van Schouten. The Cape was named for Hoorn, a town in the Netherlands where Willem was born: it was the name also of a companion vessel, commanded by Willem's brother Jan, which had earlier caught fire and sunk.

Isla Hornos, which is the southernmost point of the Americas, is Chilean territory. On a green hilltop to the east stands a small meteorological station manned by four or five naval ratings: ships approaching close usually call them up by radio and seek permission to sail within territorial waters. There are also a chapel and lighthouse and, on a headland close by, a striking monument of cast aluminium with a cut-out representing an albatross in flight. This was erected in 1992 as a memorial for seamen who have lost their lives in rounding the Horn.

With Chilean permission and calm weather it is possible to land below the station. The ship lies off the northeast corner of the island, where the Zodiacs can run into a sheltered cove. A steep wooden staircase leads up the cliffs. At the top of the staircase take care to turn left: turning right leads you into a minefield that the Chileans laid in the early 1980s under threat of Argentine invasion. No one seems very clear whether the mines are still functional; do not become the one who finds out. You can visit the station and chapel, meet the meteorologists and their two or three large, amiable woolly dogs, buy souvenirs, sign the visitors' book, and walk an easy path to the albatross memorial. The vegetation is wind-sculptured scrub, waist-high and usually muddy underfoot. Watch out for Magellanic penguins in the undergrowth.

## Heading south

From Cape Horn we head south across the Southern Ocean. Wind and swell are usually from the west, which is a good recipe for rolling. However, 'west' can mean anywhere from southwest to northwest, and that makes quite a difference. If they are from southwest, we may be partly heading into them, which slows us down and can be uncomfortable. Northwesterly wind and sea help us along, and shorten the journey by a few welcome hours.

The crossing takes anything from 40 to 60 hours, depending on sea (Figure 4.2), swell, wind—and economics. Ships seldom travel at their fastest speed: each has an economical cruising speed that gives good progress without overspending on fuel. Then good timing is essential: there would be no point in travelling fast just to reach our destination in the middle of the night. You can mark progress by going up to the bridge (most cruise ships have an open-bridge policy, which makes you welcome there) and checking the chart. The navigation officer will have marked in the course he hopes to take, and every few hours—usually at the end of each 4-hour watch—one of the officers will have marked in the position actually reached along the course.

The bridge is very much a working space: do not mistake it for the ship's social centre. You will be welcome on it so long as you observe the normal courtesies. Enter and leave without banging the doors (a small point, but stand on the bridge for half an hour when people are coming and going, and you'll see why).

**Figure 4.2**   *The Drake Passage may be flat calm, but more often strong winds and swell combine to give rough seas. Be prepared for two days of rolling and pitching. If you take pills to ward off sea sickness, take them before you reach this stage, which is 7–8 on the Beaufort Scale (opposite).*

Bid good-day to those on watch, speak quietly, and keep out of the way. Don't fiddle with any of the switches, buttons or knobs: one passenger I knew set off the engine-room sprinkler system, and doused the Chief Engineer. Entertain your friends elsewhere: a noisy conversation can be very disruptive.

Ask questions only when everything is quiet—not when the officers are preoccupied with something else. As in any other business, expect different responses from the people you meet on the bridge. Some officers may welcome a chat (and if foreign, a chance to try out their English), and an opportunity to explain their work. Others may need to think, or brood, or simply to concentrate on the job. It is their space: let them make the running.

There is usually a great deal to do on board. On a well-run cruise you will receive plenty of guidance about what to do and when to do it. Find your way to the lecture room, library and bar. Stay alert for announcements over the loud-hailer system. Make friends: there are interesting folk aboard. Attend as many meals, lectures and briefings as you can. Read the daily handouts. Get out on deck as much as possible. Watch the birds and try to identify them. Learn the Beaufort Scale of wind strength (Box 4.1), so you'll know when a gale is blowing. Keep an eye open for whales.

If you are feeling seasick, be glad you are not on a slow, creaking sailing ship on a diet of salt pork, hard tack and weevils, watching the rats chasing the cockroaches around your cabin. Your ordeal will last only for hours. If you have nothing better to think about, work out how much it is costing you per minute. Does that make you feel better or worse? Endure it with the certainty of better times to come.

## Box 4.1  Beaufort wind and sea scale

This scale was invented in 1805 by Commander Francis Beaufort RN, who wanted to set standards of wind force at sea. He had no means of measuring wind speeds, so the original scale was based entirely on how winds of different strengths affected sailing ships and disturbed the sea surface. The scale has been used and developed over the years since then, and still provides a very good way of estimating wind strength from sea conditions.

Conversions:  knots (nautical miles per hour) to statute miles per hour,  multiply by 1.15
knots to kilometres per hour,  multiply by 1.84
knots to metres per second,  divide by 2
metres to feet,  multiply by 3.3

| Beaufort No. | Wind speed (knots) | Description of wind | Sea No. | Wave height (m) | Description of sea surface |
|---|---|---|---|---|---|
| 0 | <1 | Calm | 0 | 0 | Sea like a mirror |
| 1 | 1–3 | Light air | 0 | 0 | Ripples like scales, without foam crests |
| 2 | 4–6 | Light breeze | 1 | 0–0.3 | Small wavelets: crests appear glassy but do not break |
| 3 | 7–10 | Gentle breeze | 2 | 0.3–0.6 | Large wavelets: crests begin to break. Foam glassy, scattered white horses |
| 4 | 11–16 | Moderate breeze | 3 | 0.6–1.2 | Small waves becoming longer: fairly frequent white horses |
| 5 | 17–21 | Fresh breeze | 4 | 1.2–2.4 | Moderate waves, lengthening: many white horses, slight spray |
| 6 | 22–27 | Strong breeze | 5 | 2.4–4 | Large waves start to form: white foam crests extensive everywhere, moderate spray |
| 7 | 28–33 | Near gale | 6 | 4–6 | Sea heaps up. White foam from wave tops blown in streaks along wind: spindrift appears |
| 8 | 34–40 | Fresh gale | 6 | 4–6 | Moderately high waves, lengthening. Edges of crests break into spindrift. Foam is blown in streaks along the wind |
| 9 | 41–47 | Strong gale | 6 | 4–6 | High waves: dense streaks of foam along the wind. Sea begins to roll: spray limits visibility |
| 10 | 48–55 | Storm | 7 | 6–9 | Very high waves with long crests: large patches of foam blown in streaks along wind. Sea rolls markedly, surface appears white: spray limits visibility |
| 11 | 56–63 | Violent storm | 8 | 9–14 | Exceptionally high waves: sea covered with long patches of foam: edges of wave crests blown into foam: spray limits visibility |
| 12–17 | >64 | Hurricane | 9 | >14 | Air filled with foam and spray. Sea surface white with driving spray: visibility seriously limited |

## Landings

On the evening before the first landing, the expedition leader will give a briefing on landing procedures. This is another important occasion, not to be missed. A very few landings will be at quays or jettys, where you walk ashore dry-shod. But these are expedition cruises: you are far more likely to be landing from Zodiacs (inflatable boats), on beaches or rocks, which can be daunting and dangerous if you are ill-prepared, but easy enough when you know how.

You will be told how to dress—warmly, with waterproof pants and gumboots, wearing the special inflatable life jackets that usually hang in the cabins, with cameras and binoculars safety stowed in backpacks or under clothing. It is important to keep hands free for holding on. You'll be briefed on how to wait in the foyer, descend the gangway (Figure 4.3) holding on with both hands, and wait at the bottom until the boat crew are ready to help you. Stepping from gangway to boat is easy in calm conditions, a little more tricky if there is a swell and the ship is rolling. You'll be shown how to grasp forearms, not hands, as you are helped into the boat, and sit down immediately where you are directed.

**Figure 4.3** *Landing. The gangway is lowered: the order has been given. Dressed warmly and booted for a wet landing, with cameras safely stowed in pockets and backpacks, passengers have descended and are ready to move off in the Zodiac inflatable boat.*

**Figure 4.4**  *Zodiac preparing to land. These boats (generally called Zodiacs, though made by several manufacturers) are driven by a powerful outboard engine. Very stable, with several separate airtight compartments and an excellent safety record, they carry 12–14 passengers.*

A Zodiac holds about a dozen passengers and driver (Figure 4.4). There is a can of high octane fuel aboard, so strictly no smoking. The driver, operating a powerful outboard, is in charge. He or she will ask you not to stand up, for example to take a photograph, without asking permission, particularly when the boat is moving. Zodiacs are much safer than they look, and remarkably stable. But if a dozen people stand up together and the driver swerves, everyone ends up in cold water.

Landing is usually easy. The driver runs up to the shore, where boat handlers are waiting to hold the boat, and everyone slides along to swing out in turn over the bow. If there is a strong surf, they may bring the boat in stern first. Either way, you will be told exactly how and when to get out between waves, and avoid filling your boats with water.

## Further reading

Reader's Digest. 1985. *Antarctica: Great Stories From The Frozen Continent.* Surrey Hills NSW, Reader's Digest Services Pty.

# Chapter Five

# The Falkland Islands and South Georgia

## Introduction

Though distant from continental Antarctica, these islands are often included in Antarctic cruise-ship itineraries, and provide ecological stepping-stones to the much colder, barer lands of the far south. Geographically the Falklands stand in the South Atlantic Ocean and are cold temperate islands. South Georgia, though only slightly farther south, stands in the Southern Ocean and is a periantarctic island. The important marine boundary called the Antarctic Convergence (Map 2) runs diagonally between them.

Climatic differences between the two groups are due primarily to differences in temperature of the surrounding seas, which directly or indirectly influence their mean temperatures, levels of permanent snow, lengths of growing season, soils, vegetation, and many other aspects of their ecology. Both islands appear green at sea level, but the Falklands have a much wider range of soils, habitats and plants. Both support huge colonies of breeding birds, but missing from South Georgia are the wide variety of land-feeding birds that twitter from every Falkland's bush. All but four species of South Georgia's birds feed exclusively at sea.

The Falklands are currently farmed and support a population of about 2000, plus a military garrison of similar size to keep the Argentines at bay. South Georgia was never farmed, though horses, cattle and sheep were grazed from time to time, pigs were kept under cover to feed the whalers, and introduced deer are flourishing. However, it was formerly the centre of a substantial whaling industry. Its current population is a small army garrison (again to keep the Argentines away), plus four or five civilians including a harbour master and museum guides. These may be replaced by a predominantly scientific group.

## The Falkland Islands

### Geography

Lying 600 km (370 miles) east of Patagonia, this is a compact group comprising two large islands, East and West Falkland, fringed by myriad lesser islands—officially over 400 (Map 4). Extending 260 km (160 miles) from east to west and 140 km (87 miles) from north to south, they include about $12\,000\,\text{km}^2$ (4690 sq. miles) of land. The islands are low-lying and far from exciting at first appearance. The rocks are ancient (palaeozoic and mesozoic) sediments, mainly quartzites,

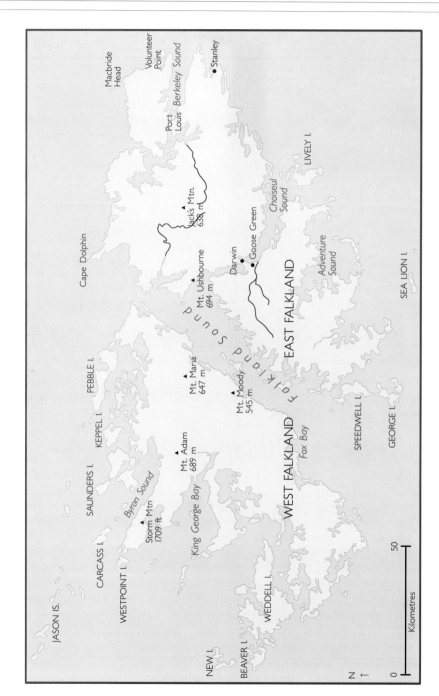

**Map 4** *The Falkland Islands.*

sandstones, mudstones and shales, planed and smoothed by weathering to rolling moorlands. Their highest points are Mount Usborne (705 m, 2312 ft) on East Falkland and Mount Adam (700 m, 2297 ft) on West Falkland.

Steep cliffs 100 to 200 m high (330 to 660 ft) form the western coasts of many of the western islands. Eastern coasts tend to have gentler shores, including many kilometres of white sandy beaches. Between lie rolling moorlands interspersed with bare rock outcrops: guidebooks ask you to note especially the 'stone rivers' of rock fragments extending downhill from many of the higher peaks, a distinctive feature of the islands. The hills become snow-covered in winter but there is no permanent ice. Former glaciation seems to have been restricted almost entirely to the highlands. The moorlands are peaty (below) but there are only a few thick deposits: like earlier Falkland settlements, Stanley was sited on the shores of a sheltered harbour with good peat—the islands' only fuel—on the nearby hills.

## Climate

These are cool temperate islands, damp and windy, with mean annual temperature 5.8°C, range of monthly mean temperatures 7.1°C. Annual precipitation is 60 cm, much of which falls as fine rain, sleet, hail or snow: expect one or the other—quite possibly all four—practically every day. Snow falls frequently, but seldom settles for long except on the uplands. Winds are strong (annual mean about 17 mph, 7.6 m/sec) and persistent, usually from west or northwest. Travellers who arrive in summer during one of the frequent depressions, encountering hail, sleet and half a gale, go away wondering how the 'kelpers', as Falkland Islanders are called, manage to survive in so miserable a climate. If summers are like that, what on earth are winters like? In fact the seasons are fairly similar, with mean temperatures only slightly lower in winter, and winds only slightly stronger. At any time of the year may come a bonus of clear sunny weather, almost windless, with brilliant blue skies—ideal for tramping over moorlands or beachcombing. Experience one or two of those, and you'll understand why the kelpers quite enjoy their islands.

## Soils and vegetation

Thin soils, and thick, patchy deposits of peat support heath, scrub and grassland close to the coast, and moorland or fellfield of low-growing shrubs and cushion plants on higher ground. On ungrazed islands stands of tall tussock grasses line the shores and lower slopes: most of the Falkland Islands must have looked like that before they were burnt and heavily grazed. There are no native trees: the tallest vegetation is shrubs of boxwood or fachine growing 2–3 m (6–9 ft) high. The flora includes many algae, lichens, mosses and ferns. There are 164 species of native flowering plants, notably tussock and other grasses, rushes and shrubs, with many tiny but attractive flowering plants including marigolds, sea pinks, marsh daisies, orchids and yellow pansies. The native flora competes with over 90 species of flowering plants introduced accidentally or for forage. Coasts are fringed with beds of marine algae, including spectacular forests of giant kelp that grow over 50 m (160 ft) long.

## Birds and mammals

The 63 species of birds that breed on the Falkland Islands include six species of penguins (probably more than anywhere else in the world), 12 species of albatrosses and smaller petrels, and over 30 species of land-feeding birds. The seabirds form spectacular colonies, now mostly on the western islands remote from Stanley. The land birds show strong affinities with species on the South American mainland, from which most are clearly derived.

A single species of land mammal, the warrah or native fox, disappeared from the main islands during the 19th century, due to hunting. Introduced mammals include rats, mice, rabbits, hares, Patagonian foxes, marine otters, guanacos, sheep, goats, pigs, horses, cattle, and domestic dogs and cats.

Marine mammals ashore on rocky coasts include southern sea lions and Falkland Island fur seals: on beaches look out for southern elephant seals. In the harbours and among the islands you may see leopard seals, killer whales, long-finned pilot whales, dusky and hourglass dolphins, Peale's and Commerson's dolphins, and spectacled porpoises.

## History

The islands were discovered in 1592 by a British mariner, John Davis, and subsequently visited by sealers and fishermen from many countries. French fishermen from St Malo called them Iles Malouines, from which the current Argentine name Islas Malvinas is derived. A French settlement was established in 1764 at Port Louis, followed by a British settlement at Port Egmont in 1766. A year later French interests in the islands were sold to Spain, which in 1770 evicted the British colonists and established Spanish colonists in their place. The Spanish settlement closed in 1811, leaving cattle, horses and other domestic animals roaming ferally.

Following wars of independence in South America, Daniel Jewitt, an American adventurer, established a settlement at Port Louis in November 1820 on behalf of the newly-formed Provincias Unidas de Sud America. His colony quickly disappeared. In 1829 the Provincia de Buenos Aires renewed both the claim and the colony, appointing Louis Vernet as governor. In 1831 Vernet made the political mistake of seizing three US sealers and demanding hunting fees from them. On 31 December of the same year the US naval sloop *Lexington* stopped by, evicted the governor and his entourage and dismantled the settlement. The Provincia sent out a new governor, whom the disgruntled settlers murdered. In December 1832 Captain John Onslow, in HMS *Clio*, revisited Port Egmont and re-asserted the almost-forgotten British claim to sovereignty.

The current settlement originates from a British occupation that began at Port Egmont in 1833. The first British colonists included Scottish crofters, who made use of peat for domestic fuel, grew potatoes, raised cattle, pigs and horses, and cropped sheep wool for export. Gorse and fast-growing conifers were introduced to provide windbreaks and fencing. Burning and grazing made severe inroads into the original vegetation, including the arcades of tussock grass that were once a feature of island coasts. In 1845 the seat of government moved to the capacious harbour of Port Stanley which, during the late 19th century, became an important naval base and a focal point for shipping en route for Cape Horn and the west coast of the Americas. The colony's prosperity declined after the Panama Canal opened in 1914, and the population, by then numbering about 2000, found itself isolated and impoverished.

Argentina's claims to the islands precipitated an armed invasion on 2 April 1982. After an occupation lasting 74 days (John Smith's (1984) book *74 Days* tells the story of the occupation) a British task force liberated the islands on 14 June. A large military airport was built and a garrison installed, and British funding was provided to broaden the economy, supporting offshore fisheries control and tourism. The Falkland Islands currently remain a Crown Colony of the United Kingdom, administered by a Governor-in-Council and locally elected Executive Council. The population are predominantly British and determined to remain so. About half live in Stanley, the rest are spread in farming communities across the 'camp' or countryside. Sheep farming is still the major industry, though important revenues now come from leasing fishing rights and servicing the fishing fleets of other nations. There is known to be oil in the maritime area surrounding the islands—no doubt a consideration in the sovereignty issue. The Falkland Islanders did not relish being invaded, and their hostility to Argentina dies hard. Only recently has a total ban on visits to the islands by Argentinians been lifted, and a direct air link re-established. Argentinians are equally determined that the Islas Malvinas are theirs.

## Landings on the Falkland Islands

### Clearance to land

All ships need to obtain customs and immigration clearance before landing parties on the Falkland Islands. Yachts are required to seek landing permission from Port Stanley. For cruise ships approaching from South America that want to visit West Falkland first, an official is usually flown out to await the ship at the first point of landing.

All land on the islands is owned privately or publicly, and permission has to be obtained from owners before parties can be landed. In the West Falklands visitors are made welcome by arrangement currently at three islands—New, West Point and Carcass. In the East Falklands landings are possible in Port Stanley, the islands' capital and only town, at Volunteer Point (Figure 5.1), where there are Magellanic and gentoo penguins and a small but spectacular colony of king penguins, and at Bleaker and Sea Lion Islands off the east coast.

### New Island

In the southwest corner of the group, New Island is a narrow, convoluted island some 12 km (7.5 miles) long, low along its eastern shore but rising to steep, 200 m (600 ft) cliffs in the west. The landing is on a sheltered, sandy beach at the Settlement, a cluster of small houses and sheds that are the only human habitation. Visitors are likely to be welcomed by one or both of the island's owners,

**Figure 5.1** *Magellanic and gentoo penguins await the early-morning arrival of a cruise ship at Volunteer Point, Falkland Islands. This is usually the calmest time of day: later heavy surf may make landing on the beach difficult or impossible.*

Ian Strange and Tony Chater, both naturalists, artists and writers, who live on the island in summer and are always pleased to show visitors around.

New Island has a long history of human occupation. In the late 18th century it became one of several centres used by American whalers and sealers. Nearby Coffin, Penn, Fox and Barclay islands were named for prominent Quaker seafaring families. About 1812 Captain Barnard of Nantucket built a stone shed ashore, a few hundred metres north of the Settlement, which still stands and is probably the Falkland Islands' oldest historic building. Throughout the 19th century sealers took fur seals and oil-hunters took penguins from the extensive colonies. From the 1860s the island was leased for farming: sheep and cattle were liberated to graze the moorlands. In 1908 a small whaling station was built in South Harbour, the bay south of the Settlement, by Salvesen and Co. of Leith. It was not a success, and much of the equipment was in 1916 shipped to South Georgia.

Since 1971, when New Island was acquired by its present owners, the grazing stock has been progressively reduced. From 1977 Ian and Tony have administered it independently as two reserves, New Island North and New Island South, with slightly differing management objectives but a common desire to see the island protected in perpetuity and used only for education, field research, and the appreciation of ecology and conservation. Both owners have publications and other mementos to sell in aid of their conservation work. Count yourself lucky if you can buy signed copies of Ian Strange's (1992) *Field Guide to the Wildlife of the Falkland Islands* and Tony Chater's (1993) *The Falklands*, both excellent books.

New Island is rich in wildlife, with over 35 species of breeding birds. Along the

**Figure 5.2**   *Part of a mixed colony of several thousand rockhopper penguins and black-browed albatrosses, breeding together in a gully on the weather side of New Island, one of the western Falkland Islands. The albatrosses take off from the cliff tops: the rockhoppers have a long walk to reach the sea.*

shore look out for fur seals, southern sea lions, and gentoo and Magellanic penguins. From the Settlement there is an easy 20-minute walk over the moors to a spectacular, steep-sided amphitheatre in the western cliffs, lined with the nests of several thousand rockhopper penguins and black-browed albatrosses (Figure 5.2). During the walk watch out for predatory striated and crested caracaras, browsing upland and ruddy-headed geese, shrill-voiced pied and black oystercatchers, and diminutive tussock birds, Falkland thrushes and long-tailed meadowlarks.

## West Point Island

This is a rounded, rolling island some 8 km (5 miles) long, lying in the Wooly Gut, a deep tidal channel off the north-west corner of West Falkland. Formerly called Albatross Island, it was well known to 19th-century sealers and penguin hunters, and in the late 1870s was one of the first of the outlying islands to be occupied and farmed. The pioneer settler, Arthur Felton, ran sheep, cattle and horses on land that turned out to be unusually fertile. His great-nephew, Rod Napier, continues the tradition by grazing some 1500 sheep, which produce an annual crop of fine wool.

On a warm sunny day West Point Island has the feel of South Devon or the Kerry coast. Rod and his wife Lilley live in the family homestead, tucked securely alongside a natural harbour on the north shore. Homestead and farm buildings are ringed by gorse hedges, that blaze throughout December with brilliant, scented blooms. Beyond the hedge is a barely discernible airstrip, used by inter-island aircraft to bring visitors, and keep Rod and Lilley within easy reach of Stanley. Isolated they may be, but seldom lonely: West Point in summer is a popular port-of-call for cruise ships and visiting yachts.

At anchor off the harbour, watch out for Peale's dolphins, fur seals and sea lions, all of which seem to use Wooly Gut as a freeway. It is an easy landing at a concrete jetty close to the shearing shed, or on the cobbled beach alongside: this is one of the few landings where it is possible to step ashore dry-shod. A short walk up a grassy slope leads to the homestead, with flagstaff and sheltered garden. From there several paths—little more than sheep-tracks—head off around the island.

The recommended excursion is a leisurely walk of about 30 minutes over close-cropped turf to the wilder, western side of the island, where there are steep cliffs and colonies of rockhopper penguins and black-browed albatrosses. Rod provides Land-Rover transport for all but the last few hundred metres. A further 10-minutes' walk takes parties to a point where they can overlook a small breeding colony of fur seals. Here the wind is usually strong, raising a powerful swell that beats against the foot of the cliffs. On the walk back the wind is usually behind us, and the prospect of a generous homestead tea beckons.

### Carcass Island

Named after one of the two Royal Navy ships that established the first British settlement on the Falkland Islands (January 1776), this is a small but typically beautiful island of the western group. Some 10 km (6 miles) long, it lies off the north-western corner of the Falklands, steeply cliffed at its western end but lower and more accessible in the east. The island is owned and farmed by Rob and Lorraine McGill, who live in a cottage homestead close to the beach, tucked into the corner of a bay on the sheltered southern shore. The homestead is surrounded atypically by a shelter-belt of introduced pine trees, within which nest a colony of native black-crowned night herons. Rob and Lorraine welcome visitors who come by prior arrangement, and lay on a splendid afternoon tea.

The best way to appreciate Carcass Island, especially on a fine day, is for parties to land on the broad sandy beach close to the southern point, and wander in a desultory way toward the homestead (Figure 5.3). There are many good things to be seen on the way. The beach itself is a haunt of Magellanic and gentoo penguins, steamer ducks, two species of oyster catchers, Falkland skuas, Dominican gulls and kelp geese. The strandline is marred by plastic fishing nets, ropes, banding and squeezy-bottles, mostly from the fishing fleets that work offshore (Figure 5.4). But fossick about and you will soon be joined by completely fearless tussock birds and Cobb's wrens, which feed on sand-hoppers. They appreciate having some of the debris moved so they can get at the hoppers.

In the belt of tussock grass above the strand look out for slightly smaller southern grass wrens. Move slowly and quietly through the tussock, and you will almost certainly come across groups of Magellanic penguins (Figure 5.5), taking the air at the mouths of their burrows. Shy birds, they disappear underground if they see you first, often to lie in the entrance to their burrows, twisting and turning their heads. Do not be tempted to put your fingers within reach: they have very

**Figure 5.3**   *Landing on Carcass Island, western Falkland Islands. This is one of many small islands with steep cliffs forming the western, weather shore (Figure 5.2), and sandy beaches in the east. A stroll through the tussock grass brings you to colonies of Magellanic and gentoo penguins.*

**Figure 5.4**   *Plastic debris accumulates on the beaches of the Falkland Islands, most of it attributable to offshore fishing fleets. Among the debris, watch out for nesting oyster-catchers, snipe, and very tame wrens and thrushes foraging for sand-hoppers.*

**Figure 5.5** *Magellanic penguin with half-grown chick. These are timid birds, that wander freely across the beaches, but disappear quietly among the tussock grass if you approach. Sit still for a few minutes and watch, and you may see one emerge, like this, with one or two chicks.*

sharp, serrated bills. Seemingly unoccupied burrows may contain nests and brooding birds. Again do not be tempted to explore: the burrows are usually longer than an arm's-length, and often full of fleas.

On the hillside is a colony of gentoo penguins, nesting in the open in full visibility. These are similar to gentoos you will see in Antarctica, but a slightly larger northern subspecies. A few hundred metres beyond are the sand dunes that mark the northeastern side of the island. Return in the direction of the southern shore, then head across the grazed pasture toward the homestead. You will have walked a few kilometres over fairly easy firm ground, and earned your splendid tea. On the way back to the ship you may well be picked up and escorted by a posse of Peale's dolphins.

## Volunteer Point

A low sandy spit on the approaches to Stanley Harbour, Volunteer Point has a single claim to fame: it is the site of the Falkland Islands' most celebrated colony of king penguins. Formerly the islands had many communities of kings, but all were destroyed by oil-hunters during the 19th century. Today there are several small colonies in out-of-the-way places, known only to local naturalists who keep quiet about them. Volunteer Point has the one acknowledged colony—currently of about 220 breeding birds, which has grown from a tiny nucleus over a period of about 30 years. This is an exposed site—a length of pale golden beach without a semblance of shelter, where any kind of wind or swell produces spectacular rollers. Landing for visitors is never certain: the most likely conditions are to be found in the early morning after a few hours or days of calm weather—all too rare on the Falklands. Ashore are gentoo and Magellanic penguins, oystercatchers and kelp geese: watch out for flightless steamer ducks, that swim in small family groups just beyond the surf.

There is a raised strand line sculptured by winter storms, and beyond it a broad plain of turf, well mown by sheep and geese. Tread carefully and keep in line, for the sandy soil is riddled with shallow burrows of Magellanic penguins. There are several colonies of gentoos and plenty of plovers, oystercatchers, gulls and land birds trying to distract your attention. A kilometre or so farther inland is gathered the single group of king penguins that most people have come to see.

Kings stand about 75 cm (30 in) tall, a whole size larger than the gentoos and Magellanic penguins nearby. They breed in the open on grassy sward or bare soil (Box 5.1). Come prepared with plenty of colour film. Singly or en masse, king penguins in fresh plumage are unbelievably photogenic, with blue-grey suits, white and golden-yellow shirt fronts, black head, golden-orange throat patches, brown eyes, and black bills with pink and purple plates (Figure 2.10). Garish? Well, you and I wouldn't get away with it, but they do. Nobody complains: everybody photographs them madly.

Theirs is a complex breeding cycle, basically because they are large birds that take over a year to rear their chicks. Their colonies are not, therefore, so tightly synchronized as those of most other species, with everyone nesting, courting, laying, incubating and tending chicks at the same time. At Volunteer Point in October and November you see large woolly brown chicks left over from last season (Figure 5.6), some already growing their juvenile plumage. Tending them are adults in old worn plumage, others in full moult with feathers flying in all

**Figure 5.6**   *King-penguin chicks about 1 year old, in the final stages of moulting from brown overwintering down to seagoing juvenile plumage. For an account of the complex breeding cycle of this species see Box 5.1.*

## Box 5.1  King penguins breeding

King penguins have a complex breeding cycle. Because they are large birds, their chicks take between 10 and 12 months to mature from egg to independence. Chicks are nurtured by their parents through the winter, sometimes well into spring. Most parents cannot therefore breed annually like other penguins. Early-season visitors to a colony in October and November will thus see chicks in brown woolly down from the previous season, almost fully grown but as yet unmoulted or only partly moulted, being fed and preened by parents in shabby old plumage. Alongside them will be adults in full moult, and others again in smart new plumage, that have started the new season's courtship, laying and incubating.

Moulting birds are easily recognized. Penguins change all their feathers at once, taking 2 to 3 weeks over it. New feathers push the old ones out, so the moulting bird stands in a pool of tattered old feathers, looking thoroughly self-conscious and uncomfortable. Only at this point do you realize just how many feathers go to make a penguin. On several species I have counted there are about 11 per square cm (70 per square inch), with far denser coverage on neck, shoulders and head. When the last feathers have been replaced, the penguin goes to sea, feeds for about a week, and comes back ready for action.

Courtship takes 2 to 4 weeks. The newly returned birds find partners and display, crowing ecstatically, walking tall with necks extended, heads flagging from side to side and orange patches flashing. They mate frequently, the female lying prone, the male balancing precariously on her back. Between bouts of activity they find quiet corners and sit in companionable silence, like lovers the world over. There are no nests: soon after it appears, the single egg is taken over by the male, who holds it on his feet under a fold of feathered skin, slumping into a relaxed position that is easy to identify. Father holds the egg for 2 to 3 weeks while mother recovers at sea. Thereafter the parents alternate, until the egg hatches at around the 54th day.

Eggs laid early in the breeding season (say mid-November) hatch in late December or early January. Throughout this period the colony changes: last year's chicks moult into juvenile plumage (a pale, washed-out version of adult plumage: Figure 5.6) and leave for the sea. Relieved of responsibility, their parents moult, fatten and court: if it is still only February, March or April, they may lay again, though late-hatched chicks have little chance of surviving the winter.

Chicks of early breeders grow quickly, graduating from a first coat of grey-brown plush to brown woolly down which lasts them through autumn and winter. The colony in winter consists almost entirely of these chicks, whose parents return to feed them at 2 to 3-weekly intervals. Not surprisingly they lose weight, and only those that were fat enough in May or June will survive to spring. Parents that loose their chicks become the early breeders of the following season.

directions, and others again in smart new suits, already well into courtship, mating and incubating. The order behind this seeming disorder is explained more fully in Box 5.1.

## Stanley

Founded in the mid-19th century on the western shore of a fine enclosed harbour, Stanley (for long Port Stanley, though nowadays the 'Port' is usually left off) has remained the only settlement above hamlet size on the islands. A town of slightly more than 1000 inhabitants, it retains the feel of a working village that has striven for a time to grow, then thought better of it (Figure 5.7). The site was chosen for its inner and outer harbours (which between them could accommodate half the Royal Navy) and proximity to extensive peatbeds that provided the domestic fuel. In sailing-ship days the sweet smell of burning peat wafted far out to sea, warning fog-bound mariners that the Falklands were close at hand.

A street plan of Stanley shows a simple grid of roads, with everything in walking distance. Several stores sell groceries, chocolate, wines and spirits, stout boots, waterproofs, and items of cold-weather clothing that you may have forgotten to bring with you. There are shops that sell locally designed woolly jumpers, hats and gloves, books and souvenirs. Well-informed philatelists head straight for the post office, where there are usually new issues of stamps to be bought, both for the Falkland Islands and for the Falkland Islands Dependencies and British Antarctic Territory too.

**Figure 5.7** *Part of the waterfront, Stanley, Falkland Islands. In the foreground is the Anglican cathedral. The islands have no native trees, but conifers and other tough trees have been introduced to grow among the buildings, helping to create windbreaks.*

Several pubs sell warm beer or cold, and restaurants provide good fish and chips (this is, after all, a British community) and more exotic fare. A stroll along the harbour road takes you past Edwardian brick villas, painted wooden houses, and the rotting hulks, spars and guns of sailing ships that came into harbour and never left it. There is a mini-cathedral with an arch made of four converging whale ribs. Across the harbour lies the old naval dockyard, now disused, with the names of visiting ships picked out in white-painted stones. Beyond the head of the harbour stand the hills from whence, on 14 June 1982, came the army that liberated Stanley from the Argentine occupation force.

On the waters of the harbour you may see giant petrels, coveys of steamer ducks, and possibly cape petrels, that sometimes come in with the fishing boats. The hulks are usually decorated with roosting shags: on the foreshore look out for gentoo penguins, Falkland skuas, two species of oystercatchers, red-billed dolphin gulls, and the larger, more raucous Dominican or black-backed gulls.

The road winds on past a recently built war memorial that commemorates those of the British Forces who died in the Argentine war. There is a new hospital, and a sprawling villa that might house a suburban golf club, but is actually the colonial Governor's residence. Walk on toward the satellite dish that marks the communications centre, where you can telephone home. From the headland beyond rises an older war memorial, commemorating the naval Battle of the Falkland Islands, that occurred early in World War I. Just beyond the memorial, on the left, stands a brown wooden chalet that the Argentines built in 1982 to house their own governor. He hardly stayed long enough to appreciate it, so the chalet has become an excellent little museum (Figure 5.8) and a rewarding end-point to the walk.

**Figure 5.8**   *Stanley Museum. Built as a residence for the Argentine governor, the building houses a museum of Falkland Island history, life and wildlife. The collection owes much to the enthusiasm and care of its founding director, John Smith. Photograph: Ann Stonehouse.*

# South Georgia

## Geography

South Georgia is a banana-shaped island over 200 km (125 miles) long and up to 35 km (22 miles) broad, in the north-eastern corner of the Scotia Sea (Map 5). Approaching from the Falkland Islands, the first indications of land are a group of isolated outliers, Shag Rocks and Black Rock, some 250 km (156 miles) from the western end of the main island. Later appear Clerke Rocks, Willis Island, Cooper Island, and finally South Georgia itself (Figure 5.9). First impressions from the sea are of dark, looming cliffs interspersed with ice fields. On days of fog and low cloud (which are sadly all too common), that may be all the visitor sees. Most ships shape a course along the northern side of the island, which is better charted, more scenic, and less ice-infested than the colder southern coast. It also gives direct access to King Edward Point, the island's administrative centre, where a customs and immigration officer comes aboard.

Fine weather reveals the true majesty of the island. This is a block of serrated mountains like alps in mid-ocean: the highest point, Mount Paget, rises to 2934 m (9624 ft), and several other peaks of the central Allardyce Range rise above 2000 m (6500 ft). A central ice cap, constantly renewed by snowfall, merges into valley glaciers that descend to sea level. Fjords and bays, headlands and glaciers alternate along a deeply indented coast. Of a total area of 3750 km$^2$ (1464 sq. miles) about 60% is ice covered. This proportion is currently diminishing. Many glaciers that within living memory came down to the sea have now retreated several kilometres

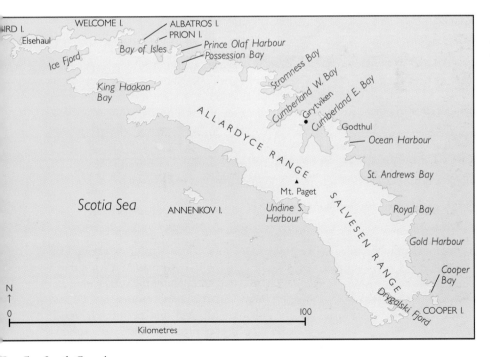

**Map 5** *South Georgia.*

**Figure 5.9**   *South Georgia's main settlement. In the foreground stands the government centre, King Edward Point. In the background is Grytviken, a derelict whaling station (see Figure 5.10). A memorial cross to British explorer Sir Ernest Shackleton stands on the hilltop to the right.*

inland, leaving extensive coastal moraines and shallow ponds. This is especially so on the warmer north side of the island.

South Georgia forms part of the Scotia Ridge, a series of folds in Earth's crust that effectively continue the Andean Cordillera southward. The folds pass through Staten Island (east of Cape Horn), continue eastward under the sea as the submarine Burdwood Bank, reappear at Shag Rocks and continue in a southeasterly direction through South Georgia. Thereafter they turn southward through the South Sandwich Islands, and westward through the South Orkney and South Shetland Islands and Antarctic Peninsula (Map 3). The rocks are mostly volcanic shales and tuffs, metamorphosed, folded, twisted, faulted, and heavily eroded by sea, frost and foul weather.

## Climate

Though in latitude similar to the Falkland Islands, South Georgia is surrounded throughout the year by water that is 6 to 7° cooler. In consequence it has a much colder climate. The weather is cool, wet and windy throughout the year, with mean annual temperature 1.9°C, range of mean monthly temperatures 6.8°C, and 140 cm of rain and snow annually. Winds blow strongly and persistently, much influenced by local topography. Damp westerlies hitting the windward coast rise over the mountains to become dry, gusty downslope winds on the east side. Snow may fall in any month. Close to sea level it accumulates thickly between May and

October, but disappears quickly in summer. Sea ice forms occasionally in sheltered bays during the winter, but seldom lasts more than a few days.

## Soils and vegetation

The island supports only 26 species of native flowering plants, ferns and club mosses. Tussock and other grasses form meadows in a narrow band along the coast, accumulating thin, peaty soils fertilized by sea spray and seabird droppings. Poor drainage gives rise to bogs in which rushes and mosses predominate. Beach sites are currently being invaded by expanding colonies of elephant seals, fur seals and penguins, all of which destroy the vegetation locally. On higher ground small shrubs, moss cushions and lichens form heathland, giving way to feldmark close to the snowline.

## Birds and mammals

Spectacular colonies of king, gentoo and macaroni penguins, together with albatrosses, mollymawks, and huge flocks of smaller petrels, breed among the tussock grass and scree slopes. Elephant seals and fur seals breed on many of South Georgia's beaches, both having recovered from 19th-century commercial hunting. Fur seals have made a remarkable comeback, from an estimated few hundred at the end of the 19th century to well over a million today.

There are no native land mammals. Norway rats and house mice introduced by sealers flourish among the coastal tussock. Whalers brought in cattle, sheep, rabbits, horses and reindeer. Fortunately only the reindeer survive: three herds browse freely on lowland vegetation and appear to be spreading.

Elephant and fur seals are the commonest seal species. Elephant seals form breeding groups in September and October. By the time summer visitors arrive in November much of the excitement is over and pups are leaving for the sea. Adults remain plentiful on the beaches and among the tussock, many accumulating in wallows to moult. Be alert for lone elephant seals if you are walking through the tussock. They have come ashore to sleep and do not appreciate being disturbed. Despite their bulk they are surprisingly agile.

Fur seals breed later, mature males coming ashore from early November. Pregnant females swarm ashore in late November, give birth, re-mate, and feed their pups during December and January. Young males that are excluded from the breeding colonies form clubs among the tussock grass. Take care to keep clear of fur seals: they bite each other hard, and will bite you if you stumble into them, however inadventently (p. 52).

Leopard seals are often seen hunting off penguin colonies. Some 15–20 Weddell seals are usually to be found lying on snowbanks in Larsen Harbour, off Drygalski Fjord, at the southeastern end of the island. This is the northernmost breeding area of a species that typically breeds on fast ice far to the south.

## History

The island was probably discovered during the 17th century, but was charted, named and claimed for Britain by Captain James Cook in 1775. From about 1790 it was exploited by sealers, whose hunt for fur seals and elephant seals continued sporadically throughout the 19th century. Elephant sealing under license continued until 1964. In 1904–05 South Georgia became an important centre of whaling, with several stations operating for different periods up to 1965.

South Georgia has no permanent human occupants, but has been occupied continuously since the opening of the first whaling station at Grytviken in 1904, and the nearby seat of government, King Edward Point. In 1925 the Discovery Committee established a scientific station at King Edward Point for studying whales being processed at the whaling stations. British Antarctic Survey operated a biological station at King Edward Point from 1969 to 1982, and a station for bird and seal studies continues to operate on Bird Island.

Claimed by both Argentina and Britain, South Georgia was invaded by Argentine forces in April 1982. The British task force relieved it after brief fighting some 3 weeks later. It is administered by the United Kingdom as a dependency of the Crown Colony of the Falkland Islands. Hence the small garrison and civilian administrative unit which is due to be replaced soon by scientists and a civilian administration.

## Landings on South Georgia

### Grytviken and King Edward Point

It is usually necessary for visiting ships to call first at these twin settlements, to obtain clearance from the customs and immigration officer. They lie in Cumberland Bay, a fine sheltered harbour halfway along the north side of the island. Grytviken was South Georgia's first whaling station, set up in 1905 by an Argentine and Norwegian consortium (Figure 5.10). The name means 'pot harbour'; the beach on which the station was built had been a campsite of early 19th-century sealers, who left some of their cast iron pots there. King Edward Point, just across the bay, was the seat of government, established in the following year. On the Point lived the magistrate, policeman, customs officer and postmaster, who between them maintained law and order and collected revenues from whaling.

Whaling ceased at Grytviken in 1964–65. The station was finally abandoned in 1971, and the few remaining whale-catchers, together with a floating dock, were scuttled at their moorings. The last magistrate left King Edward Point in 1969. Shore-parties from deepsea-fishing boats and other unauthorized visitors subsequently looted the whaling station and destroyed equipment. The Point continued as a scientific centre until the Argentine invasion of 3 April 1982, when, after a short, sharp battle, the tiny garrison of Royal Marines surrendered and they and the resident scientists were removed. A liberating force retook the Point on 25 April, but thereafter only the garrison and a few civilian staff were returned to the island. The wreck of an Argentine Puma helicopter, shot down during the invasion, remains on Brown Mountain, a short walk up from the whaling station, and defensive positions dug by the invaders can still be seen around King Edward Point. Special permission is usually needed to visit the Point.

The immigration and customs officer comes aboard, often accompanied by men

**Figure 5.10**   *Grytviken. Founded in 1905 and built up through the first half of the century, the station was active until the 1960s, processing many thousands of whales into oil and bonemeal. Take care as you walk around: many of the buildings are unsafe, shedding their corrugated iron in strong winds.*

and women from the garrison, who bring a portable post office that sells stamps and souvenir postcards. Ashore visitors may spend an agreeable half-day wandering through the abandoned whaling station and visiting the restored manager's villa, which has been converted to a museum (Figure 5.10). A souvenir shop sells mementoes, and behind the station stands a small white church, built in 1913 and now maintained by the garrison (Figure 5.11).

With the help of leaflets obtainable from the museum it is possible to see much of how the station worked. If you regard all whalers as thugs and whaling as the ultimate evil you will probably not be interested. However, here was practised— under great difficulty and with much ingenuity—an industry that was honoured in its time, employed many honest, hardworking folk (and probably a few rogues), and provided commodities that, for five or six decades, the world badly needed and was glad to accept. Take great care in your wanderings around the station: many of the buildings are unsafe and should not be entered.

Walk out along the southern shore toward the sealers' and whalers' graveyard. Watch out on the way for elephant-seal pups, that play wide eyed and solemnly in the freshwater culverts and streams: less than 2 months old, they are already up to 2 m ($6\frac{1}{2}$ ft) long. Some may still be feeding: their mothers come back from time to time to tend them. There are usually a few adult male elephant seals in wallows behind the beach, moulting, grumpy, and smelling memorably: if you take photographs, avoid using flash, which is said to disturb them, and try not to stand above them, which they interpret as a threat. On fine days there are often king and gentoo penguins, and shy pintail ducks in the tussock pools.

**Figure 5.11** *Whalers' church, close to Grytviken station. Built in 1913 in the Norwegian tradition, it provided services for the whalers, who were mainly from Norway, the Shetlands and Argentina. One of the few buildings remaining intact, it is currently maintained and used by the British garrison.*

**Figure 5.12** *Grave of Sir Ernest Shackleton, Grytviken. The explorer, who died here in 1922, is buried in the whalers' graveyard. The cross on the hill (Figure 5.9), visible as you enter the harbour, was built as a personal memorial by his shipmates.*

The stranded hulk is *Louise*, a three-masted sailing ship built in 1869, that brought the first consignment of coal to the station and was beached in 1904. She remained intact for many years, but was burnt out when members of the garrison played war games around her. Blue-eyed shags often perch on her remaining timbers, hanging their wings out to dry. In the cemetery are graves dating back to the early 19th century. At the back stands a granite pillar marking the grave of Sir Ernest Shackleton (Figure 5.12), who died here in his expedition ship *Quest* on 5 January 1922. His shipmates erected a memorial cross at Hope Point, which can be seen just beyond King Edward Point as you leave the harbour. The isolated cross on the hillside above the cemetery commemorates Walter Slossarczyk, third officer of the German expedition ship *Deutschland*, who was lost from a small boat in Cumberland Bay on 26 November 1911.

## Cumberland Bay

In the excitement of visiting Grytviken the splendour of Cumberland Bay itself is often overlooked. There are many alternative pleasant landings in both the eastern and western arms of the bay—Jason Harbour, Carlita Bay, Maiviken and Moraine Fjord, for example—and the vast, crumbling front of the Neumayer Glacier is worth several hours of anyone's time. On the far side of the eastern arm stands Barff Peninsula, an attractive, hilly stretch of country with many easy landings and pleasant walks. On fine days it is possible to ramble along streams, past lakes and tarns, across cols with splendid views of the bay on one side, the open sea on the other. Herds of reindeer, alien, damaging, but attractive to see, graze on the uplands. Sadly, official permission is needed, and cruise itineraries seldom allow the time and flexibility of schedule required for walking parties.

## Other whaling stations

South Georgia's other abandoned whaling stations have a lot to offer the industrial archaeologist, but are of limited interest to lesser mortals who have seen and absorbed Grytviken. Jason Harbour has little more to show than the remains of a small hut. Godthul represents the most primitive stages of processing, in which blubber was stripped from the whales alongside floating factories, with minimal on-shore facilities. Ocean Harbour was a more advanced station, with more permanent buildings, holding tanks and even a miniature railway. Both stations, in bays on the seaward side of Barff Peninsula, can be reached on foot from East Cumberland Bay. Prince Olav Harbour represents a still more advanced stage, with a plan or platform for cutting up the whales ashore, oil-storage tanks, and well-constructed timber buildings for the machinery and barracks for the several hundred seasonal workers. Leith Harbour and Husvik have all the elements of permanent, advanced stations that can now be seen more clearly (and safely) at Grytviken.

Stromness is richest in alternative interests. It is the station to which Sir Ernest Shackleton, Frank Worsley and Tom Crean descended after crossing South Georgia from King Haakon Bay on 19–20 May 1916. The waterfall that finally soaked the party is in there at the head of the valley, and the manager's villa is still standing, though only just. This is another good place for walking—idyllic on a fine day.

Reindeer browse peacefully among the abandoned ships' propellers and stacked harpoon heads: there is a gentoo colony on the hill behind the station, and a small, family-sized colony of fur seals breeds by the stream at the northern end of the beach. The colony will no doubt grow, but this is currently a place to see new-born pups without undue risk of a mauling.

Whaling stations (Box 5.2) were built in bays well known to earlier generations of sealers, whose camps, trypots (iron pots used to extract oil from blubber, and graveyards can still be found among the tussock grass. Many of these early relics that were clear during the whaling days are now becoming overgrown by tussock grass: within decades many will be lost altogether, and the early human history of South Georgia will be all the more difficult to read.

### Willis Islands and Bird Island

These islands at the western end of South Georgia were named by Captain Cook in 1775—the Willis Islands after the midshipman of HMS *Resolution* who first sighted the main peak, Bird island because of the 'vast numbers' of birds seen upon it. Passing cruise ships occasionally take time off to visit them, especially if there are ornithologists aboard; official clearance is needed. The Willis Islands are reputedly the home of some five million golden-crested Macaroni penguins, as well as innumerable grey-headed and black-browed mollymawks, wandering albatrosses, light-mantled sooty albatrosses, giant and lesser petrels, brown skuas, Dominican gulls and shags. The bird cliffs at the eastern end of Bird Island provide memorable views of mollymawks nesting and in flight. Many of the birds, including huge flocks of cape petrels, prions, storm and diving petrels and other small fry, feed locally in spectacular flocks that skim and settle around the ship.

Bird Island is an important centre of biological research. Bird and seal studies began in 1958–59 under biologist Lance Tickell, at a camp in Jordan Cove. The present station, run by British Antarctic Survey, has operated continuously since 1978. It is the site of important long-term studies of wandering albatrosses, mollymawks, macaroni penguins and other birds, and also of fur seals. A few cruise-ship visits to the station are allowed each year, when scientists are happy to explain their work and outline the global significance of their studies.

### Elsehul

In whaling days this harbour was an overnight haven for whale-catchers at the western end of the island. Bad weather gave crews an hour or two to go ashore and collect penguin eggs for breakfast, with never a fur seal in sight. In the 1960s it became a study site for British Antarctic Survey botanists, whose semi-derelict hut you see on the beach. Now Elsehul is a slum, epitomizing the explosion of fur-seal stocks and the damage that this engaging but overwhelming animal inflicts on the environment.

Fur seals visiting cities in Europe or North America might reasonably comment on humans in very much the same terms. However, the rich lowland vegetation that the botanists were studying has been almost completely destroyed by breeding animals, and the tussock right up to the skyline is heavily infested with immature

### Box 5.2   The whaling stations

After the initial success of Grytviken, Norwegian and British companies established further whaling facilities in harbours along the north coast of South Georgia—Husvik and Stromness in 1907, Godthul in 1908, Jason, Ocean and Leith harbours in 1909, and Prince Olav Harbour in 1911. Requirements were a sheltered deep-water harbour for mooring ships, flat ground for building, and a reliable supply of freshwater. Some began as sites for servicing floating factories and developed no further than sheds on the beach: others became fully manned processing stations.

Whale stocks around South Georgia were quickly depleted. Ocean Harbour closed in 1920 and much of its equipment was shipped to Stromness. Old-style floating factories were replaced by new factory ships with internal slipways. Jason Harbour was not used after 1926, Godthul closed in 1929. The 1931 depression hit the remaining land stations hard: Prince Olav Harbour and Husvik closed, and Stromness stopped processing whales to become a ship-repair yard. In World War II many of the tankers, transport and factory ships of the British and Norwegian whaling fleets were sunk or diverted to more urgent uses: Leith Harbour closed and only Argentine-owned Grytviken remained in operation.

The post-war years saw renewed demand for whale products: both Husvik and Leith Harbour reopened, and the three stations, together with Stromness, operated in friendly rivalry for almost two decades. Their end came during the 1960s, when cheaper substitutes for whale oil were found in a range and variety of vegetable oils. Stromness and Husvik closed in 1961, Grytviken in 1964 and Leith Harbour in 1965.

males. While their presence make it virtually impossible for visitors to land, Elsehul still provides superb Zodiac runs. The seals cavort and play happily among the kelp forests, and display their seemingly chaotic but obviously effective family life along the shore. Giant petrels float on the calm waters: some 5000 macaroni penguins and hundreds of mollymawks breed on the steep slopes by the harbour entrance. Look out for small groups of king penguins; they seem to be starting tiny breeding colonies in quiet corners that the fur seals have not found.

### Welcome Islets

Usually judged too steep for landings and dangerous in rough weather, on a calm day these provide another excellent Zodiac run (Figure 5.13). About 20 000 macaronis nest on the islands, together with shags, gulls and breeding fur seals—all very visible from boats close inshore.

### Rosita Harbour

Lying immediately behind the protecting arm of Cape Buller, this is another whaler's haven and anchorage, sheltered from westerly winds at the western end of Bay of Isles. Cruise ships occasionally anchor overnight, allowing a full day's exploration of the bay. On a still night there are interesting sounds to be identified:

**Figure 5.13** *Zodiac cruise in the Welcome Islets. Exposed to open ocean swells, these islets offer few safe landing points. On a fine day their teeming wildlife, including thousands of macaroni penguins not readily seen elsewhere, is well worth an extended Zodiac cruise.*

the yelping of adult fur seals on the nearby beach, the high-pitched howls of their young, and the musical braying of king penguins in their colonies on distant Paul Beach and Salisbury Plain.

## Prion and Albatross Islands

The Bay of Isles is wide open to swells from the north, which occasionally make landings difficult. Both popular landings, these islands can usually be approached from their southern side, where the swell may be less. However, within the past 2 or 3 years breeding seals have taken over their beaches, and it is not always possible to find a site where the local territory holders permit landing. Parties that get ashore face a climb up a stream bed through shoulder-high tussock grass (often wet: wear waterproofs) onto the windswept, rolling tops of the islands (Figure 5.14).

On the way up keep an eye open for pipits, South Georgia's only passerines or perching birds, that twitter like sparrows among the grasses. Introduced rats have driven them from the mainland, so you see them only on the islands. Look out too for incubating or brooding giant petrels: they nest in areas with a clear take-off run, and are readily disturbed, so keep well away from any you see. The tarns and lakes usually support delicate little South Georgia pintails, that quack engagingly like ducks the world over. On the tops hold onto your hat and keep clear of the cliff edges, not only to avoid being blown off (always an embarrassing experience) but because burrowing petrels nest there, and boots damage burrows. On a fine day

**Figure 5.14**  *Guides mark out a safe path through shoulder-high tussock grass on Albatross Island, Bay of Isles, South Georgia. Unlike the main island, the offshore islands are free of rats, and home to land birds, notably pipits and pintails, as well as many seabirds.*

either islet provides a splendid panoramic view of ice-capped Mount Ashley (1154 m, 3785 ft) and the Lucas and Grace glaciers that fall from it.

Then be prepared for an extraordinary experience—a close encounter with wandering albatrosses, the world's most majestic birds (Figure 5.15). Several dozen wanderers nest on either island: from a distance you see them as widely spaced white dots among the tussock. Magically for us, an approach by slow-moving parties of human visitors or individuals does not seem to worry them, or alter their behaviour in any way. On a fortunate day you will see couples and trios engaged in balletic courtship, adults incubating or resting on empty nests, and large, almost fully-fledged chicks from the previous year, anxiously watching the sky for parents bringing their next square meal.

Sit quietly at a reasonable distance from a nesting bird; stop talking, forget your camera, binoculars and troubles, and give these huge, wonderful birds a few minutes of your life—a few hours if the schedule allows. Be still, and you will do them no harm (Figure 5.16). They in return offer a curious tranquillity that may last a long time—perhaps for the rest of your life. Very few come away unmoved from a visit to the wandering albatrosses.

## Salisbury Plain

South of Albatross Island lies the long, exposed beach of Salisbury Plain. This often provides the wettest of wet landings, so make sure that cameras, chocolate bars and

**Figure 5.15**    *A wandering albatross incubates contemplatively among the tussocks on the rolling top of Albatross Island, South Georgia. Both partners take turns to incubate their single eggs for over 60 days, between watches making long foraging flights across the Southern Ocean.*

**Figure 5.16**    *Whether courting, nest-building, incubating or brooding chicks, wandering albatrosses pay only passing attention to visitors. Their chicks, fed at long intervals by both parents, take over a year to grow.*

**Figure 5.17** *Colonies of king penguins numbering tens of thousands are found in several of South Georgia's bays and harbours. The population has expanded rapidly in recent decades. Here three adults, seemingly indifferent, size each other up at the start of the breeding season.*

other valuables are safely tucked away in plastic bags. Scramble ashore wet or dry onto the sandy beach, and you will immediately perceive the attraction you have come to see—a vast colony of king penguins (Figure 5.17).

How many are there? Counting kings is notoriously difficult because of their curious breeding pattern (Box 5.1), and nobody so far as I know has recently estimated this colony, which extends across the plain and high up the hillside beyond. My guess is a total of well over 30 000 pairs. Visitors in November and December see wild-looking brown individuals (once thought to be a separate species of 'woolly penguin') that are chicks from last season. They are waiting for their parents to return from the sea with cropfuls of fish, squid, krill, or whatever else passes for breakfast. Side by side with the chicks are suave adults in full breeding plumage, whose preoccupation is quite clearly to make provision for the next crop of chicks: courtship and mating are rife on all sides.

Eggs appear from early November onward, the incubating birds forming nuclei of peace and quiet within the colony. If you wander into the colony area, keep clear of groups of birds that are standing together a flipper-length apart, in slumped postures. Each is incubating a single large egg on its feet. Some will be awake but drowsy, others fast asleep. A sleeping bird that wakes suddenly, to see something new and unexpected nearby, may drop the egg in panic and run: so will its neighbours, leaving eggs on the ground as a feast for skuas.

Take care not to leave, as I once did, a small camera unattended among incubating kings. Any that have lost their eggs tend to take up stones or other foreign objects from the ground to hold in the brood pouch, and a small 35 mm

**Figure 5.18** *King-penguin chicks hatch between December and March, and remain in the colonies throughout winter. By the following November they are almost ready to moult into juvenile plumage (Figure 5.6) and leave for the sea. Photograph: Ann Stonehouse.*

camera seems to fit very well. Playing guess-who's-got-the-camera with a dozen or a hundred sleepy king penguins can take up a lot of your day.

Adult king penguins, like scientists at Antarctic stations, have generally too much on their minds to bother with visitors. Chicks are less sophisticated, and at this stage exemplify insatiable curiosity toward anything new in the colony. Sit still for a moment and they will gather round, inspecting your shoelaces, pecking gently at hair, rucksack or gloves (Figure 5.18). They seem happy to meet you, and not to mind having their photographs taken, but soon grow bored and move on (Figures 5.19 and 5.20).

### Possession Bay

Cruise ships sometimes call in because this is the bay where Captain James Cook landed in January 1775, claiming South Georgia for his sadly troubled monarch George III. No on-the-spot evidence of his visit has been reported from the beach. Cook was born near Whitby, Yorkshire, in a northern latitude close to that of South Georgia in the south. He would have had reasonable expectation of finding, in such a latitude, a land not unlike his homeland, with rich potential for colonization. Instead he found '... a savage and horrible country', where '... not a tree was to be seen, nor a shrub even big enough to make a toothpick'.

He was puzzled that '... an island no greater than this, situated between the latitude of 54° and 55°, should, in the very height of summer, be in a manner wholly covered many fathoms deep with frozen snow ...', and speculated on the existence of a vast, cold continent awaiting discovery in the south. Though still

**Figure 5.19**  *Hungry king-penguin chicks, having survived on meagre rations throughout winter, rely on frequent visits from their parents to fatten in spring. Here a yearling, already well fed, pesters its parent for more.*

**Figure 5.20**  *King-penguin chicks, waiting for their parents to return with food, are often curious and ready to approach humans. This one has an interest in boots. The photographer has learnt to sit still in a corner of the colony and let the penguins approach her.*

hopeful of finding the continent, Possession Bay and South Georgia convinced him that, '. . . to judge of the bulk by the sample, it would not be worth the discovery'.

## St Andrews Bay and Gold Harbour

Toward the southern end of South Georgia, these two very similar bays accommodate large colonies of king penguins. Each has a glacier, a stream, a broad sandy beach, a hinterland with a few kilometres of ground suitable for walking, and a headland to the north that affords some protection from prevailing winds. Both are wide open to swell, and can be visited only on relatively calm days. Both are well worth a visit, if only because breeding fur seals have not yet worked their way so far south, and the beaches are relative free of them. The seals that grace the shore are elephant seals. Despite being ugly, grumpy, and smelly, they are less aggressive and make far better company.

If you see a much thinner, sleeker seal with large head, slim body and narrow flanks, it is likely to be a leopard seal. Usually solitary, they attach themselves to colonies and prey on penguins. You will almost certainly see evidence of their hunting in empty skins washed up along the strand. Ashore they are not aggressive to people or penguins, but treat them with respect and keep clear. A seal that can figure out how to skin a penguin could shake you out of your parka in no time at all.

## Royal Bay

Between St Andrews Bay and Gold Harbour lies Royal Bay, site of yet another king-penguin colony, and also of gentoo penguins and blue-eyed shags. Visitors sated with birds (do such exist?) might prefer an excursion to Moltke Harbour, in the north-east corner of the bay, where a German geophysical and biological expedition led by Dr K. Schrader spent an industrious year in 1882–83. The expedition formed part of the International Polar Year, a cooperative programme of research later to be echoed by the International Geophysical Year 1957–58.

The party landed on 20 August 1882 from the three-masted naval steam corvette *Moltke*. Over 100 men cleared a site of snow and built a prefabricated station, leaving 11 scientists and technicians to complete a full year's observations of meteorology, tides, astronomy, magnetometry, gravimetry and a dozen other disciplines. The station stood for over 50 years: its remains can still be traced among the invading tussock.

## Cooper Bay

Off the south-eastern corner of South Georgia stands Cooper Island, named by James Cook for his First Lieutenant, Robert Palliser Cooper. You cannot land there—it is a scientific reserve. The channel that separates it from the mainland is Cooper Sound, and on the mainland itself lies Cooper Bay, a complex of three shallow bays of great beauty and interest (Figure 5.21). On low, grass-covered cliffs along the northern flank of the bay are several colonies of macaroni penguins, some of the few on South Georgia that can readily be visited without a steep scramble.

**Figure 5.21** *Though most chinstrap penguins breed farther south in the Scotia Arc, one large colony occurs in Cooper Bay, toward the eastern end of South Georgia. The colony has expanded from a few hundred in the 1950s to several thousands, creating space for itself among the tussocks.*

On the southernmost point is a colony of chinstrap penguins, which are rare on South Georgia and again not easily visited. The bay between has a hinterland of rolling grassy plains and uplands—altogether a delightful corner for picnicking on a fine day.

## Drygalski Fjord and Larsen Harbour

The southern end of South Georgia is made up of parallel chains of mountain peaks aligned north-west–south-east, of which the highest form the Salvesen Range. Ice-capped Mount Carse (2331 m, 7649 ft) and the twin tops of Mount Macklin (about 1860 m, 6100 ft) tower above spectacular Drygalski Fjord, a deep enclave 13 km (8 miles) long, less than a mile wide and sheer-sided, terminating at the junction of Risting and Jenkins glaciers.

Near the entrance to the fjord lies the narrow, bent finger of Larsen Harbour, a far narrower channel that winds into the heart of the mountains on the southern side of the fjord. This was the haven for whale-catchers working the rich whaling grounds east of the island. Buoys moored in the entrance were used for the temporary attachment of whale carcasses. 'Buoy-boats' (usually superannuated catchers) collected and towed the carcasses to the whaling stations, while the catchers went off for more.

Not far inside Larsen Harbour lives a small but surprisingly constant population of 20 or more Weddell seals, a species that is elsewhere found almost entirely on the fast ice of much colder Antarctic coasts. Several of them, in grey or brown dappled coats, are usually to be seen sleeping—practically always on snow banks—on either side of the channel.

Beyond the harbour the channel shallows quickly, providing an interesting Zodiac run to the cliffs of Philippi Glacier at its head. This excursion on a fine sunny day, followed by a slow cruise down Drygalski Fjord, makes a memorable ending to a South Georgia visit.

## Further reading

Carr, T. and Carr, P. 1998. *Antarctic Oasis: Under the Spell of South Georgia.* New York and London, W. W. Norton & Co.

Chater, T. 1993. *The Falkland Islands.* St Albans, Penna Press.

Davis, T. H. and McAdam, J. H. 1989. *Wild Flowers of the Falkland Islands.* Bluntisham, Bluntisham Books.

Headland, R. K. 1984. *The Island of South Georgia.* Cambridge, Cambridge University Press.

Murphy, R. C. 1948. *Logbook for Grace.* London, Robert Hale.

Rankin, N. 1951. *Antarctic Isle: Wildlife in South Georgia.* London, Collins.

Shackleton, E. H. 1919. *South.* London, Heinemann.

Smith, J. 1984. *74 Days.* London, Century Publishing.

Strange, I. 1992. *A Field Guide to the Wildlife of the Falkland Islands and South Georgia.* London, Harper Collins.

Wild, F. 1923. *Shackleton's Last Voyage: The Story of the Quest.* London, Cassell.

Worsley, F. A. 1940. *Shackleton's Boat Journey.* London, Hodder and Stoughton.

# Chapter Six

# South Shetland, South Orkney and South Sandwich Islands

## Introduction

These three island groups fringe the eastern and southern edges of the Scotia Sea. Together with South Georgia and linking submarine mountains, they form a major mountain chain, the Scotia Arc or Ridge, that loops from Staten Island, Tierra del Fuego to the tip of Antarctic Peninsula (Map 2).

Both sea and arc were named after *Scotia*, the ship of the small but effective Scottish National Expedition, led by geographer William Bruce, that sailed these waters in 1902–04 and set up a research station on the South Orkneys. The names of the island groups are much older. James Cook named 'South Sandwich Land' in 1765 for the fourth Earl of Sandwich, who was First Lord of the Admiralty at the time. (Yes, the same Fourth Earl invented the sandwich, so he could play cards continuously without stopping for meals: a dedicated man.) The South Shetlands and South Orkneys, discovered in the early 19th century, were named after their counterparts in equivalent latitudes off northern Scotland.

## Geology and ice

All the big islands and many of the smaller ones are mountainous and ice covered (Figure 6.1). The Scotia Arc represents a contorted line of pressure between the edges of neighbouring sea-floor plates—pressure that repeatedly in the past has resulted in intense heating, metamorphism (heat-induced changes in the rocks) and volcanic activity. Currently only Deception Island (South Shetlands), possibly the isolated Bridgeman Island in Bransfield Strait, and eight of the South Sandwich islands are volcanically active. From time to time parts of the submarine ridge burst into activity, releasing shoals of pumice and forming new seamounts to keep the hydrographers busy.

The rocks are mainly brown and grey mudstones and volcanic lavas, agglomerates and tuffs, contorted, folded, faulted, altered by heat, and punctuated by volcanic plugs of dark basalt. They include fragments of fossil leaves and wood, dating from the Jurassic onward.

About 90% of the total land area lies under permanent ice, with active glaciers and more passive ice shelves descending to the sea. Ice cliffs form much of the coastlines, alternating with rocky headlands and beaches.

**Figure 6.1**    *Eastern King George Island, South Shetland Islands. Ice-clad mountains, low ice caps, coastal glaciers, nunataks and dark rocky headlands characterize many of these coasts, but the weather is seldom so clear and sunny as this. Photograph: Ann Stonehouse.*

## Sea ice

Each winter fast ice forms round the South Shetlands and South Orkneys, extending far out to sea. Southern South Sandwich Islands are invested in pack ice, much of which grows elsewhere but drifts in to surround them. After the ice forms, mean temperatures on the beaches fall 9–10°C below freezing point. Late-spring visitors see remnants of the fast ice in bays and harbours: Whalers' Bay in Deception Island sometimes keeps its ice sheet as late as November, though by that time it is soft enough for even a Zodiac to become an icebreaker.

## Climate

All the islands stand north of the Antarctic Circle, so the sun comes up every day, though low and often hidden by cloud. Snow falls persistently in winter, replenishing the ice caps and mantling the rocks, beaches and sea ice 1 to 2 m deep. From late September the sun climbs higher, the sea ice disperses, the land warms, and snow turns to sleet or rain. However, gloomy, wet and windy weather prevails even in summer, with mean temperatures near freezing point.

Despite lying further north, the South Orkneys are slightly colder than the South Shetlands, because of cold air and ocean currents from the Weddell Sea. The South Sandwiches too are colder than their latitude would warrant, though there are no long-term records to say just how much colder.

## Vegetation and wildlife

Vegetation is mostly algae, lichens and mosses. The green alga *Prasiola crispa* (Figure 2.1) often forms extensive mats in early summer, especially on soils that are enriched in nitrogen by bird droppings. Mosses grow wherever there is moisture, usually in scattered tufts among the rocks, but occasionally in extensive beds covering several hectares of sandy beach or moorland. Lichens take several forms. Some grow as red, yellow, grey or black incrustations on rock surfaces: others with leaf-like form grow from rocks, or among mosses and other vegetation. The two species of Antarctic flowering plants, hair-grass and pearlwort, grow sparsely among the mosses. The grass sometimes forms a few square metres of greeny-brown lawn inviting enough to sit on. Sadly, Antarctic Treaty regulations require you to 'keep off the grass', though they do not yet stop you enjoying the earthy scent.

All the Scotia Arc islands are rich in marine wildlife. Elephant seals breed on many of the islands in early spring, fur seals slightly later. Both were reduced by hunting that began in the late 18th century and continued intermittently for over 100 years. Both seem now to be increasing. Whales were abundant until the early 20th century, when competitive hunting severely reduced stocks: again they are now recovering. Weddell seals breed along the fast ice of the coasts, crabeater seals breed offshore on the sea ice, and leopard seals haunt both coasts and pack ice in summer. Breeding seabirds are especially prominent, notably penguins, albatrosses, petrels (see Box 6.1), skuas, Dominican gulls, shags and sheathbills.

## Politics

The three groups of islands, together with South Georgia, are claimed by both Argentina and Britain. Chile claims only the South Shetlands and South Orkneys, which lie within the Antarctic Treaty area, while the South Sandwiches and South Georgia do not (Chapter 11). Britain's claims, based originally on discovery, were renewed and reinforced by licensing and administration during the whaling period, from 1904 onward (see Box 6.2). The most tangible consequence of these rival claims is the rash of stations, huts and navigation beacons that appeared during the late 1940s and 1950s, many of which are now disused or derelict.

## South Shetland Islands

Outliers of the Antarctic region, and often the visitor's first landfall, these are a chain of eleven major and many smaller islands off the north-western flank of Antarctic Peninsula (Map 6). They include a western group comprising (east to west) King George, Nelson, Robert, Greenwich, Deception, Livingston, Snow and Smith Islands, and a more compact eastern group including Gibbs, Elephant and Clarence Islands, extending toward the South Orkneys.

Captain William Smith discovered the islands in February 1819 when his brig *Williams*, trying to round Cape Horn, was blown off course to south and west. He probably sighted Livingston Island, which rises almost to 2000 m (6600 ft).

## Box 6.1   Giant petrels

*Almost the size of albatrosses and equally graceful in flight, these are curiously ugly birds with huge bills, domed heads (to accommodate the massive jaw muscles) and often disconcerting pale-grey eyes. There are two species, rather misleadingly called northern and southern, though both breed only in the southern hemisphere. Northern giant petrels, mostly grey or grey-brown, with dark reddish-tipped bill, breed mainly on the Southern Ocean islands and South Georgia. Southern giant petrels, which generally breed south of the Convergence but also on the Falkland Islands, may be any colour from white through grey-brown to black, with a pale, green-tipped bill.*

*These are predators and scavengers, feeding at sea or ashore on virtually any animal matter that they can tear apart and swallow. On shore and close by we see them gorging on dead seals and penguins: flotillas of giant petrels often wait offshore when young penguins are entering the water for the first time, and particularly vulnerable to attack. Like all other petrels they have difficulty in walking on land. Despite their fearsome appearance they are curiously timid when humans approach. Because they are heavy, they need a long take-off run to launch themselves into the air: it makes sense for them to be wary.*

*They lay a single white egg. Nesting birds that are not used to people readily leave eggs or chicks and fly off if approached: then they may take a long time to land, often some distance away, and waddle back to the nest. Skuas quickly learn to move in and grab whatever is going.*

*If you find yourself approaching a giant petrel colony, walk slowly and watch the nearest birds closely: you may be sure they will be watching you. If accustomed to visits, they may well sit tight. If not they will become restless, stand up and possibly start to move away. At any sign that you are disturbing them, back off slowly and walk round. That will keep you, them, your cruise director and everyone else happy.*

*Should you see a small unaccompanied giant petrel chick on a nest, do not be tempted either to comfort it or take a close-up photograph. Petrels of all kinds leave quite young chicks unattended, allowing both parents to forage simultaneously. If hassled, the chicks use a devastating secret weapon: they vomit their breakfast in a well-aimed jet, like a miniature fire hose. Biologists who need to band and weigh petrel chicks take a trash-can lid as a shield.*

*It may well be yesterday's breakfast, or even the day's before. It will certainly be oily and smelly, and will stick to your clothes for the rest of time. Friends on board will not want to know you. You will not want to know yourself. It will serve you right for dodging the guidelines and getting too close.*

He made a rough survey, claimed the islands for King George III, and reported his discovery of 'New South Britain' to the British Admiralty. In the following year he returned, bringing Edward Bransfield, a naval hydrographer, to chart the new group properly. Smith's name is perpetuated in the westernmost island of the group, Bransfield's in the strait between the South Shetlands and Antarctic Peninsula.

The islands quickly became known to sealers from Britain and the United States,

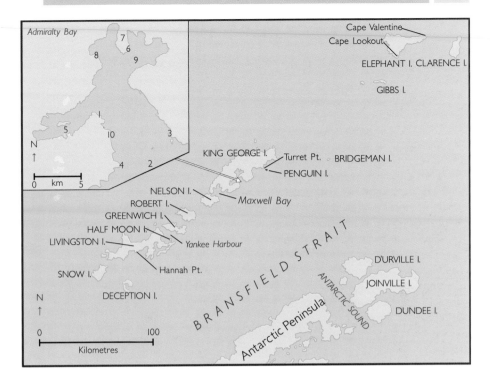

**Map 6**  *The South Shetland Islands. Key to inset: 1 Arctowski Station, 2 Bransfield Strait, 3 Cape Vaureal, 4 Demay Point, 5 Ezcurra Inlet, 6 Ferraz Station, 7 Keller Peninsula, 8 Machu Picchu Station, 9 Martel Inlet, 10 Pieter J. Lenie Station.*

who explored every beach and cove first for fur seals, later for elephant seals. By the mid-19th century many thousands of both had been taken, and little remained of either stock. Beaches and caves still bear remnants of sealing camps, including trypots (the iron pots used for extracting oil from blubber) and the brick or stone hearths on which they were mounted.

Early 20th-century whalers combed South Shetlands waters for right and humpback whales. Tax revenue from whaling subsidized research on the biology of whales and the Southern Ocean, and also hydrography and survey. From this period dates much of the accurate mapping and charting of the group. After inshore whaling died the South Shetlands lost their importance and were left in peace. Then toward the end of World War II, political rivalry between Argentina and Britain brought both nations back to the islands, soon to be joined by Chile. All three nations set up stations and refuge huts partly for science, but mainly as a statement of political ownership and involvement.

From the 1957–58 International Geophysical Year more nations became interested in the South Shetlands. Since then King George Island especially has become a centre for scientific work, hosting the research stations and 'refuges' (now often semi-derelict huts) of no fewer than 11 nations. The Chilean station Teniente Marsh (actually a village-sized complex of three stations) is equipped with

Box 6.2   *Scotia Arc whaling*

Once established on South Georgia, whaling spread quickly to the South Shetlands. Under licence from the government of the Falkland Islands and Dependencies, in 1906–07 a Norwegian-Chilean company operated the floating factory Gobernador Bories at Whalers' Bay, Deception Island (p. 133), with two catchers to hunt the whales and tow them in. The venture proved profitable: within a few years up to a dozen floating factories from South America, Newfoundland and Norway worked in Deception and other South Shetland harbours, notably Admiralty Bay.

At first only the outer layer of skin and blubber was processed, leaving the carcasses to drift and rot. From this period date the whalebones—mainly ribs, vertebrae and skulls—that still lie scattered along many of the island beaches (Figure 6.2). Later more advanced floating factories were brought in to recover oil, protein and bonemeal from the discarded carcasses. The early factories were converted liners with additional boilers and equipment for grinding and drying.

Processing required freshwater, which was gathered from dammed glacial streams and carried to the ships in water boats—simple, flat-bottomed wooden scows, built on the spot from prefabricated parts. Crude dams can still be seen at the old whaling sites,

**Figure 6.2**  A Weddell seal drapes itself comfortably among whale ribs and vertebrae, in the shelter of a decaying waterboat—both remnants of the whaling industry that flourished in these waters during the first half of the 20th century.

and fragments of boats remain among the whalebones. Oak barrels and barrel staves also litter the beaches where whalers worked. These were made up on the spot by coopers, for transporting the oil and meals to market.

In 1910–11 a British administrator was appointed for Deception Island, to supervise the activities of four floating factories. A magistrate replaced him in the following year, and the number of floating factories increased to nine. In the same year floating factories began operating at Powell Island and Signy Island in the South Orkney Islands, and enterprising Norwegians began searching the South Sandwich Islands for likely harbours. The shore factory on Deception Island was built in 1912–13.

Inshore whaling continued in the South Shetlands, mainly from Deception Island, throughout the 1920s. Elsewhere it was less successful. On the South Sandwich Islands it proved impossible: there were no suitable harbours. South-Orkneys operations were chancy, due to the harsher climate and more persistent sea ice. This led, however, to the development that launched the industry in a new direction. When late ice in 1912 kept the ships from their South Orkney harbours, three of them, Falkland, Thule and Tioga, operated instead alongside the ice edge. So began Antarctic pelagic whaling, which gave the whalers three important advantages: it required no harbours, involved no regulations, and attracted no taxes.

Carcasses at that time were still stripped and dismembered alongside the floating factories. At sea this worked only where conditions were calm, for example in ice fields where floes damped down waves and swell. In the summer of 1925–26 came Lancing, designed for pelagic operations in the Ross Sea, and incorporating a stern slipway through which carcasses could be hauled for inboard processing. Within 2 or 3 years new-style ships were busy throughout the Southern Ocean, killing and processing whales so fast that the markets for their products were flooded.

Inshore whaling on the South Shetlands declined during the depression years and finished altogether in 1930–31. At the end of that season the Deception Island station closed, the magistrate went home, and the old floating factories, now outmoded, sailed away to the scrapyards.

**Figure 6.3**  Deacon Peak, Penguin Island. Though not known to have been active in historic times, the twin peaks of red scoria and reefs of consolidated lava suggest an island of recent volcanic origin. It is the home of chinstrap and Adelie penguins, giant petrels, skuas and Antarctic terns.

an airstrip capable of accommodating transport and passenger aircraft, and a hotel for visitors.

The northern sides of the islands receive the full force of northwesterly gales. Bestrewn with rocks, reefs and islets, and subject to heavy seas, they are no place for casual visitors. Cruise ships sail instead along Bransfield Strait, visiting the more sheltered harbours and landings on the southern sides of the islands.

## Landings on the South Shetland Islands

### Penguin Island

Off southern King George Island, at the eastern end of the South Shetlands chain, Penguin Island is often the first landing point for cruise ships from South America. Penguins abound on every Antarctic coast, so many other islands have received the same name. This, however, is the original, genuine Penguin Island, named by hydrographer William Bransfield on 22 January 1820 before any others were known, or at least recorded on published maps.

Pear-shaped, and about 1.4 km (0.9 miles) in diameter, Penguin Island is a volcano, currently inactive. Winter snows disappear suspiciously early from its surface, suggesting that it may still be warm from activity within the last couple of centuries. The northern half is flat and covered with scoria (cinder-like rocks): the southern half rises to Deacon Peak, a cone of red scoria and black lavas (Figure 6.3). The summit, 170 m (560 ft) high, is the highest point along the rim of a caldera over 60 m (200 ft) deep. Wave action from the west is rapidly eroding the side of the main cone, giving an impression of impermanence: Is the whole structure no more than a few hundred years old, with only a few more centuries to go? A second vent, probably more recent, forms a circular lake 300 m (1000 ft) across near the eastern shore of the island.

On seaward sides the island is flanked with cliffs of black lava and scoria up to 10 m (33 ft) high. Visiting ships usually lie off in deep water to east or west, and visitors land on cobbled or sandy beaches along the northeastern or northern shores. Over the northern plain you can walk easily in any direction. Much of it is bare sand and scoria, but algae, mosses and lichens flourish in moist patches. You will see both species of Antarctic flowering plant, hair-grass in abundance, pearlwort more scarcely. Reefs of hard, jagged lava rise above the scoria, decorated with orange, grey, green and black lichens.

On the east coast near the lake are three chinstrap-penguin colonies, totalling about 2000 nests. Their occupants patter busily back and forth to the sea: it is important not to stand in their way (Figure 6.4). Scattered about the north-western quadrant of the island are nest circles, guano and other traces of extensive old penguin colonies, abandoned some hundreds of years ago—possibly during an eruption, which must have puzzled the penguins. Antarctic terns nest in a slight depression near the centre of the island, warning visitors of their presence by noisy mobbing. This is a sensible precaution: the eggs and chicks, solitary and nestling in tiny hollows, almost exactly match their background. Though difficult to see, they are remarkably easy to walk on. When the terns give warning, retrace your steps

**Figure 6.4** *Chinstrap penguins, each with a crop full of food for hungry chicks, take precedence over human visitors. It is important not to disrupt their journey. They are programmed rather than determined. If diverted, they may delay their visit, or return to sea without visiting their chicks.*

and make a wide sweep around the area. These are delicate, elegant birds, easily harmed by blundering.

Skua nests are scattered thinly all over the island. Skuas too give warning when you approach a nest: the sitting bird makes a high, wailing call, to which the partner responds by attacking (Figure 6.5). Do not provoke them into attack: it upsets them and wastes their energy. It may even spoil your day: diving skuas hit hard enough to draw blood, to break spectacles, to knock a camera out of your hand, or to damage your eyes. Respect their warnings and keep clear: they have plenty to worry about, without having to cope with humans as well.

Many of the lava reefs house giant-petrel nests: we estimate a total population of about 2000 nests (Figure 6.6). These again need to be approached with care. Giant petrels quickly become accustomed to visitors, but in the early season especially are liable to abandon their nests if approached too closely, and that gives the skuas a chance to steal their eggs.

In the south the plain rises, gently at first then steeply, to the slopes of Deacon Peak. It is a popular walk: by mid-summer there are usually well-marked tracks from the western landing sites across the island, round the crater rim and up a ridge to the top. On a clear day the peak provides a panoramic view of King George Island from Cape Melville in the east to Twin Pinnacles and Lions Rump in the west.

Beyond the peak, in the south-west corner of the island, about 400 pairs of Adelie penguins nest in two compact colonies. Gentoos are not known to nest on

**Figure 6.5** *Brown skuas greet intruders, whether other skuas or humans, with alarm calls and wings spread. If you have caused the display, back off: you are in their territory, and there may be a nest or chicks nearby. If they attack, they will swoop repeatedly, and may hit you quite dangerously.*

**Figure 6.6** *Giant petrel nesting among volcanic boulders. Despite their size, these are often timid birds (see Box 6.1, p. 114). If unused to visitors, they may take off and abandon their eggs or chicks, giving predatory brown skuas the opportunity of a quick meal.*

the island, but Adelies, chinstraps and gentoos can often be seen together on the beaches. They may even pose obligingly together, so you can get all three in one frame. Blue-eyed shags, that nest close by at Turret Point, fly past in skeins of six to a dozen, and feed in shallow waters just off the rocks.

Weddell seals breed in September on the winter fast ice between Penguin Island and Turret Point. Breeding is over and the pups have gone by the time cruise ships arrive, but two or three adults usually haul out near the landing beaches, along with elephant seals, young male fur seals, and occasionally leopard and crabeater seals. Humpback, minke and killer whales are often seen offshore. This must once have been a whaling area: skeletons and skulls of humpback and smaller whales litter the northern beaches of the island. Beachcombers may spot the spars, masts and hull of a small sailing scow, wooden towing toggles (used in towing whales to the factory ship) and two buckled harpoon shafts that may well have come ashore in stranded carcasses.

## Turret Point

A rocky peninsula on the southern flank of King George Island, Turret Point lies across a narrow channel from Penguin Island, forming the east side of King George Bay. Its name comes from the high turreted rocks that form the south-western point of the main headland. The earliest recorded visit was by Edward Bransfield, the hydrographer accompanying Captain William Smith, of the brig *Williams*. On 22 January 1820 Bransfield landed first on Penguin Island (see p. 118), then on the nearby shore of King George Island to collect water. Bransfield's journals described freshwater streams and lakes, penguins and basking elephant seals—all still-recognizable features of Turret Point. There is no on-site record of these historic landings.

The landing sites are beaches of cobbles and boulders, one facing westward into King George Bay, the other facing south-west toward Penguin Island. During strong southwesterly swells, when surf breaks on both beaches, there is a third possible landing along the eastern side of Mersey Spit, a low shingle bank off the south-east corner of the point.

Ashore there are wide expanses of raised beaches, and a hinterland of gently sloping shingle and rock platforms, faulted and cut by steep-sided valleys. The ground rises gently from sea level to high points around 50 m (164 ft) in the north-east corner. The rocks are lavas and breccias, volcanic but very much older than those of Penguin Island, dipping gently to east and north-east. Three shallow lakes, the largest 120 m (400 ft) across, occupy the high north-eastern plateau. Above the lakes and highest rocks rises the main ice cap of King George Island. The ice is usually snow-free from mid-to-late summer, and relatively safe for guided parties to walk on. From the edge of the ice cap flow three fast streams, that cross the area and join to form a single torrent that pours into King George Bay.

Though not quite so rich as Penguin Island, Turret Point offers plenty of wildlife. At least 2000 pairs of Adelie penguins nest in a group of colonies north of Mersey Spit, and several hundred chinstraps occupy the rocky 'turrets' of the south-western corner, along with a few dozen blue-eyed shags. Several hundred giant petrels (Box 6.1) nest in groups on the uplands, usually on windy points where they can easily take off and land. Skuas, terns and Dominican gulls nest in scattered colonies.

Turret Point lies on a spectacular stretch of coast, with extensive ice cliffs and glaciers on either flank and the ice cap rising behind. It was a haunt of 19th-century sealers: remains of at least one sealing camp have been identified in the lee of the large reef close to the southern beach. There are enough whalebones and debris along the beaches to suggest that, in the early 20th century, it was a centre for whaling, with a factory ship harboured close by (see also Penguin Island, p. 118).

## Admiralty Bay

A huge, branching inlet in the southern flank of King George Island, Admiralty Bay (Map 6, inset) has provided shelter and sustenance for generations of Antarctic mariners. Shelter lies in its many harbours and inlets, sustenance in its concentrations of penguins and seals, some of which have the good sense to live there all the year round.

Should you be faced with shipwreck but allowed to choose your venue (admittedly an improbable combination), Admiralty Bay would be a sound choice. Some 8 km (5 miles) across at the entrance and 16 km (10 miles) deep, its ink-blue waters and backdrop of glaciers would compensate for much discomfort. More practically, you could be sure of a welcome and hot coffee at a selection of friendly research stations, speaking a surprising variety of languages (see Box 6.3).

## Commandante Ferraz Station

Why a Brazilian station in Antarctica? Brazil joined the Antarctic Treaty in 1975, and became a Consultative Party in 1983. Brazilian scientists have shown a strong commitment to Antarctic research, particularly in glaciology, geophysics, terrestrial and marine biology, astrophysics and meteorology. Commandante Ferraz Station was built on Keller Peninsula in February 1984. Like most modern stations the buildings are prefabricated metal containers, well insulated and linked by passages, with comfortable accommodation for 25 in summer and 13 in winter. Water comes from two glacial lakes nearby: a septic-tank system deals with sewage, and sludge is removed to avoid local pollution. The station managers have laid out an easy trail of length about 1600 m (just less than a mile), that starts at the landing point in Martel Inlet and leads in a counter-clockwise direction around the site. Turn sharp right at the landing and head 600 m (2000 ft) northward along the coast to a point where, on a patch of grassy sward, lies the skeleton of a large baleen whale. It is in fact bits of several whales, all victims of harpooning and flensing, whose bones came to rest on the foreshore during the early days of the 20th century. However, it is a good use for old bones, conveying an impression of size and making an interesting photograph.

Beyond the skeleton the path turns left and retraces itself at a higher level over typical South Shetland vegetation—algae, lichens, mosses and grass, growing from thin soils and often completely arid by mid-to-late summer. Reflect that in winter

## Box 6.3  Stations in Admiralty Bay

*Admiralty Bay is the site of an early British station, Base G, built in 1948 on the east side of Keller Peninsula, at the head of the Bay. Don't count on them for coffee: they closed in 1962, and the huts, all but the foundations have been removed. Close by is Commandante Ferraz, a Brazilian station built in 1984, very active and far more likely to be hospitable. Westward across Mackellar Inlet, at Crépin Point, stands Machu Picchu, a summer-only Peruvian station dating from 1988. Facing it across the harbour on Point Hennequin is an Ecuadorian camp, built in 1989 and used only occasionally for summer field parties. Half-way down Admiralty Bay on the west side, at Point Thomas, stands the Polish station Henryk Arctowski, erected in 1977 and currently one of Antarctica's best-known and busiest stations, and the one most hospitable to visitors. Three kilometres (2 miles) south of Arctowski, at Llano Point, stands a small US summer station, officially Pieter J. Lenie but generally known as Copacabana. Started in 1978, it houses summer-only ornithological research parties.*

*Cruise ships may land at any of these points except Copacabana, which stands in a Site of Special Scientific Interest and does not welcome casual visitors. The most likely landings are Point Thomas and Keller Peninsula. Under a joint Polish and Brazilian initiative Admiralty Bay has recently (1996) become an Antarctic Specially Managed Area. An important facet of the management strategy is to develop Arctowski, and possibly also Commandante Ferraz, as sites where visitors from cruise ships are welcomed, shown around, and given rare opportunities to learn more of Antarctica and Antarctic research.*

all this lies under a metre or more of snow, and indeed that the whole of Admiralty Bay is iced over for several months. The path leads to the site of the old British station, Base G, much of which was removed in 1995. There remain rows of concrete foundation blocks, which lichens are doing their best to camouflage.

The trail continues past the lakes from which the station draws its water, past the remains of a British radiosonde hut and a modern meteorological installation, then doubles back past a sundial (yes, the sun shines occasionally in the South Shetlands, but not often) and to the door of the main station complex. The Brazilians are hospitable to visitors who have applied beforehand to visit the station and, not surprisingly, offer the best coffee for miles around. If you feel like a longer walk, turn right at the sundial and take a coastal path that leads to a stream and a small, unexciting refuge hut.

## Henryk Arctowski Station

Built in 1977 on a triangular sand flat south-east of Point Thomas, Arctowski represents a generation of stations between 'traditional' Base G and modern Commandante Ferraz, with prefabricated buildings, spread over a wide area. Operated by the Polish Academy of Sciences, it is named for Henryk Arctowski (1871–1958), a Polish geologist who served with the *Belgica* expedition of 1897–99, and was thus one of the first ever to winter in Antarctica: his portrait hangs in

the station. Arctowski accommodates up to 70 in summer and 20 in winter. The
yellow and brown building close to the flagstaff is the main residence: outbuildings
along the shore provide laboratories and additional living space, and the buildings
behind the station house workshops, generators, boats and other equipment for a
busy, multidisciplinary community (Figure 6.7).

Poland has always welcomed visitors to Arctowski, which accordingly receives
more ships and tourists than any other station. A trail 1600 m (almost a mile) long
encircles the station area. From the landing point by the lighthouse turn left around
the rocky cliff. On a sandy patch just beyond the cliff both hair-grass and pearlwort
grow abundantly. Head northward along the shore. The cobbled beach is littered
with whalebones, including the skull and vertebrae of several large rorquals (Figure
6.8). Keep an eye on the lagoon alongside and the shore itself. One or two black-
necked swans usually spend a summer vacation here: it makes a change, after all,
from the bustle of South America. Other occasional visitors include white-rumped
sandpipers, Magellanic penguins, and bewildered cattle egrets searching everywhere
for cattle.

At the far end of the beach, by the foot of the rocky point, is a damp hollow that
usually contains a dozen or more moulting elephant seals. Just beyond is the start
of a large colony of Adelie penguins, that extends up the ridge and far beyond. This
is also the north-east corner of the neighbouring Site of Special Scientific Interest,
that extends 6 km (3.7 miles) along the coast to Demoy Point, and 3 km (1.9
miles) inland.

The trail turns right by the elephant seals and winds along the foot of the hill.
The electric winch is the business end of a ski lift, that the Polish scientists use for
recreation in winter. On your left lies the northern end of the SSSI, an area rich in

**Figure 6.7**   *Part of Henryk Arctowski Station, Admiralty Bay, facility of the
Department of Antarctic Biology, Polish Academy of Sciences—a friendly station with
a stylish information centre, where visitors are welcome. Safe walks have been marked out
around the station and in the hills behind.*

**Figure 6.8** *Remnant of the early 20th-century industry, this fragment of whale skull is one of many lining the beaches of Admiralty Bay, South Shetland Islands. In the early days, only the blubber was stripped off for processing, allowing the carcasses to drift away and rot.*

natural history that the scientists have set aside for study. On the hills above is a grave marked with a cross. This is the grave of Wlodzimierz Puchalski, a distinguished Polish nature photographer, who died while filming at the station in 1979. It is by any standards a fair place to rest. From here on a fine day there are splendid views across Admiralty Bay to the head of the harbour, Hennequin Point and Cape Vaureal. On a bad day you'll be lucky to see the far side of the station area.

The path leads on across rich grassy sward and over a stream, then downhill to the back of the station area. Head over toward the greenhouse, close by the main station building, which formerly grew flowers and fruit. Under the Antarctic Treaty importing seeds and plants is now banned, so the greenhouse, rather sadly, has become a research facility. You are usually welcome in the living quarters and information centre, unless there is a conference or some other event to keep visitors at bay. Few other modern stations have the homely, comfortable atmosphere of Arctowski, so savour it if you have the chance. Close beneath the lighthouse is the Visitors' Centre, one of the few buildings in Antarctica with a claim to elegance and originality of design.

## Maxwell Bay

Some call it an Antarctic slum, an eyesore, an insult to Antarctica. Others berate it as the logical outcome of Antarctic Treaty policy. To paraphrase Treaty wording, a

Contracting Party shall be entitled to participate in Treaty meetings during such times as it '. . . demonstrates an interest in Antarctica by conducting substantial research activity there . . .'. The generally accepted form of demonstration is to set up a station, and ease of access has made Maxwell Bay a prime target (Box 6.4). If five or six nations want to work in one accessible area, is it better to have them all together, or scattered in five or six different localities?

In fact the stations making up the complex are well run and tidy. Ships usually anchor off the station complex and Zodiacs land passengers on a gently sloping beach (Figure 6.8). A half-hour saunter takes you through the Chilean township of Puerto Frei (actually three linked stations), past the bank, post office, supermarket, school, hospital and stylish Catholic church (yes, this is still near-Antarctica, believe it or not), past the family quarters called Villa las Estrellas, up the hill to the airfield and hotel (Teniente Rodolfo Marsh).

If you still feel energetic and have an hour or more to spare, turn back to the crossroads and take the road to the right, over the hill to Hydrographer's Cove and Great Wall Station (Figure 6.10). Keep to the road and you will not get lost: you may, however, be run over by trucks commuting on who-knows-what business between the stations. Once out of town, you can see some of the natural beauty and the wealth of vegetation that, long ago in 1967, earned Fildes Peninsula the status of Specially Protected Area.

Otherwise it is an easy stroll back to the beach: return the way you came, or divert to the left and wander through Bellingshausen Station. The Russians, currently in dire financial difficulties, have adopted capitalist ethics in a big way. Several may invite you to visit their back-room boutiques and gift shops, and offer all kinds of bargains from vodka to fur hats.

Behind the kitchens you will meet half a dozen fat, prosperous-looking skuas. Their interpretation of the new capitalist ethic is to hang around the back door for

---

### Box 6.4  Stations in Maxwell Bay

First to move into the Maxwell bay area was Argentina, which in 1947–48 set up Jubany, a small station in Potter Cove, and in 1953 Ballvé, a refuge on Ardley Island. In 1967 Fildes Peninsula, the ice-free western tip of King George Island, was declared a Specially Protected Area under the Antarctic Treaty. However, in the same year USSR built substantial Bellingshausen Station in the middle of it. Chile followed closely in 1969 with Presidente Eduardo Frei Station, and a refuge beyond Suffield Point. In 1972–73 USSR cut a road 1.2 km (0.75 miles) east to a neighbouring cove, where they built a bunkering depot large enough to supply oil not only to the station, but to the Soviet fishing fleet as well.

In 1979 Chile built air station Teniente Rodolfo Marsh adjacent to Presidente Frei: it included a 1200 m (3900 ft) airstrip that has since been extended to 1500 m (4900 ft), and a small hotel. In 1981–82 Chile built a refuge on Ardley Island, and Argentina enlarged Jubany for permanent occupation. In 1985 Uruguay built Artigas Station beyond Suffield Point, and China built Great Wall Station in Hydrographer's Cove. In 1988 South Korea moved in with King Sejong Station, on the south shore of Marion Cove.

**Figure 6.9**   *Maxwell Bay, King George Island, the site of Chilean and Russian research stations, and a Chilean Air Force base, with family living quarters, supermarket, bank, hospital, church, school and other amenities. An airstrip capable of landing C140s lies over the hill behind.*

handouts. You will seldom have a chance to see skuas closer: notice their size— much larger than they appear in the air—and their curious combination of webbed feet and curved talons.

Most of the Maxwell Bay stations can be visited by prior arrangement. Some, like Great Wall (Figure 6.10), will give you a quick account of their work and purpose, but no more. Others will show you accommodation, workshops and laboratories, even videos of their activities. Practically all of them these days sell T-shirts, postcards, pins, badges and other trinkets, which passengers, deprived of shopping for as long as 3 or even 4 days, seem only too glad to buy.

### Aitcho Islands

Between the ice cliffs of Greenwich and Robert Islands lies English Strait. At its north-eastern end stand Aitcho Islands, a group of flat, slab-sided islands, neither exciting nor distinguished, but easy to reach from the south and recently increasing in popularity. Who was Aitcho? A Peruvian admiral? A South Korean president? Neither: British hydrographers who named the islands during the 1960s simply ran out of inspiration, and gave them the initials of the Hydrographic Office. Before that their identity was uncertain, and their history difficult to trace.

Cecilia Island, named for a 19th-century sealing ship, is one of the two southernmost islands that are most often visited. From cobbled beaches there are easy climbs through the cliffs to a smooth rolling plain. Only recently, perhaps

**Figure 6.10**    *Great Wall Station, a government research facility of the Republic of China. A short walk from Maxwell Bay, it is open to visitors by previous arrangement, though the scientists are usually too busy to talk.*

within the last few hundred years, have these islands emerged from an ice cap that probably covered the whole group, bridging the northern end of English Strait, and bulldozing the islands beneath. Colonies of chinstrap penguins, with a few pairs of gentoos on the outskirts, occupy open ground, probably where winter snows lie thinnest and disappear early in the season. Shortly after the spring melt, when the gravel is still damp, these plains grow mats of intense green *Prasiola*, an alga that flourishes for a few days or weeks, then dries and is stripped off by the wind.

## Yankee Harbour

Tucked into the southern flank of Greenwich Island lies Yankee Harbour, an almost circular haven roughly 1 km (0.6 miles) in diameter. Protected by a narrow shingle spit 1.2 km (0.75 miles) long, it is backed to north and east by an ice cliff up to 30 m (100 ft) high. The entrance is a channel less than 500 m (1600 ft) wide. Though sealers were glad of it, cruise ships usually anchor outside and send in the Zodiacs.

Why Yankee Harbour? American sealer Nathanial Palmer was probably the first to use it in 1820. British charts called it Port Williams after Smith's brig (p. 121), and also Hospital Cove: some ailing sealer may have recuperated or died there. After 1821, when an American sealing fleet used it as a depot and base, it was called both Yanky Harbour and Fanning's Harbour, the latter after Captain E. Fanning who led the sealers. After years of confusion, only recently has general agreement been reached on Yankee Harbour.

The approach is from McFarlane Strait, between Greenwich and Livingston Islands: just to confuse matters this was formerly known as Yankee Sound. Despite the narrow entrance, ships under sail found it an easy harbour to enter or leave in almost any wind. Even when conditions are rough in the Strait, there are usually calm, sheltered water and easy landings within. Fast ice covers the harbour in winter, and may persist late into November. Deep snow lasts from May to October, then disappears rapidly during November and December. Yankee Harbour appears to have a milder climate than neighbouring Half Moon Island (see p. 130).

This is a place where visitors can walk without passing out of sight or getting into difficulties. The south-eastern shore is a broad strand with raised beaches, fronting a steep mountain ridge just over 300 m (1000 ft) high. Parties often land on the spit, which is made up of raised beaches overlying a glacial moraine. A leisurely stroll toward the mainland takes 20 minutes, or longer if they beachcomb. The outer, exposed shore often yields the more interesting finds: on different visits we have found storm-washed seaweeds, starfish and other invertebrates from the seabed, parts of crabeater-, Weddell- and leopard-seal skeletons, towing toggles and old spars from the whaling period, and less welcome plastic crates, bottles and fishing nets from more recent ships.

At the base of the spit within the harbour are the remnants of a sealer's camp. Look out for a damaged cast-iron trypot, and the red bricks that once formed the hearth on which it and probably other pots were mounted. In sealing days there would have been a tented camp, timbers and piles of barrels nearby, but little else: the sealers were poor folk, with little to bring.

From this point there are further walks north-eastward toward the moraines and ice cliffs, either along the shore, or at a higher level through the gentoo-penguin colony. Beyond the colony lies a refreshing area of terraced beaches, with a small meandering stream, ponds, mosses, and patches of soil and grass turf, where half a dozen elderly elephant seals—probably pensioners—sleep away their days. In clear weather an easy scramble up the lower slopes of the ridge yields spectacular panoramic views of the harbour, McFarlane Strait, and the south-eastern corner of Livingston Island.

The colony contains about 2000 gentoo-penguin nests. Chinstrap penguins are occasionally seen in the area, and may breed there from time to time. Blue-eyed shags feed in the harbour and roost along the spit, gathering at dusk and flying in skeins to their breeding colony on Half Moon Island, 5 km to south-west. Giant petrels are not known to nest in the area, but several dozen gather in the harbour close to the penguin colony from late January onward, preying on fledgeling gentoos. Toward evening Wilson's storm petrels flutter over the scree slopes, and cape petrels and snow petrels nest far out of reach on the heights above.

About 50 pairs of brown skuas nest along the spit and in scattered nests among the gentoos. A few scavenge in the colony, while the rest seem to feed at sea or along the shore. Similar numbers of Dominican gulls nest around the harbour, mainly in groups toward the ice cliff. Two or sometimes three pairs are the sole tenants of the Chilean 'refuge'—a picturesque hut built in 1953 from old packing

**Figure 6.11**   *Chilean refuge at Yankee Harbour, Greenwich Island, a remnant of the 1950s, when three governments promoted their claims to this sector of Antarctica. It is built of old packing cases. Gentoo penguins now nest in the living room, and Dominican gulls have taken over the roof.*

cases, and now long past its sell-by date (Figure 6.11). While fast ice remains in the harbour as many as 30–40 Weddell seals may congregate on it, making use of holes and cracks for feeding. After the ice has gone, Weddell, crabeater, leopard and elephant seals haul out on either side of the spit. Humpback, minke and killer whales are often seen offshore in McFarlane Strait.

Yankee Harbour is visited by a few cruise leaders who know it, and ignored by others. Half Moon Island (see below), with its chinstrap colony and Argentine station, provides a strong counter-attraction close by. However, on days when the latter is shrouded in fog, western Greenwich Island including Yankee Harbour is often bathed in sunshine. When Half Moon Island is thickly covered with early-season snow, or when it already has visitors, Yankee Harbour may be an attractive alternative.

## Half Moon Island

Across McFarlane Strait, in the lee of Livingston Island, stands small, crescent-shaped Half Moon Island. It looks like the remnants of a volcanic caldera, but geologists advise us to see it instead as a group of craggy islets joined by a curving sweep of shingle beaches (Figure 6.12). It is a popular landing place. The high point toward the eastern end overlooks a colony of about 2000 chinstrap nests.

**Figure 6.12** *Half Moon Island, South Shetland Islands. Melting snow reveals a pattern of raised shingle beaches, representing former sea levels. The Argentine station Teniente Cámara is on the far right, and the ice cliffs of eastern Livingston Island lie across the channel beyond.*

Terns, skuas, sheathbills and Dominican gulls nest close by, and the easternmost point of the island, accessible on foot at low tide, has about 30 pairs of blue-eyed shags.

Clearly visible as you approach from McFarlane Strait are the buildings of a small Argentine station, Teniente Cámara, formerly naval but now civilian operated. Built in 1953, it is a comfortable old station with accommodation for about 20 scientists. The hangar once housed a seaplane, but is now used for storage.

Most operators land close to the penguin colony and leave passengers free to wander along the point. When you have seen enough of the chinstraps and shags, walk back toward the station and cross over to the western shore of the island. On the beach immediately below the crest we once saw a moulting Emperor penguin—rare for these latitudes. Bear right and walk northward along the shore behind the station. On a fine day Livingston Island provides a wonderful backdrop to the ice-strewn channel. Weddell and elephant seals, and occasionally leopards, haul out on the beaches. Minke whales often post up and down the channel, and there is a convenient collection of whalebones where you can sit and admire the scene.

Half an hour's walk brings you to the northern end of the island, a delightful area of lagoons, streams and rock pools. Cruise operators seldom visit this area, though there are good Zodiac landings close to the northern point. Energetic folk can climb to the top of the hill, for a good panoramic view of the island and McFarlane Strait. Watch out for skuas: over 50 pairs breed up on top, and as always you need to keep clear of their nests and chicks.

## Hannah Point

On the south-west coast of Livingston Island, this is the bent tip of a ridge that sweeps down from the crest of the island. On either side lie icefields, terminating in the ice cliffs of Walker Bay and South Bay. Formerly called Black Point, Hannah Point was renamed for a 19th-century sealing ship that sank nearby. In foul weather it has an ominous look, as though biding its time to sink a dozen more ships. Good weather reveals gentler qualities: there are few more enjoyable places to visit than Hannah Point on a sunny day.

Most parties land on a small cobbled beach on the northern side of the Point (Figure 6.13), immediately below extensive chinstrap and gentoo-penguin colonies. Its main attraction for cruise leaders is the eight or nine pairs of macaroni penguins (Figure 2.15) that nest among 900 pairs of chinstraps. Over 3000 visitors per year land at this one point, bearing heavily on the small area, and on the shoulders of a few small penguins.

Macaronis are by no means the only attractions. Competing for attention are nesting sheathbills in caverns by the shore, and Dominican gulls on the crags immediately above. Visitors walk uphill past small groups of nesting chinstraps, with larger colonies of both chinstraps and gentoos to left and right, plus a small group of nesting shags within easy reach. There are usually young male elephant seals and fur seals on the landing beach, and large elephants haul themselves up the slope to a malodorous wallow at the top. Over the cliff close by you may see more elephants swimming in the rock pools below.

**Figure 6.13**  *Hannah Point, Livingston Island. Giant petrels nest among the crags in the foreground: in the background is the low-lying Point itself, covered with gentoo and chinstrap-penguin colonies. The square-cut bay on the right is the most popular landing site.*

From the first slope it is usually possible to thread your way westward along the hillside toward Walker Bay. Immediately above is a colony of about 80 nesting giant petrels; immediately below are the main colonies of chinstraps and gentoos, and it is important to avoid disturbing either. Gentoos hatch in mid- to late-December, chinstraps a week or two later. It is safe to walk between their colonies during incubation, hatching and brooding, but later, when the chicks leave their nests and young, non-breeding birds enter the colonies, walking without disturbing becomes more difficult. There is usually a way through on higher ground, keeping below the crags where the giant petrels nest.

In calm weather both Walker Bay and South Bay offer alternative landings, giving better access to the bays and taking pressure off the penguins. Both bays provide excellent walks of several kilometres over flat ground, as far as the moraines that terminate the glaciers at either end. There are raised beaches, moss beds, ponds, streams, breeding colonies of giant petrels and Dominican gulls: Weddell, crabeater, leopard and elephant seals have all been seen there. South Bay has additional attractions of small gentoo-penguin colonies and reefs richly covered with lichens. The ridge between the bays rises to 600 m (1970 ft) and more, but there are three or more easy crossing points for guided parties. Look out for an interesting flora of grey-green lichens at cloud level around 150 m (490 ft), and for splendid panoramas of the western Livingston Island, Bransfield Strait, and Deception Island to the south.

Hannah Point is curiously short of skuas, possibly because there are so many Dominican gulls—about 400 pairs—which replace skuas as predators on the penguin colonies. A few non-breeding skuas make a precarious living on the outskirts: should they enter the main colony areas, 10 dozen gulls yell at them and see them off. However, here I have seen skuas play a trick that I have seen nowhere else. One gets behind an incubating chinstrap and drags it off the nest by the tail, while the other grabs an egg from the front. It works every time.

Livingston Island's rocks include sedimentary layers with fossil leaves and fragments of wood, deposited in shallow water when lakes and forests covered the area. Rock fragments containing these fossils can be found in the moraines at the west end of Walker Bay.

## Deception Island

Some 26 km south of Hannah Point looms Deception Island, a ring-shaped island almost 13 km (8 miles) in diameter with an extensive internal crater. Therein lies the deception: those who discovered it thought it a dull pudding of an island, until they came to the south-east corner and discovered the capacious inner harbour, now called Port Foster. Most of the crater rim rises over 100 m (330 ft), and is ice free in summer. Mount Pond, the highest peak, rises to 548 m (1800 ft) on the east side of the island, Mount Kirkwood, the second highest, to 464 m (980 ft) in the south, and both are ice capped.

Port Foster has a long history of use, by the sealers, the whalers, and by virtually every other expedition that sailed south in this sector of Antarctica. Pioneering aviator Sir Hubert Wilkins scraped a runway along the shore of Whalers Bay, the small harbour near Neptune's Bellows, and from it made Antarctica's first survey

## Box 6.5  The 1967–70 eruptions

*Since its discovery in 1820 Deception Island has maintained a reputation for uncomfortable happenings. US expedition commander Charles Wilkes in 1842 witnessed a major eruption, reporting that 'The whole south side of Deception Island appeared as if on fire . . .'. From time to time parts of the harbour floor have risen or dropped, to the disquiet of mariners at anchor inside. A cruise in fine weather toward the north end of the crater gives you a chance to see several consequences of major eruptions that occurred in 1967–70.*

*Look first for Telefon Bay (named after a ship of the whaling period), at the north end of Port Foster. Here an eruption in December 1967 set the sea boiling, raised a column of cinder-like scoria 9000 m (30 000 ft) into the air, and left a new island 800 m (half a mile) long in the bay. A nearby Chilean station was evacuated by helicopters of their own navy.*

*Turn east to Mount Pond. Here in February 1969 a fissure 11 km (7 miles) long opened in the lower slopes, raining hot scoria and setting ablaze a new Chilean station in Pendulum Cove. Behind Whalers Bay it opened under the ice mantle, producing a flow of mud and ice blocks that swept through the British station, across the old whaling station, and broadened the shore by some 80 m (270 ft). The British party escaped carrying sheets of corrugated iron over their heads. Again Chilean naval helicopters flew in from a ship outside the Bellows, rescuing both parties.*

*In August 1970 a line of craters opened at the end of the harbour, adding a lunar effect to the foreshore between Telefon Bay and Pendulum Cove, and damaging the Argentine station Decepción. Since 1970 the island has kept relatively quiet, though subject to occasional rumblings and tremors. Two scientific stations remain in the harbour, year-round Decepción, and a nearby Spanish summer-only base. Not surprisingly, both are dedicated to the study of vulcanology.*

flights in 1928 and 1929. Today only fragments of this early history remain, for the shape of Whalers Bay, and indeed of Port Foster, was radically altered by volcanic eruptions and mud-slides between 1967 and 1970 (Box 6.5).

The outer rim of the island provides one popular landing, Baily Head (Figure 6.14), on the east side below Mount Pond. This may be quite an adventure, for the beach is steep and there is usually heavy surf. Ensure that all cameras and other expensive equipment are safe in plastic bags, that your hands are free for holding on to the Zodiac, and that you are ready to leap out and run up the beach as soon as your driver gives the word.

Once ashore you find yourself on a narrow beach of black volcanic sand, in the shadow of the towering brown cliff that is Baily Head itself. On your right is an ice cliff, striped like a zebra in wavy lines of grey and black, that runs north in a dead-straight line for over 8 km (5 miles). The bands are fine scoria, blown onto the surface of the ice each winter and covered with more snow. With you on the strand are several hundred chinstrap penguins (Figure 6.15). Many are in groups that are entering and leaving the water in a businesslike penguin way. Others are just standing and watching the curious way in which humans perform the same feat.

**Figure 6.14** *Landing at Baily Head, Deception Island. In heavy surf on this exposed shore, handlers in overall suits hold the boat, and passengers scramble out before the next wave douses them. It is good, clean fun, but make sure that your cameras and binoculars are in, safely bagged.*

**Figure 6.15** *Chinstrap penguins on the beach at Baily Head enter and leave the water with far less fuss. All they have to worry about is the possibility of a leopard seal lurking beyond the breakers. The seals, sensibly enough, tend to catch incomers loaded with food, rather than empty outgoers.*

**Figure 6.16**   *Running between the rock cliffs of Baily Head on the left, and dark gravel-ladened ice cliffs on the right, this valley drains a huge amphitheatre where tens of thousands of chinstrap penguins nest. A steady procession of penguins passes up and down the highway.*

From the beach inland runs a penguin highway, with busy two-way traffic (Figure 6.16). Politically minded observers may note that, more often than not, the birds keep to the left, demonstrating beyond doubt their British affinities. Follow them 100 m inland and you will see what this is all about. The path opens up to a broad amphitheatre several kilometres across that is one enormous penguin colony. Nesting penguins extend as far as you can see on the distant hillsides and even beyond. How many? There is no reliable way of counting. Estimates vary, as well they might, but here are at least 100 000 pairs of chinstraps, and possibly more. There may well be bigger colonies on some of the South Sandwich Islands, but this is as big as most people can absorb.

Should you lack something to think about as you lie awake at night, consider how much food must be caught within swimming distance of the island, to feed all these birds and their one or two growing chicks. That is just one rough indication of Southern Ocean productivity during the summer months.

Passing through Neptune's Bellows is a second adventure. What may seem like a narrow passage is in fact even narrower, because of a reef in the middle. Look out for the wreck on the southern, left-hand or port-side beach, of a whale-catcher that failed to make it. Most cruise ships are more successful, and come to anchor safely in Whalers Bay. Ashore close by are the remains of the whaling station, now partly submerged under a flow of mud and gravel which, following the eruptions, descended from the hills behind. Walk first in the direction of the derelict aircraft hangar, built in the 1960s when there was a British research station in Whalers Bay.

Behind the hangar stands the fuselage of a de Haviland Otter, destroyed like everything else in the eruption and flood. Do not walk any further in this direction: here starts a Site of Special Scientific Interest, where biologists are studying the settlement of plants on the new ground. Returning through the old station, stroll along the beach toward Neptune's Window, the deep, prominent nick in the crater wall. If the tide is low the beach will be steaming: dig a small hole in the sand, but take care—the water a few centimetres down may be far hotter than you expect. At mid-tide it is possible to bathe. If you see flocks of gulls and cape petrels feeding close inshore, take a closer look: they are probably picking up parboiled krill (small pink shrimps) and other plankton killed by the hot water.

Walk on past foundered huts, piles of oak barrel staves and other debris from the whaling days. Think, perhaps, of a dozen floating factories moored side by side just a few metres offshore, belching steam and an overpowering, rancid-gravy smell. Note the remnants of dams, and the water boats sunk in the stream beds, from which water was constantly drawn to feed the boilers. On the cliffs by Neptune's Window look out for cape petrels nesting on open ledges, and Wilson's storm petrels fluttering over nests buried deep in the scree slopes.

Along Port Foster the hot springs at Pendulum Cove provide another popular landing, for the sole purpose of bathing (Figure 6.17): the area immediately behind, including the burnt-out Chilean station, is a no-go Site of Special Scientific Interest.

It can be fun: take shoes to protect your feet from the hot water, and a dressing gown to protect the rest of you from cold air when you emerge. They will probably give you a certificate, to remind you of the moment when you bathed voluntarily in

**Figure 6.17** *Deception Island's warm springs extend in a line along the shore. Here in Pendulum Cove, hardy bathers wallow in warm shallows cut from the black volcanic sand. It is warm in the water, but cold enough for gowns, parkas and hot punch when you emerge. Photograph: Sally Stonehouse.*

the Southern Ocean. Only you can judge whether it is worth remembering, or best forgotten.

## Elephant Island

The eastern group of South Shetland Islands lie off the main route from Ushuaia to Antarctic Peninsula, and so are seldom visited. The most popular landing is Cape Lookout, the southernmost point of the island, where several bays and spits of land, backed by steep black cliffs 200 m (650 ft) high, provide a range of alternative sites to suit wind and swell (Figure 6.18). There are gentoo, chinstrap and a few macaroni penguins, and usually huge flocks of cape petrels and storm petrels feeding close inshore. Both species breed in the screes and on the crags immediately above the penguins.

Why the name Lookout? It is hard to say. The cape was charted and named in 1822 by the British sealer and navigator George Powell. Certainly if anyone needed to keep watch over this corner of the Southern Ocean, there could be no better place, but who did? I have heard it represented as the place where Shackleton's stranded party wintered and kept a lookout for their rescuers. A good story but not true.

More difficult to reach, but of greater historic interest, is Cape Valentine, the easternmost point of the island. Here Sir Ernest Shackleton landed with his party of castaways on 15 April 1916, making their first landfall since the loss of their expedition ship *Endurance.* The narrow beach under towering cliffs afforded them

**Figure 6.18** *Red parkas among nesting penguins at Cape Lookout, Elephant Island, South Shetland Islands. The cliffs and scree slopes are home to thousands of breeding cape petrels, which descend to form huge feeding flocks in the waters nearby.*

shelter for 2 days, before they moved to a safer and more sheltered site on the north side of the island.

That site was Point Wild, named for Frank Wild, the expedition's second-in-command. Here a party of 22 men settled to winter under two upturned lifeboats, while Shackleton and five others sailed off in a third boat to seek help from South Georgia. It is not a hospitable site—a spit of rock and shingle, possibly 200 m (650 ft) long, terminating in a rocky point—and the party was ill-equipped after its long and hazardous trek. Under Wild's leadership they survived for over 4 months until 30 August, when Shackleton returned.

After an unavailing search for a more suitable ship, Shackleton borrowed *Yelcho*, a Chilean naval tender of 150 tonnes, hardly fit to work out of harbour, and crewed by naval volunteers. The gallantry of 'Piloto' Lt. Luis Pardo, its commander, is recognized by the bronze bust that now stands, incongruously but entirely fittingly, on the beach at Point Wild.

## South Orkney Islands

East of the South Shetlands, the South Orkneys form a compact group comprising Coronation, Signy, Powell and Laurie Islands and many smaller islets (Map 7). Their total area is over 600 km$^2$ (234 sq. miles) of which over 90% is ice covered. The rocks are ancient gneisses, schists and limestones, overlain by sedimentary mudstones, shales and conglomerates. Climatically they are similar to the South Shetlands, but colder and with longer and harsher winters.

First sighted by sealers George Powell and Nathaniel Palmer in December 1821, they were charted, named and claimed for Britain in the following year by a third sealer, William Weddell. Sealers scoured the islands throughout the 19th century. From about 1910 the surrounding waters were hunted by whalers. In 1920 a small

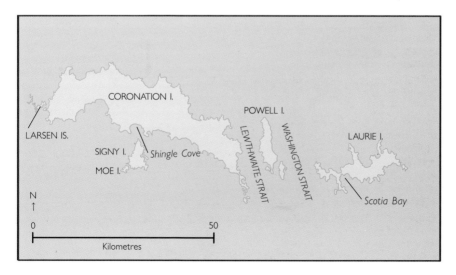

**Map 7**   *The South Orkney Islands.*

whaling station was established on one of the smaller islands by Captain Peter Sørlle and run for a few seasons. The site became Factory Cove, and Sørlle called the island Signy after his teenage daughter. The factory did not prosper and was soon closed. In 1947 a British scientific station was built in the same cove, later to become Signy, British Antarctic Survey's main base for terrestrial biological studies.

## Landings on the South Orkney Islands

### Orcadas

In 1903 the Scottish explorer William Bruce wintered his ship *Scotia* in Scotia Bay, and established a meteorological observatory on nearby Laurie Island. The station was taken over in the following year by the Argentine Meteorological Office. Renamed Orcadas, it has been manned continuously ever since, providing the longest uninterrupted record of Antarctic climate. Orcadas remains a small, comfortable station for up to a dozen scientists. In a pleasant setting very typical of the islands, it can be visited by arrangement.

### Shingle Cove

Neither Signy Station nor the island on which it stands are open for visits, but scientists from the station are sometimes happy to meet visitors at this attractive site on Coronation Island, just across the channel. The cove forms part of Iceberg Bay, which usually contains small bergs broken off from the neighbouring ice shelf. Fine shingle beaches provide several possible landings, with easy walks up through the cliffs to the penguin colony above (Figure 6.19). About 4000 pairs of Adelies nest

**Figure 6.19** *Adelie penguins in Shingle Cove, Coronation Island, South Orkney Islands. Slightly colder than the South Shetlands, with longer winters due to persistent sea ice, the South Orkneys are no less hospitable to breeding birds, including several species of penguins and petrels.*

in the colony, scattered in about 20 well-spaced groups. The hut in the middle is a refuge for scientists who may visit the colony from Signy and find themselves stranded.

Among the penguins nest a few pairs of brown skuas, and a colony of Antarctic terns seems to own parts at least of the rough ground immediately behind: if you visit, take care where you walk, because their eggs and chicks are so well camouflaged as to be almost invisible. North of the colony lies a stream-cut valley, with a steep-sided moraine left by the glacier that has now retreated to Iceberg Bay. From the top you can see over the penguin colony and along the coast. If you have time, search along the cliffs for nesting cape petrels, remembering to keep a respectful 5 m (15 ft) from any you find.

## South Sandwich Islands

A north-to-south chain extending over 350 km (220 miles), the South Sandwiches include 11 large islands and several smaller ones with a total land area of about 300 km$^2$ (120 sq. miles), of which some 85% is ice covered (Map 8). James Cook charted the southern islands of the group in 1775: hence the English names Thule, Bristol, Montagu, Saunders, Candlemas and Vindication. Thaddeus von Bellingshausen added three northern islands in 1819: hence Zavodovski, Leskov and Visokoi. The names of both discoverers have quite rightly been added to the list.

Ten of the islands form an arc along the eastern extremity of the Scotia Ridge. The eleventh island, Leskov, lies some 56 km (35 miles) west of the main arc. Rising from an ocean floor over 3000 m (9800 ft) deep, each island is an eroded volcanic peak, formed relatively recently. Only Visokoi, Montagu, Bristol and Cook Islands rise above 1000 m (3300 ft). Immediately north-east of the arc the ocean floor descends into the South Sandwich Trench, a steep-sided gash over 8000 m (26 200 ft) deep.

The islands are made up of solidified basaltic lava and looser scoria, eroded by wave action and glaciation. There are no sheltered harbours, and the cliffs on all sides make landing diffi-cult. Eight of the islands—Leskov,

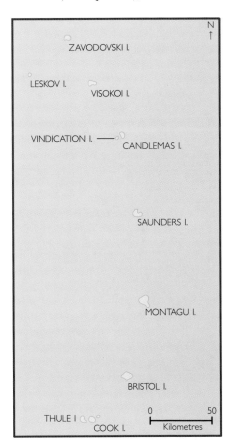

**Map 8**   *The South Sandwich Islands*

Zavodovski, Viskoi, Candlemas, Saunders, Bristol, Bellingshausen and Thule—have shown volcanic activity within the last century, ranging from fumaroles to full eruption. A submarine eruption 56 km north-west of Zavodovski Island in March 1962 produced a mass of pumice and a previously unrecorded shoal only 27 m below sea level.

Sealers visited the islands during the 19th century, and 20th-century whalers hunted profitably in the disturbed, fertile waters downstream (eastward) from them. The southern islands, lying within the northern limit of pack ice, may experience harsher winters and shorter summers than the northern islands, but both climatic and botanical data are few. All the islands are windswept and bare, with little soil, standing water or vegetation. Their most prominent inhabitants are penguins. Nobody has counted them properly—it is doubtful if they could—but estimates indicate that some 5 000 000 chinstraps predominate, tens of thousands of Adelies, and just a few thousand gentoos and macaronis. Millions of petrels and other seabirds breed on the islands, feeding in huge flocks in the surrounding waters.

Both Argentina and Britain claim the islands. A large Argentine naval station established at Ferguson Bay, Thule in November 1976 was evacuated and destroyed by Britain in January 1982. Adelie, chinstrap and gentoo penguins nest philosophically in the ensuing mess, which neither nation has made more than token efforts to clear.

## Landings on the South Sandwich Islands

On calm days when the swell and wind are down it is possible to land by Zodiac at rocky points on several of the islands. However, such days are rare, like penguins' teeth: cruise operators cannot rely on them and have no time to wait around. Hence only ships with helicopters visit the South Sandwiches with any certainty of putting people ashore.

### Ferguson Bay

On the south-east corner of Thule Island is the most sheltered of all South Sandwich sites for landing. That is why the Argentines built their station there. Hewison Point is a consolidated lava flow of fairly recent origin, predominantly black, with brown and grey overlying scoria. In the cliffs behind are bands and patches of black, fawn and bright red scoria, representing successive erruptions. The lava is difficult to walk on, there is very little beach, and only meagre vegetation of algae and lichens. However, there is a large colony containing all three pygoscelid penguins—Adelies, chinstraps and gentoos. Look around, and you will find places where the three nest together within a single camera frame. Nesting space seems to be short: around the colony perimeter chinstrap penguins nest on snowdrifts, sinking almost a metre below the surface from their own body heat (Figure 6.20).

So penguins are crazy? Another feature of Hewison Point is the wreckage of Thule Station, a large, elaborate military and scientific base with quarters for over

**Figure 6.20** *A late spring fall of snow on an overcrowded colony on Thule Island, South Sandwich Islands, forced these chinstrap penguins to lay on a wind-packed snow surface. Their body heat has melted the snow, and the chinstraps are incubating uncomfortably in ever-deepening holes.*

100 men. Built by one power at enormous cost, destroyed by another at considerable cost just 6 years and 2 months later, then left to desecrate the landscape into an indefinite future (Figure 6.21): Now that *must* be crazy.

## Other islands

The South Sandwich Islands lie outside the Treaty area and landings are not always reported. Nattriss Point, south-eastern Saunders Island, has a large area of scoria hills for walking, and extensive colonies of chinstrap and macaroni penguins. Blackstone Plain, the northern point of the same island, is an extensive lava field with black lava cones that are former sea stacks. Both provide good views of Mount Michael, the island's rounded summit, with its constant plume of steam. Candlemass Island is a complex of several volcanic cones, the southern half high and ice capped, the northern half bare, with lakes and scoria flats between. On rugged Clapmatch Point, the southernmost corner, is a lively colony of fur seals, best viewed from Zodiacs. Zavodovski, the northernmost island, is almost ice free. Volcanically one of the liveliest, it has a reputation for emitting noxious gases. Avoid if you can Noxious Bluff, Stench Point and Acrid Point in the west, Reek Point in the north and Pungent Point in the east. Settle with confidence for the south-eastern coast beyond Fume Point, where there are miles of scoria hills, an interesting rugged coast, and the smells are animal—due mostly to chinstrap, macaroni and gentoo colonies, breeding fur seals, and wallowing elephants.

**Figure 6.21** *Chinstrap and adelie penguins nest among the tangled remains of a military research station at Hewison Point—built by Argentina and destroyed by Britain—on Thule Island, southernmost of the South Sandwich Islands.*

## Further reading

Fuchs, V. E. 1982. *Of Ice and Men.* London, Anthony Nelson.
Huntford, R. 1985. *Shackleton.* London, Hodder and Stoughton.

# Chapter Seven

# Antarctic Peninsula and Palmer Archipelago

## Introduction

Antarctic Peninsula marks the southern end of a long chain of mountains that runs almost continuously from Alaska down the western side of the Americas to Tierra del Fuego, and on through the Scotia Arc to Antarctica. The underlying force is an east–west collision between Earth's crustal plates, raising the rims of the continental plates that carry the Americas and West Antarctica. The result in the far south is an alpine peninsula 800 km (500 miles) long, with a complex of off-lying islands called Palmer Archipelago.

The archipelago, separated from the peninsula by Orléans Strait and Gerlache Strait, includes Trinity, Hoseason, Liège, Brabant, Wiencke and Anvers Islands, extending south to Bismarck Strait. One other large island, Adelaide Island, occupies a similar position further south, with the Biscoe Islands between. The peninsula curves from north-east to south, disappearing in the far south under the ice of West Antarctica (see inside back cover).

## Geology and ice

Rocks are mainly sediments and volcanic debris, deposited in an ocean basin and subsequently consolidated, injected with molten rock, uplifted, faulted, and eroded to form the mountains we now see (Figure 7.1). Some strata include fossil leaves, wood, and marine and freshwater shells, confirming that the land mass from which they originated was subtropical and forested, with warm lakes, swamps and warm shallow seas close by. Several of the northern islands have been volcanically active within the past million or so years, some within the past few thousand.

The major channels and waterways are due to block-faulting and erosion: huge blocks of mountains have been upthrust or dropped in relation to their neighbours, and water and ice have eroded the planes of weakness between. One striking erosional feature is the high plateau, now ice capped, that can clearly be seen running almost the whole length of the peninsula, and probably planed by glaciers in a previous cycle of uplift. Ice currently covers most of the peninsula and islands, pouring off the tops in glaciers and forming piedmont shelves along the shores. Annual snowfall replenishes the ice, of which thousands of tonnes are shed each year into the sea. Lively glaciers calve to form only small bergs, bergy bits and brash ice. The big tabular bergs you may see in Bransfield Strait are mostly from much larger and more extensive ice shelves; for example, those calving into the Weddell or Bellingshausen Seas.

**Figure 7.1**   *Distant sunshine lights up the ice-covered mountains and central plateau of Graham Land, Antarctic Peninsula. While most of Antarctica lies entirely under ice, the Peninsula has a relatively high proportion of exposed rock, including headlands and beaches.*

## Sea ice

Fast ice forms all around the peninsula and islands from late April or May each year: with packed snow on top it may reach a metre or more (3–4 ft) thick (Figure 7.2). The ice sheet weakens and disperses from September, and by October or early November forms huge rafts of drifting pack ice, which may by its sheer bulk impede even ice-strengthened ships. Gerlache Strait and Lemaire Channel, the main highways south, are usually open by mid-November, at least as far as the Argentine Islands. Farther south the pack ice continues to disperse through December and January, though remnants accumulate in particular bays and in constrictions like The Gullet, between Adelaide Island and the peninsula. Experienced captains know the alternatives and take no risks.

There are 'good' years when the ice disperses early and 'bad' years when it hangs about, and there is some evidence of long-term cycles affecting the peninsula. Pessimists say we have enjoyed more than a decade of good years, and that we may expect a higher proportion of bad years from now on. Well, I guess that is what pessimists are for. Meanwhile the ice of the peninsula area is negotiable and reasonably safe for ice-strengthened ships with experienced masters.

## Climate

The western flank of the peninsula is by far the mildest corner of continental Antarctica. Mean July (winter) temperatures fall to about −12°C over the whole

**Figure 7.2** *Scientists working over the side from a research ship study the character-istics of a large floe in year-old sea ice, snow-covered and well over 1 m thick. In the background are pressure ridges, caused by wind-induced movements between the floes.*

area: mean January temperatures rise to around freezing point along most of the western side, even far into Marguerite Bay. The east side is colder and more icebound, which is why cruise ships seldom penetrate far down that way. The hardy folk who conduct their research on Antarctica's high plateau, or in the higher latitudes of McMurdo Sound, write off the peninsula as Antarctica's banana belt.

Depressions track across the peninsula, bringing heavy snow in winter and sleet or rain in summer. Winds pack the snow into drifts that persist well into summer, and keep the ice caps topped up. Many low-lying islands along the peninsula are ice domed and have ice cliffs all round: only a narrow shingle beach at low tide indicates a rock core.

## Vegetation and wildlife

The western peninsula has vegetation similar to, though generally slightly poorer than, that of the South Orkney and South Shetland Islands. The two species of flowering plants, which are often taken to indicate the best conditions, are sparse in the north and much sparser in the south, reaching southern limits on islands in southern Marguerite Bay. Colder conditions on the east side restrict vegetation severely. Birds and seals show similar distributional gradients: the warmer western side is better populated than the east. Elephant seals, fur seals, and chinstrap and gentoo penguins venture only about halfway down the peninsula. Weddell seals and Adelie penguins continue well beyond, to a limit that is probably set by persistence of fast ice, rather than cold.

A small colony of Emperor penguins breeds on the Dion Islands, in northern Marguerite Bay, and there is almost certainly another colony, as yet undiscovered, in the region of Snow Hill Island (p. 155).

## History

The peninsula was the first part of Antarctica to be seen by man, around 1820, and the first to be explored systematically. That expeditions of many nations have helped to chart it is clear from multilingual place names. Though indications of a peninsula were clear by the mid-19th century, its exploration followed directly from a resolution made at the Sixth International Geographical Congress, which met in London in July 1895: '... exploration of the Antarctic Regions', declared the geographers, '... is the greatest piece of geographical exploration still to be undertaken'. Within a decade Belgian, British, German, Swedish, Scottish and French expeditions were on their way to Antarctica, all but the British and German concentrating their attentions on the peninsula (Box 7.1).

The most significant charting was done by the Belgian and two French expeditions between 1897 and 1910. Much was later added by Norwegian whalers who worked this area from about 1910 to the 1930s, and British Discovery Expeditions that undertook hydrographic, oceanographic and whaling research both here and elsewhere in the Southern Ocean. Later still the British Graham Land Expedition, the last major British expedition in the area under private enterprise, mapped extensively in the southern half of the peninsula. The Falkland Islands Dependencies Survey (which arose from Operation Tabarin) and its successor British Antarctic Survey have since mapped and completed geological and biological surveys from a string of stations throughout the area. Argentine and Chilean national expeditions have done similar work, mainly in the north.

## Politics

The area is claimed by Argentina, Britain and Chile. To Britons it is an interesting but remote colonial territory, maintained perhaps from a sense of tradition and duty—a curious anomaly in times of rigorous economies in national expenditure. Argentines and Chileans see it as the southern extension of their own countries. While all three subscribe to the Antarctic Treaty, none shows the least inclination to surrender its claim to the others or to the world at large. Significantly, British and Argentine stations in this sector of Antarctica retained normal friendly relations during the 1982 struggle over the Falkland Islands. South Georgia and the South Sandwich Islands became involved, but not Antarctica within the Treaty area.

## Landings in the northern peninsula area

Cruise-ship itineraries and landings in this area are determined very much by the day-to-day movements of drifting pack ice, and of the ships themselves. Cruise leaders compare notes frequently by radio, reporting weather and ice conditions, and trying to keep out of each others' way. This maintains an illusion, treasured by some passengers, of being alone in the wilderness. Less romantic and more realistic travellers are always interested to see another ship and more passengers: they wave to each other and wonder who is having the better time.

## Esperanza

On the north-eastern tip of the peninsula (Map 9) lies Hope Bay, a magnificent natural harbour and a site of both historic and current interest (Figure 7.3). Here stands another of Antarctica's small towns, the Argentine military and scientific station Esperanza (Figure 7.3). The settlement, an orderly collection of scarlet chalets housing a few dozen military families and scientists, borders a much larger township of Adelie penguins estimated to include some 50 000 nests. Behind towers Mount Flora, a conical peak named not for its present-day vegetation, but for a fossil flora of leaves, seeds and fragments of wood discovered at the turn of the century in one of its outcrops.

Esperanza is usually open for visits by previous arrangement. You may be met at the quay by a ranger in khaki uniform with lemon-squeezer hat, who hands out information on the station and its environs. One of the first buildings along the main road is a small stone hut, restored and ringed by a rope-and-post fence, where three men of Nordenskiöld's Swedish expedition wintered involuntarily in 1902–03 (Figure 7.4). From their hopes of rescue came the name Hope Bay (Box 7.3). On a rise overlooking Esperanza stands an old British station, built in February 1952 and

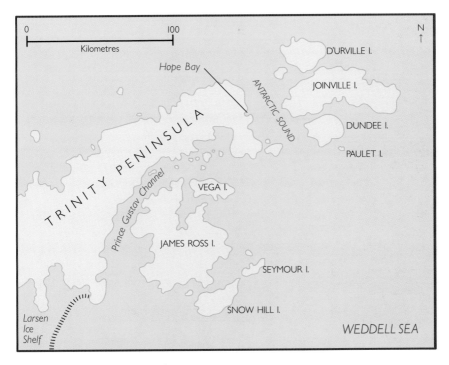

**Map 9**   *The Trinity Peninsula.*

Box 7.1 Historic expeditions

| | |
|---|---|
| 1820 | Captain William Smith and Edward Bransfield charted 'Trinity Land', now Trinity Peninsula, on the northern tip of Antarctic Peninsula. |
| 1820–21 | US sealer Nathanial Palmer discovered 'Palmer Land': his discovery is recognized in Palmer Archipelago. |
| 1832 | British sealers John Biscoe and George Avery discovered Adelaide Island and Graham Land, 1832. |
| 1838 | A French naval scientific expedition led by Jules-César Dumont d'Urville in Astrolabe and Charles-Hector Jacquinot in Zélée discovered Orléans Channel and d'Urville and Joinville islands, off the tip of the peninsula. |
| 1843 | Captain James Clark Ross in HMS Erebus, accompanied by Francis Crozier in HMS Terror, discovered land that is now called James Ross Island. |
| 1874 | Captain Eduard Dallman in the German steam sealer Grönland, hunting for seals and whales, charted Bismarck Strait and nearby coasts. |
| 1892–93 | Four Scottish whaling ships from Dundee (Balaena, Active, Diana and Polar Star) with scientist William Bruce aboard, and the Norwegian whaling ship Jason (Captain Carl Anton Larsen), independently explored the northern peninsula area to investigate possibilities of commercial whaling. |
| 1893–94 | Norwegian whaling ships Jason (with Captain C. A. Larsen), Castor and Hertha explored widely along Antarctic Peninsula: no whales caught, but returned with seal skins and oil. |
| 1897–99 | Belgian Antarctic Expedition. Lt. Adrien de Gerlache de Gomery in Belgica explored Palmer Peninsula and western Antarctic Peninsula whilst overwintering in pack ice of Bellingshausen Sea. |
| 1901–04 | Swedish South Polar Expedition, led by Dr Nils Otto Nordenskiöld, wintered at Snow Hill Island and surveyed the Prince Gustav Channel area. After their ship Antarctic was crushed by ice in the Weddell Sea, parties wintered at Hope Bay and Paulet Island: they were rescued by the Argentine naval sloop Uruguay. |
| 1903–05 | French South Polar Expedition, led by Dr Jean-Baptiste Charcot, wintered in Français at Booth Island, Palmer Archipelago, exploring and charting south to Adelaide Island. |

1908–10     Second French South Polar Expedition, led by Charcot, wintered in Pourquoi pas? at Petermann Island and explored southward into the Bellingshausen Sea, discovering Marguerite Bay and Charcot Land.

1910–11     Exploratory voyages for floating factories along the peninsula: annual whaling expeditions followed.

1911–12     German South Polar Expedition, led by Dr Wilhelm Filchner, intended to cross Antarctica. A base established on Filchner Ice Shelf had to be evacuated when the shelf calved; their ship Deutschland was beset for 9 months in pack ice.

1921–22     Thomas Bagshawe and Maxim Lester wintered at Waterboat Point, surveying and recording meteorology, tides, geology and breeding of gentoo penguins.

1925–27     Start of Discovery Expeditions, which for many years undertook research on whales, marine biology and hydrography, especially in the Scotia Arc and peninsular sector of Antarctica.

1928–29     Wilkins-Hearst Antarctic Expedition. Attempting to cross Antarctica by air, Sir Hubert Wilkins overflew Antarctic Peninsula and Weddell Sea from Deception Island, South Shetlands, to Hearst Island (71 °S).

1929–30     In a second attempt to cross Antarctica, Sir Hubert Wilkins flew from Deception Island over the north end of the peninsula, then south over Charcot Island and Bellingshausen Sea to 73° S.

1934–35     Preparing for an aborted attempt to cross Antarctica by air, US explorer Lincoln Ellsworth overflew part of Trinity Peninsula from Snow Hill Island.

1934–37     British Graham Land Expedition, led by Australian John Rymill, explored the west coast of Antarctic Peninsula from bases in Argentine Islands and Marguerite Bay, sledging south to King George VI Sound with air support.

1935–36     Lincoln Ellsworth overflew West Antarctica from Dundee Island to Bay of Whales (Box 7.2).

1939–41     United States Antarctic Service Expedition. Western party led by Commander Richard Byrd established base on Stonington Island, Marguerite Bay, exploring plateau and southern peninsula area by sledge and air.

1943–44     Operation Tabarin. First permanent Antarctic research station established by British naval expedition at Port Lockroy, Wiencke Island. Forerunner of many British, Argentine and Chilean stations in the peninsula area.

**Figure 7.3** *Part of the Argentine research station Esperanza, at Hope Bay, Antarctic Peninsula. Like the Chilean station in Maxwell Bay (Figure 6.9), this is a military base with scientists attached. The station has living quarters for families, a school, shops, and other amenities of civilization.*

**Figure 7.4** *Swedish explorer Otto Nordenskiöld and two companions pitched their tent on the empty beach of this bay in late summer 1903, waiting vainly for their relief ship* Antarctica *to arrive. Eventually they built this stone hut, and spent the winter in it, calling their location Hope Bay.*

**Figure 7.5** *Base D, a British station of Operation Tabarin, was built at Hope Bay in March 1945. It was destroyed by fire in November 1948, with the loss of two lives. Both British and Argentine bases have since been built at Hope Bay. The site of the tragedy, never cleared up, is now a rubbish dump.*

closed 12 years later. Below on the foreshore are the remains of an older British hut, the original Base D of Operation Tabarin, built in 1945 and tragically destroyed by fire in November 1948. The site has never been tidied and could be mistaken (as indeed it clearly has been) for a rubbish dump. Close by are graves of two young scientists, Canadian meteorologist Dick Burd and British geologist Michael Green, who died in the fire (Figure 7.5).

## Antarctic Sound

From Esperanza, cruise ships often head south-eastward through Antarctic Sound (named for Nordenskiöld's ship) toward Erebus and Terror Gulf (named much earlier for Ross's ships). Known locally as 'Iceberg Alley', the sound is usually littered with tabular icebergs that have calved from ice shelves much farther south, and drifted north with the clockwise circulation of the Weddell Sea.

A few miles south of Esperanza stand the steep cliffs of Brown Bluff, made up of brown tuffs and breccias (airborne volcanic deposits) capped by dark lavas—a reminder, should we need one, of the ancient volcanic history of this area. Adelie penguins nest along the foot of the bluff. This makes a pleasant landing, a wilderness alternative to the bright lights of Esperanza. Across the sound lie ice-capped D'Urville and Joinville Islands, charted by the French expedition of 1837–40 that later discovered Terre Adélie, on the far side of Antarctica (Chapter 9).

## Box 7.2   First flight across Antarctica

*Lincoln Ellsworth, a wealthy US explorer inspired by the spirit of frontiersman Wyatt Earp and the polar adventures of Richard Byrd, was determined to make the first flight across Antarctica. His first attempt, starting in the Bay of Whales in 1933–34, failed when his aircraft was damaged in offloading from the expedition ship (called Wyatt Earp after his hero). His second attempt, starting from Snow Hill Island 1 year later, was foiled by bad weather. In November 1935 he was successful: Ellsworth and Canadian pilot Herbert Hollick-Kenyon took off from the ice cap of Dundee Island, and overflew the unknown interior of West Antarctica. He discovered Eternity Range, at the base of Antarctic Peninsula, and Sentinel Range farther south, then crossed miles of featureless plateau before descending to the Ross Ice Shelf.*

*Running out of fuel, they landed a few miles short of Bay of Whales and walked on to the ruins of Byrd's abandoned Little America II station. There they camped, to be picked up by the British research ship* Discovery II *and transferred 4 days later to* Wyatt Earp, *which had steamed round to collect them. Sentinel Range, which includes Vinson Massif (5140 m, 16 863 ft), Antarctica's highest mountain, forms the western bloc of what are now called the Ellsworth Mountains: the ice-covered plateau beyond is Hollick-Kenyon Plateau. Ellsworth claimed his discoveries for the United States, but the claims were never ratified.*

Neighbouring Dundee Island, named by the 1893 Scottish whaling expedition, is almost entirely ice capped except for Welchness, its westernmost point. Behind the point nestles a small, summer-only Argentine base, Petrél Station. This too makes an agreeable landing, used sometimes when Esperanza and Brown Bluff are icebound. Dundee Island provided the airstrip for the first-ever trans-Antarctic flight (Box 7.2).

In mid-sound stands tiny Rosamel Island, 416 m (1365 ft) high, a volcanic remnant with the section of a crater clearly visible in the south-east corner. Ships usually pass east of it, skirting the ice cliffs of Dundee Island, rounding Cape Purvis, and heading toward Paulet Island, more clearly a volcanic cone, that looms ahead.

### Paulet Island

About 3.5 km long and 2.5 km across (2.2 × 1.6 miles) this is a relatively recent volcano with red-brown scoria cone. Evening sunshine highlights colours on the western slopes, making them glow as though still cooling. The cone, which may well have risen within the last 1000 years, rests on a foundation of lavas, forming cliffs 200 m (660 ft) high at the southern end, much lower in the north. Its rim, 353 m (1160 ft) high, hides a small summit crater, and there is an older crater on its western flank.

Paulet Island is home to several 100 000 pairs of Adelie penguins—about as many as you are ever likely to see together—which nest on every available beach and well up the sides of the cones. Clearly this island stands in a very rich area of sea, with few alternative nesting grounds available. The island supports also a few

**Figure 7.6** *This small corner of a very large Adelie-penguin colony on Paulet Island includes another historic hut, in which 22 shipwrecked survivors of Nordenskiöld's Swedish expedition spent the winter of 1903. In some years the colony extends to include the hut as well.*

hundred pairs of blue-eyed shags, and Weddell seals are particularly abundant on the beaches and off-lying pack ice.

Of more human interest is the remains of a hut, about 200 m (660 ft) inland from a small cove on the north-eastern side of the island (Figure 7.6). Measuring about 12 × 8 m (40 × 26 ft), with stone walls 1–2.5 m (3.3–8 ft) high, this was built by 20 castaways from Nordenskiöld's expedition ship *Antarctic*, which was crushed in pack ice some 40 km (25 miles) offshore in late February 1903 (Box 7.3). The party was rescued after a hard winter by an Argentine naval ship. The grave of Ole Christian Wennersgaard, a seaman of the expedition who died during the winter, lies close to the shore some 300 m (980 ft) from the hut, marked by a cross and now completely overwhelmed by penguin nests.

## Snow Hill and Seymour Islands

These two islands lie in line astern some 80 km (50 miles) south of Paulet Island, in an area where pack ice and tabular bergs often make navigation difficult: in consequence they are not often visited. Seymour Island, a bare, rugged island, is noted for its outcrops of fossil-bearing strata in which Swedish geologists initially, and many others since, found remains of plants, penguins and primitive whales. The most recent finds include fragments of small land mammals. In a bay on the northern flank of the island stands Vice-Commodoro Marambio, an Argentine air

## Box 7.3   The Swedish South Polar Expedition 1901–04

*Otto Nordenskiöld, an established Arctic explorer, sailed south in 1901 to investigate the east coast of Antarctic Peninsula, bordering the Weddell Sea. His ship* Antarctic *was commanded by C. A. Larsen, a whaling captain with experience at both ends of the world. In summer 1902 Nordenskiöld set up a small base on Snow Hill Island. During the following winter and spring he and his companions sledged and surveyed south to 66°S along the ice-bound eastern flank of Antarctic Peninsula, and north to Prince Gustav Channel, filling in many empty spaces on the maps.*

   Antarctic *wintered in South Georgia. In the following summer Larsen tried to relieve Snow Hill, but failed due to heavy pack ice. In late summer* Antarctic *became caught and crushed in the pack ice, sinking off Paulet Island. Larsen led the crew of 22 to the island, where they built a stone hut, roofed it with sail canvas, and spent a crowded, uncomfortable winter. Meanwhile three men that Larsen had landed at Hope Bay found themselves stranded there, wintering in a tent which they surrounded with stone walls. In November 1903 all three groups were rescued by the Argentine naval ship* Uruguay.

station complete with small airstrip. Native inhabitants include a colony of about 20 000 pairs of Adelie penguins.

   Southwest of Seymour Island looms Snow Hill Island, larger and mostly ice capped, with an ice-free north-eastern peninsula on which stands the isolated hut of Nordenskiöld's expedition. Built in 1902, this is Antarctica's oldest dwelling, contemporary with Scott's *Discovery* hut in McMurdo Sound. Argentine museum staff have repaired and tidied it. If you visit, please take great care to shut the door when you leave, so that the hut does not fill with snow during winter blizzards.

   The Adelie colony has grown, but otherwise changed little, since first described by Nordenskiöld's biologist K. A. Andersson. This is a very likely area for seeing emperor penguins: keep a good lookout on pack ice, especially for groups of grey woolly chicks that represent the final stages of colony life. Almost certainly a colony forms somewhere in this area every winter, on a site as yet undetected. Chicks floating on ice floes are not necessarily at a disadvantage: parents may well be with them, perhaps swimming nearby in search of food. This is also a good area for snow petrels—perhaps the most elegant of all Antarctic birds. Almost inevitably they appear when pack ice is around, floating in flocks of several dozen like black-eyed ghosts.

## Bransfield Strait

Ships' captains tend to dislike this ice-strewn corner of Antarctica, and are glad to return through Antarctic Sound to Bransfield Strait. After a day spent off the northern tip of the peninsula they usually head westward along the strait overnight, keeping well out from the land to avoid reefs and small islands. Of these, plenty are marked on the charts, but there are probably many more unmarked, so it is safest to keep to deep water. Landings are possible on both Astrolabe Island and Tower Island, though there is little to see on either. Mikkelsen Harbour on Trinity Island and Murray Harbour on Bluff Island were both used to anchor whaling factory ships between 1912 and mid-1920s, though again there is little to see on the spot.

## Landings in the mid-peninsula area

This may be an all-night leg of the cruise, but from late November to mid-February there is reasonable light even at midnight. If the weather is clear, it is far too good to miss: you may find it worth while to stay up on watch. By early morning southbound ships have usually entered Gerlache Strait (Figure 7.7), a channel 40–50 km (25–30 miles) wide between Palmer Archipelago and the Danco Coast (Map 10). Now you are entering what many regard as Antarctica's most beautiful area. It is especially striking in early morning light, before the sun climbs high and flattens the relief.

At first there is not much to see—just an inky sea strewn with ice floes and smallish tabular bergs, with a line of distant mountains in either side. As the channel narrows the mountains come closer, the mainland peninsula to port (left), the islands of Palmer Archipelago to starboard. Most ships keep over to the west, taking Croker Passage between Liège Island and Two Hummock Island: on the latter note Palaver Point, so named for its colony of disputatious penguins. Off the Enterprise Islands, in Gouvernøren Bay, lies the wreck of a Norwegian whaling

**Figure 7.7** *Moving slowly through thin remnants of pack ice and bergy bits, a cruise ship heads toward Antarctica. Though blessed with clear weather and a calm sea, the master will still proceed with caution. These seaways are well charted, but fragments of ice can hide reefs and other hazards.*

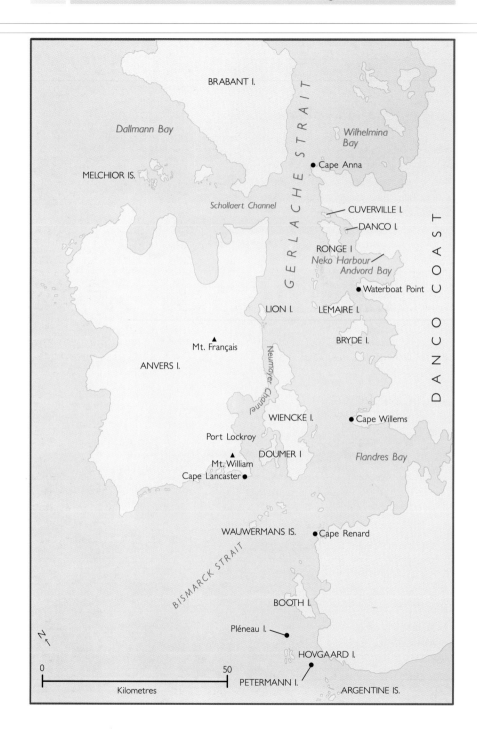

**Map 10**   *The Danco Coast.*

**Figure 7.8**    *Antarctic Peninsula on a fine day, with sparkling seas, brilliant ice, and a prospect of distant mountains. Within hours this can turn to heavy overcast, with strong winds, blowing sleet, flying spray, and lectures or videos on board instead of landings.*

transport ship, *Gouvernøren*, which burnt and sank there in 1916. Half the wreck is beached; the other half is clearly visible on the seabed, surrounded by whale bones.

By Brabant Island the strait narrows to 16 km (10 miles), restricted on the mainland side by Reclus Peninsula, Nansen Island and Arctowski Peninsula. Now the mountains stand closer, rising in jagged ranks to heights of 2000 m (6560 ft) and more. We see the undulating line of the peninsula plateau, the ice-mantled island peaks and ridges, the high ice fields and the glaciers tumbling from them (Figure 7.8). There are no landings hereabouts: ice shelves line the shore on either side, terminating in white cliffs over 30 m (100 ft) high. Immediately beyond lies Errera Channel, an L-shaped passage some 4 km (2.5 miles), which for many forms the highlight of their cruise (Box 7.4).

## Cuverville Island

A small, domed island in the mouth of Errera Channel, Cuverville has a northern face of striking black rocks, streaked and capped with green). The capping is a thick layer of moss, growing abundantly on well-watered ledges along the upper face of the cliffs. The moisture comes from an ice cap that rises behind, covering the highest point of the dome, and providing constant irrigation of melt water throughout summer. Below the cliffs a wide cobbled beach is home to some 4800 pairs of gentoo penguins—Antarctica's largest-known colony of the species.

This is a popular landing for many reasons. For a start, Zodiacs approaching the beach must often wind through a sculpture park of stranded bergy bits, calved from

Box 7.4   German and Belgian connexions

This central area of the peninsula was first charted in 1873–74 by Captain Eduard Dallmann, a German sealer from Hamburg. Exploring for fur seals in Grönland, a small steamship, Dallmann made several landfalls around the as-yet unidentified Anvers Island, naming Bismarck Strait in the south after his head of state and Grönland Point in the north after his ship. His own name appears in Dallmann Bay, between Anvers and Brabant Islands (Figure 7.9).

Belgian names date from more detailed surveys by the Belgian Antarctic Expedition of 1897–99. Leader Adrian de Gerlache commemorated the towns of Anvers (Antwerp) and Liège and the province of Brabant for their financial support: many smaller islands and features close by are named for similar reasons. Nansen Island he named after the distinguished Arctic explorer; Wilhelmina Bay, an area of spectacular islands, glaciers and rocky headlands immediately to the south commemorates the teenaged Queen of the Netherlands, whose country also backed his expedition. Errera Channel was named after a Belgian botanist, Cuverville Island for a French admiral who helped with supplies. The Danco Coast and Danco Island commemorate Lt. Emile Danco, a scientist who died in June 1899 on the homeward voyage.

The Belgica expedition was remarkable for three non-Belgian members. Polish geologist Henryk Arctowski we have already met. The third mate was Norwegian Roald Amundsen, later to explore the North-east Passage and gain the South Pole. The doctor was American Frederick Cook, later to claim (though some say falsely) the North Pole.

**Figure 7.9**   *From the high point of Cuverville Island, we look across ice-strewn Gerlache Strait to Anvers and Brabant Islands. On the strand below are the huts and tents of the author's scientific expedition, close to part of the gentoo-penguin colony that was the focal point of our studies.*

**Figure 7.10** *Visitors wander around the Cuverville Island gentoo-penguin colony, watched by our team of observers, who check their behaviour and the responses of penguins and skuas to their presence. Well-behaved visitors, moving slowly and quietly, had little measurable impact on the colony.*

neighbouring ice cliffs, fashioned by fragmentation and melting into fantastic shapes, and now aground in shallows of the northern shore. A dozen Henry Moores at peak performance could hardly have done better. Ice is white? No way: this is where you appreciate the astonishing range of colours, from cornflower blue to emerald green, to be found in glacier ice. Is the surface smooth? You will see every texture from coarse crystalline to high gloss, every surface finish from lustre to a curious hammered-pewter effect, acquired by underwater melting and revealed when the bergs turn over.

The gentoos you meet ashore (Figure 7.10) are the largest, gentlest and most musical of the pygoscelid or brush-tailed penguins (Box 7.5). This was the colony where, for three successive summers (1992–95), my research group studied impacts of tourism on the environment, including interactions between penguins and visitors. What did we find? I have summarized some of the more important points in Chapter 11.

There is something remarkably soothing about watching penguins. Whatever time of the breeding season, they usually provide entertainment—from courtship and nest-building in November to chick rearing and moult through January and February. What they are doing they have done each year for thousands of years, possibly millions, starting long before man came down from the trees. They demand from us no intervention, approval or disapproval, no subsidies, recognition, assistance, or granting of rights. They will continue long after we have worried and legislated ourselves into our graves.

## Box 7.5   The brush-tailed penguins

*Adelie, chinstrap and gentoo penguins belong to the genus* Pygoscelis: *the name means 'brush-tailed', and it is not difficult to see why they earned it. Though distinctive in dress, particularly about the head and neck, they are remarkably similar in every other respect, from choice of nest sites to breeding routine. Often two of the species breed together in the same colonies, more rarely all three: in shared colonies, each species tends to keep to its own patches. Mixed couples are occasionally seen, but no hybrids.*

*Chinstraps are smallest, fiercest toward each other and the rest of the world, and noisiest. They breed almost exclusively in the South American sector of Antarctica, from South Georgia through the Scotia Arc to the midriff of Antarctic Peninsula. Adelies come next in size, breeding mainly on the continent, peninsula and southern Scotia Arc. Gentoos are largest and mildest, with a wide range extending from Antarctic Peninsula, throughout the Scotia Arc, to islands of the Southern Ocean and South America—you may have seen them near Ushuaia. While Adelies and chinstraps are similar throughout their ranges, gentoos form at least two and possibly several races. Southern gentoos are generally smaller and stockier than northern ones, with much longer breeding seasons.*

*Adelies are usually first to breed, starting in late October or early November: chinstraps and gentoos start 2 to 3 weeks later. All three species build with stones, moss, bones and whatever else they can find, and lay two eggs, incubating for about 35 days. The chicks of all species are pale silvery-grey when hatched, but quickly grow denser down, Adelies dark brown, chinstraps grey, gentoos dark grey backed with white underparts, and orange bills like their parents. Chicks grow quickly: Adelies take 7 to 8 weeks, chinstraps and gentoos slightly longer, to be ready for the sea.*

*Young pygoscelid penguins suffer very high mortality in their first and second years. Those that survive return to the colonies from their second and third years onward. They go through the motions of courtship and nesting (we call them 'play-nesters'), but do not usually breed successfully until at least their fourth or fifth years. How long do these penguins live? Probably up to 15 or 20 years. Are they intelligent? Not adaptable as mammals are, but very well programmed for dealing efficiently with their normal, fairly narrow range of experiences. Hopeless at crossword puzzles, but dedicated parents.*

*For an old but excellent account of these and other penguins read Robert Cushman Murphy's* Oceanic Birds of South America: *despite the title he includes the Antarctic species.*

Of the hundred or so pairs of skuas that nest on the island, only half a dozen prey on penguins: the rest feed elsewhere, probably at sea. Watch them landing on the colony, alert and enterprising, waiting their chance to feed. They steal eggs and chicks, but often simply scavenge for fish or krill that spill when parent penguins feed their young. Are you tempted to take sides between predator and prey? Remember that skuas too have hungry chicks waiting for supper back home.

There are several routes up the hill behind Cuverville beach: parties under guidance can find their way up in well less than an hour. Pause for breath on the

**Figure 7.11** *Many gentoos nest high on the ridges of Cuverville Island. This allows them to breed early in the season, when the ridges are clear of snow. As these deep-worn tracks indicate, high nesting requires many laborious climbs on short legs, both before and after the snow disappears.*

ridge half way up, where the highest penguins nest. So they are crazy to nest up there? No, just keen to nest early: it makes better sense at the start of the season, when the ridges are clear of winter snow, while the sites below still lie under a metre or more (Figure 7.11). From the summit in fine weather you can see across Gerlache Strait to the Solvay Mountains of Brabant Island on the right, Schollaert Channel and Dallmann Bay immediately ahead, and the crowded peaks of Anvers Island, like kings in conference, on the left. Several dozen pairs of McCormick's or Antarctic skuas nest on top: keep out of their way or they will thump you hard (Figure 7.12). On the way down, and on the journey back to the ship, watch out for humpback and minke whales in the channel.

## Rongé Island

The narrow channel west of Cuverville Island was once a whaling harbour: an islet in the middle still bears a huge, rusty mooring chain and the wreck of a waterboat, and the near end of Cuverville beach has the remains of a dam for collecting freshwater. Alongside stands Rongé Island, with small but very active glaciers. Five minutes away by Zodiac, Georges Point on its northern end has large colonies of gentoo and chinstrap penguins, and there are more chinstraps on the off-lying Orne Islands.

**Figure 7.12**   *A McCormick's (or Antarctic) skua, smaller and paler than brown skuas (Figures 2.17 and 6.5), guards a chick and two eggs on a mossy nest high on Cuverville Island. These skuas feed mainly at sea, ignoring the penguin colony immediately below.*

## Danco Island

From Cuverville, however, ships usually head south into the narrow passage of Errera Channel. Look out for a small colony of blue-eyed shags on the south-east corner of the island, as you go past. On days when swell or pack ice make Cuverville inaccessible, Danco Island provides a possible alternative. The hut is British, built in 1956 and closed only 3 years later: it is maintained in reasonable condition, marred by rubbish in both front and backyards. Dominican gulls nest in the anthracite pile by the front door. Watch out for their speckled chicks, which may run for the sea if disturbed. About 1500 pairs of gentoos and a number of particularly fierce skuas nest on the slopes behind. It is an easy climb to the top of the hill, for an all-round view of an extraordinarily beautiful channel (Figure 7.13).

## Neko Harbour

Emerging from the southern end of Errera Channel, a sharp turn to port around Beneden Head brings us to Andvord Bay, a wide, ice-lined fjord surrounded on three sides by ice-covered mountains. To either side stand steep mountain ridges, almost completely ice covered and lined with ice cliffs. At the end of the bay rises a sheer rock ridge, flanked by three magnificent glaciers. Behind it towers Antarctic Peninsula itself, rising almost sheer to 1700 m (6000 ft). Less than 16 km (10 miles) away, on the far side of its narrow ridge, glaciers begin their more gentle descent to the Weddell Sea.

**Figure 7.13** *Errera Channel, separating Cuverville Island from Rongé Island and Antarctic Peninsula. From January onward, keep a lookout for humpback whales with calves. Here a calf lies at the surface, while the mother, tail in air, disappears on a deep feeding dive.*

On the left of the fjord, three-quarters of the way along, lies a tiny harbour under the shelter of a rocky ridge. This is Neko Harbour, named for an old floating factory of the Salvesen whaling fleet that, from 1911, anchored here off and on for almost 20 seasons. Steam, smoke, cadavers, oily refuse, whale-catchers scurrying up and down—it is almost impossible to imagine so much activity, year after year, in so placid a corner. Today there is little to see save a few bones on the shore. More bones lie full fathoms five (all right—9.1 m, 30 ft) down on the seabed, gleaming in the clear water.

A small Argentine refuge hut, red-painted and in good condition, stands on the ridge. Dominican gulls and three to four hundred gentoo penguins nest on the slopes above. A pair of sheathbills—sensible birds—raise a chick or two each year in the hut porch (Figure 7.14). Weddell and elephant seals slumber on the narrow cobbled beach.

A pleasant enough corner, but why come to Neko Harbour? Cruise operators like it for a totally different reason. Most landings are on islands: here they can tell you (with perfect truth, so far as anyone knows), that the small rocky ridge forms part of the mainland. Stand on that narrow beach of Neko Harbour (well, preferably on the rocky outcrop immediately above), and you stand on Antarctica.

## Waterboat Point

West across Andvord Bay lies Duthiers Point, and west of that a narrow channel between the mainland and Lemaire Island. Ahead on the port side, on a low rocky

**Figure 7.14**   *Sheathbill: a snow-white, pigeon-like bird with pink wattled face, that scavenges on penguin colonies. Sheathbills make a living from penguin droppings, abandoned eggs, shell membranes, dead or dying chicks, and krill that is spilt when the penguins feed their chicks.*

point jutting out from the ice cliff, you see a cluster of orange-painted huts (Figure 1.4, p. 13). This is Presidente González Videla, a venerable Chilean air force station. Built in May 1951, it was occupied continuously at first and then intermittently, abandoned for a time, and recently refurbished. Summer parties still use it: if the Chilean tricolor flag is flying, there will be someone to welcome you.

The Chileans share the point with about 2000 pairs of gentoo penguins, which nest on every patch of raised ground that is not occupied by a hut. Elephant seals prefer living in the huts: half a dozen usually lie grumbling at each other in the doorless hangar by the helicopter pad, roaring in harmony if you disturb them. Take care how you walk at Waterboat Point: on rainy days the granite rocks are slippery and the ground becomes a quagmire. If you fall, you will smell strongly of penguins for the rest of the voyage. Alternatively you may smell like a farmyard: in the early days the Chileans kept pigs and cows in the station, and there is still stable litter on the ground near the old cowsheds.

The point owes its name to a waterboat that was abandoned on the beach in the early days of whaling, and occupied for a year (January 1921 to January 1922) by two young Britons—Antarctica's smallest-ever expedition. Thomas Bagshawe, a geologist, and Maxim Lester, a merchant marine officer, came to Antarctica with two others to find a site for a more ambitious expedition—one that planned to photograph the peninsula from the air, using surplus World War bombers. When the venture fell through, Bagshawe and Lester decided to stay on, camping in the waterboat which they extended with an annex of food boxes. The whalers who brought them left with serious misgivings: they returned in spring to find the two healthy and cheerful, determined to complete a full year, with an impressive record of tidal, climatic, biological and survey observations.

The waterboat existed until the 1950s, but disappeared soon after the Chilean station was built. Only the keel plate and the charred stubs of the annex doorposts remain, now marked off by rusty barrels, a ring of tattered rope and a makeshift noticeboard. The penguins do their best to honour the site, covering it with nests which afford it some protection.

## Paradise Harbour

Immediately beyond Waterboat Point the channel opens into a wide bay, circled by protecting mountains. Named by whalers who sought shelter in its coves and inlets, Paradise Harbour is still a splendid haven, often sunny, calm and reflective when the world outside is turbulent and gloomy.

The customary landing is at Almirante Brown, an Argentine station on Coughtrey Peninsula in the south-east corner of the bay. From a small quay, steps lead up to a cluster of huts which include an oceanography laboratory, store and generator shed: a larger hut close by provides living quarters for about a dozen. These are remnants of a much larger station, built in 1951 and named for a 19th-century Irish-Argentine admiral, one of the founders of the Argentine Navy. Like many other Antarctic stations, it was destroyed by fire: the story goes that someone set it on fire because he did not want to spend another winter there. Groups of oceanographers and marine biologists now spend agreeable summers at Almirante Brown, studying seasonal changes in water quality and plankton in the harbour.

As prime examples of animal adaptability, note the seven pairs of penguins that live in the foundations of the engine shed. Their nesting material includes such handy materials as coal, nails, nuts and bolts, corks, corn cobs and a discarded spark plug. In 1995–96 a pair of Dominican gulls nested happily on an oil drum just a few metres from the oceanography laboratory. Usually the most neurotic of birds, they watched with placid interest the groups of visitors queuing to buy T-shirts and postcards.

The true attractions of Paradise Harbour are best seen in Zodiac tours: against a background of magnificent peaks, glaciers and sculptured bergs, it is not unusual in a half-hour cruise to see a large colony of nesting shags, cliffs green with copper ore, crabeater and leopard seals afloat on sea ice, and both minke and humpback whales. One large female leopard seal in this harbour sometimes becomes intrigued by a slow-moving or drifting Zodiac, swimming under and around it, popping up for a closer look, occasionally taking an experimental nibble at the trailing ends of the pontoons. This behaviour provides good photo opportunities but some misgivings: I have never known a leopard seal puncture a boat, still less leap aboard, but … Revving the engine or banging the side usually sends her away.

## Neumeyer Channel

On the north-western side of Gerlache Strait, between Anvers and Wiencke Islands, runs another spectacular mile-wide rift, named by de Gerlache for Georg von

Neumeyer, the German polar geographer. Often blocked with early-season ice, it usually clears by mid- to late November, and provides a pleasing, winding run of over 30 km (20 miles). Toward the southern end look out for Damoy Point, in a harbour with a substantial hut. This has been a staging post for British Antarctic Survey: on the ice shelf close by is a runway, from which scientists could be flown south to Rothera Station and beyond without waiting for the sea ice to clear. Now BAS has a larger aircraft that can fly them direct from the Falkland Islands to Rothera. It is a pleasant area to walk around, and the hut is well maintained.

## Port Lockroy

On the far side of Damoy Point lies an ice-ringed bay, discovered originally by Charcot's first expedition in 1904, and named after a French politician who helped to finance the expedition. Like Errera Channel and Paradise Harbour, this too is one of Antarctica's set pieces—a splendid harbour surrounded by mountains, glaciers and ice shelves. Experienced operators make a point of approaching the harbour in the early evening, enjoying a barbecue on deck in the beauty of the evening light, running Zodiac tours for those who want them, and riding at anchor overnight.

This is not an ideal landing: the rocks are steep and slippery in wet weather, and the flourishing gentoo-penguin colony on Jougla Point has recently expanded to fill several areas where landings were previously possible. Penguin tracks provide the best and safest walkways, though they are seldom wide enough to accommodate penguins and visitors simultaneously, and need to be policed by guides to maintain penguin rights of way.

Watch out for a dozen pairs of blue-eyed shags nesting on ledges among the penguins (Figure 7.15). Take great care not to disturb either shags or penguins; scared chicks may leap from the ledges, and find it impossible to get back.

Goudier Island, in the middle of the harbour, is the site of Operation Tabarin's 'Base A', Antarctica's first long-term settlement. Built in 1944, the station was occupied continuously until 1962 and intermittently thereafter. The huts, clearly visible from the bay, for long lay derelict and forlorn, but the recently formed British Heritage Trust has now repaired them, and opens them annually as a museum and gift shop (Figure 7.16).

Wildlife is rich in this area. Dominican gulls and Antarctic terns nest in the back bay, and skua nests are scattered all over the area: be prepared to retreat if they mob you. Sheathbills nest close to the huts of Goudier Island. Look up to the heights above and you may see snow petrels and Antarctic fulmars: together with tiny Wilson's petrels these form large flocks that feed in the harbour and adjacent waters. Giant petrels are frequent visitors, appearing particularly in February and March when the penguin chicks take to the water for the first time.

Weddell, crabeater and leopard seals are often present. There is usually at least one resident leopard seal, attacking penguins on the approaches to the colony, and from December onward several dozen crabeaters lie out on ice floes in Peltier and Neumeyer channels.

Port Lockroy was particularly popular with whalers: local channels provided good hunting in sheltered waters, and they could moor their factory ships in the

**Figure 7.15** *Blue-eyed shag with almost full-sized chick. Laying three or four eggs, in a nest made of seaweed cemented by droppings, shags usually manage to raise two or three chicks per season. They dive for food close inshore, and in clear water may be seen hunting far below the surface.*

**Figure 7.16** *Built at Port Lockroy in 1944, this was Base A of Operation Tabarin, Britain's first 'permanent' Antarctic station (one intended to be occupied over several years). After years of disuse and deterioration, it has been refurbished and reopened, selling postcards, stamps and souvenirs.*

inner harbour, protected from drifting icebergs by a submarine bank across the entrance. You can still see their rusted mooring chains on Besnard and Smith points. Jougla Point has a litter of whalebones on the back beach; during late January and February, when the snow has gone, dozens of oak barrel staves and other remnants lie strewn in valleys across the point. The rich summer feeding that formerly attracted whales to the area seems still to exist: humpback, minke and killer whales are frequently reported, and fin whales too may be increasing in numbers.

## Palmer Station

The ice cliffs of southern Anvers Island overlook many small islets and sheltered natural harbours, opening onto Bismarck Strait. In Arthur Harbour, halfway along the coast, stands the US biological research centre Palmer Station. The harbour first housed a small British station, Base N, that was built in 1955 and abandoned 3 years later. Americans put up their first hut in 1964 and opened Palmer in January 1965. Since then the station has been an important centre for long-term research in marine and terrestrial ecology.

Shipborne visitors are welcome so long as they have booked ahead. Those accepted receive an on-board video presentation of the biological research, followed by guided tours of the station, a break for coffee and cookies, and a visit to the shop for T-shirts and souvenirs. If weather permits, these are followed by a half-hour spell on neighbouring Torgersen Island, where a large colony of Adelie penguins is being studied. If they are lucky, visitors might also see one of the research ships that work from the station in summer.

A few years ago none of this was possible. Visitors—even those cleared officially to land—were cold-shouldered by the scientists, or brushed off with poor information. All that has changed: now Palmer Station offers good opportunities for US visitors to see where and how some of their tax dollars are spent in Antarctica. Most to whom I have talked after the visits are impressed, not only with the station facilities, but with the dedication of the scientists and technicians who work there.

Between Torgersen and Janus Islands lies the rusting hull of *Bahía Paraíso*, an Argentine naval transport that on 28 January 1989 struck a reef in the channel and foundered, releasing hundreds of tonnes of fuel oil into the surrounding water. All crew and passengers were rescued by Palmer personnel, and many were taken off by the cruise ship *Society Explorer*, that diverted to give assistance. The oil caused considerable damage to intertidal flora and fauna and killed many birds, but most of its effects have now disappeared.

## Lemaire Channel

South-east from Palmer Station are scattered the Wauwermans Islands, named by de Gerlache after a Belgian sponsor. In naming individual islands of the group the British hydrographers, perhaps in desperation, seized on a copy of *The Canterbury*

## Box 7.6    The French connexion

*French names on the map south of Anvers Island are due mainly to Dr Jean-Baptiste Charcot, a wealthy Parisian medical practitioner with a flair for polar exploration. Charcot first came to Antarctic Peninsula in 1903–05 in* Français, *a small sailing barque with auxiliary engine. After searching briefly for the missing Swedish South Polar Expedition (see Box 7.3), he sailed south and wintered in a small harbour of Booth Island. During the second summer he worked southward down the peninsula, discovering and exploring the Loubet Coast north of Adelaide Island.*

*On returning to France Charcot commissioned a new, larger barque, called* Pourquoi-pas? *(Why not?). During his second expedition (1908–10) he explored the South Shetland Islands, then headed south to winter at Petermann Island, slightly farther south than before. From February 1909* Pourquoi-pas? *lay in a small harbour which he named Port Circoncision (in case you are wondering, because he discovered it on 1 January, the Feast of the Circumcision in the Christian calender).*

*Charcot's scientists built small observatories for magnetometric, meteorological, seismographic and other studies. Biologists studied gentoo penguins (here at their southern limit of breeding), Adelie penguins and other wildlife. In the following summer Charcot charted more accurately his discoveries of the previous expedition, then explored the unknown region south of Adelaide Island, including Marguerite Bay which he named after his wife. In the Bellingshausen Sea he sailed beyond Alexander Land to within sight of Peter I Øy, discovering the ice-bound island now called Charcot Land.*

*Tales* and came up with Miller, Reeve, Knight, Chaucer, Manciple, Squire, Friar, Host, Prioress and Pardoner Islands. The largest of the group, Wednesday Island, was so named because the British Graham Land Expedition charted it on a Wednesday in January 1936.

Not very interesting? Well, neither are the islands themselves, at least early in the season. Low lying and snow capped, they could be mistaken for a crop of oversized mushrooms. However, around December a strange thing happens: they start to turn red and green, and by January may be transformed into vivid psychodelic toadstools. As last winter's snow disappears, patches of red and green snow algae are exposed in the underlying ice. Thin at first and almost invisible, the algae proliferate under summer sunshine and their colour intensifies (Figure 2.2). Snow algae occur all over coastal Antarctica, but seem particularly rich in this area, from Bismarck Strait south to the Argentine Islands.

South of the Wauwermans looms Booth Island, tall and twin spired: the French explorer Charcot wintered in a bay off the south-western corner in 1904 (Box 7.6). A ship keeping Booth Island to starboard looks as though it is heading for an unpleasant encounter with the mainland coast, but not so. Between the two lies the narrow passage of Lemaire Channel, 11 km (7 miles) long and generally less than 1.5 km (1 mile) wide. Pray as you approach that it is not choked with ice, for there can be few more exquisite marine channels in the world: to reach the entrance and have to turn away is a saddening experience (Figure 7.17).

**Figure 7.17** *Lemaire Channel, a narrow passage between Booth Island and the Peninsula mainland, named for a Belgian explorer of the Congo. Enjoy the splendid scenery, and keep a lookout for humpback, minke and killer whales, which seem to be using it more and more each year.*

Passage usually takes about three-quarters of an hour. We sail between towering cliffs of alternating rock and ice, opening on the mainland side into wide, wonderful glacier-lined bays. On a still day the cliffs are mirrored in inky water. In sunshine the channel glistens and sparkles: in dull weather we move through a grey tunnel, under cloud that swirls around the peaks on either side, or drops to the level of the masthead and the flanking ice cliffs. In all but the foulest weather passengers flock on deck, lining bow, stern and spotting top. Chatterers are silenced: complainers forget dysfunctional showers and overwarm cabins, and marvel instead at Antarctica.

Only dedicated bridge players seem immune. I once observed four matrons who had played almost continuously since Ushuaia, ignoring icebergs, whales, even a spurious report of mermaids: they continued to play all the way through the Lemaire Channel, and indeed all the way back. 'My, that's pretty,' said one, glancing through the window of the card room, and adding 'three no trumps' in the same breath. Bless them; in their own way they enjoyed their voyage enormously.

This is a rich area biologically: I have seldom passed through without seeing Weddell and crabeater seals on ice floes, and whales using the channel as a combined diner and highway. Penguins and blue-eyed shags nest in two or three colonies perched precariously on the sides. Snow petrels circle the high peaks, and cape petrels flutter in flocks over the water. Pack ice adrift around the southern entrance to the channel seems to host conventions of Weddell seals in early spring, and of crabeaters later in the season.

## Landings in the southern peninsula area

Penola Strait, at the southern end of Lemaire Channel, is the southernmost point for many ships on short cruises of 8–10 days. Having reached the satisfying latitude of 65°S, and passed through the channel, they turn around immediately and head back while the weather and ice remain favourable. Those that are continuing on longer cruises bear south-west into Penola Strait, usually stopping at one or other of a chain of three islands that appear off the starboard bow.

### Pléneau Island

Northernmost and smallest of the three, this island is 2 km (just over a mile) long, low lying and almost entirely ice free. Charcot named it Pléneau Point after his photographer, thinking it was part of neighbouring Hovgaard Island: however, a narrow channel separates the two, and Pléneau is an island in its own right. From Penola Strait several easy landing points give access to a platform of ice-smoothed granitic rocks, rising gently from the shore.

If you are geologically minded, walk to the top of the island and consider the difference between the low-lying point on which you are standing, and the towering cliffs of Booth Island to the north, and of the main Graham Coast, topped by the plateau, to the east. Pléneau and its neighbours form part of a bloc of mainly coarse crystalline rocks, of Cretaceous or later age. The mountains across the strait lie on a separate bloc of younger pyroclastic (volcanic) sediments and lavas, of Upper Jurassic age. The channels separating them are the clean-cut fault planes between blocs, formerly gouged by ice and now flooded by sea. Anyway it is a splendid view (Figure 7.18).

**Figure 7.18**  *Wind-polished rocks of Pléneau Island shine in late afternoon sunlight. We look across a narrow channel—a spectacular geological fault line—to the towering southern cliffs of Booth Island.*

Pléneau has a colony of gentoo penguins, and resident Weddell seals that like to sunbathe on the rocks. In January 1994 I found a young emperor penguin moulting on its own in a sheltered hollow about 1 km north of the gentoo penguins. For some cruise leaders, however, the island's main attraction is a wallow of moulting elephant seals, which is worth seeing if you have not visited one elsewhere.

About a dozen large males, up to 6 m (20 ft) long, come to Pléneau each year and lie together like overweight clients in a particularly unhygienic sauna, complaining—as well they might—about each others' bad breath and unsocial habits. There are smaller peripheral wallows with fewer and lesser seals: clearly the main one is exclusive to elders, perhaps of managerial level. Lying together during the moult reduces their heat losses, important at a time when they are renewing their surface skin and unwilling to enter the water. This is about the southern limit for elephant seals in the South-American sector of Antarctica.

## Hovgaard Island

The middle and largest island, 6 km (almost 4 miles) long and less than half as wide, is two-thirds ice covered, rising to a central ice peak 370 m (1200 ft) high. Discovered by de Gerlache, it was named after A. P. Hovgaard, a Danish meteorologist who had helped launch his expedition. There is a landing point at the northern end, with platform beach similar to that on Pléneau Island. Cruise leaders sometimes confuse the two, landing on Pléneau but calling it Hovgaard, and indeed, Jean-Baptiste Charcot made the same mistake. There is a colony of about 500 pairs of gentoo penguins, with the usual complement of skuas, Dominican gulls and Antarctic terns.

That, so far as I know, is all that is interesting about Hovgaard Island. If you land there and find anything more exciting, please be sure first of all that you are on the right island, then write and tell me about it.

## Petermann Island

The southernmost island is roughly triangular, about 2 km (over a mile) long: it is almost as wide at its high northern end, where it rises to an ice-covered peak 133 m (436 ft) high. Dallmann first charted the island in 1873–74, naming it for A. H. Petermann, a prominent German geographer. The main Zodiac landing is in Port Circumcision (Box 7.6), where Charcot wintered his ship *Pourquoi-pas?* from early February 1909.

The ship, 40 m (130 ft) long at the waterline, fitted snugly into the harbour, moored with 10 steel cables and protected from drifting icebergs by a double-steel hawser across the entrance. Mooring points can still be found in late summer when the snow has disappeard. Nothing remains of the timber observatories built by the scientists, but the expedition's stone cairn appears prominently on the skyline of Megalestris Hill (the old Latin name for skuas) behind the harbour. Up to 1992 the cairn supported a lead plaque stamped with the names of the 30 expedition members. This was sent home to Paris for safety, and the French government is arranging for a replica (Figure 7.19).

**Figure 7.19** *Expedition cairn on the highest point of Petermann Island, where the French explorer Dr J-B. Charcot wintered in 1909. Until recently the cairn bore a lead plaque carrying the names of the expedition members. This is now in France, eventually to be replaced with a replica.*

The hut on the shore is an Argentine refuge, built in 1955 and currently allowed to deteriorate. The store hut behind scatters sheets of corrugated iron downwind, which tourist parties from time to time recover and return. Britons from the former Faraday Station, some 10 km (6 miles) to the south, have occasionally used the refuge for rest and recreation. The cross close by commemorates three who were crossing the ice of Penola Strait on foot, and disappeared when it broke up unexpectedly.

From the landings in Port Circumcision there are easy, though often slippery, walks to the refuge hut, the memorial cross and the gentoo-penguin colony that surrounds them (Figure 7.20). Note in passing the coarse crystalline bedrock surrounding the harbour, crossed with prominent bands of pink granodiorite. In summer this too is an area of vivid pink and green snow algae: you can see the clusters of tiny algal cells—not to be confused with all-pervading and equally colourful penguin droppings—in the snow itself.

In rough weather, when spray breaks over the harbour, it is possible to land on a headland about 1 km to the north, close to two colonies of shags and an extensive colony of Adelie penguins. Both landings provide relatively easy access to Megalestris Hill and the cairn. In summer on Petermann Island, remnants of the winter snowfall tend to merge with the permanent ice caps. While it is safe to walk on the snow, the ice fields can be slippery: they may also be crevassed, and terminate in cliffs that drop straight into the sea. Thus it is safe to scramble on the slopes of Megalestris Hill, but do not be tempted to continue without a guide up to the ice-covered peak of the island, or along the ridge to the south. Or be sure to have put your worldly affairs in order before you do.

**Figure 7.20** World Discoverer *lies in Penola Strait, the channel between Petermann Island (on which we are standing) and the Graham Coast of Antarctic Peninsula. The explorer J-B. Charcot wintered his expedition ship* Pourquoi-Pas? *in the small bay immediately below.*

## Argentine Islands

The British *Antarctic Pilot*, an invaluable but prosaic guide to mariners, describes these islands as '. . . a picturesque archipelago interspersed with reefs and shoals through which there are navigable channels'. Cruise ships prevented by ice from reaching Pléneau, Hovgaard or Petermann Islands instead lie off in Penola Strait and explore the navigable channels by Zodiac, a pleasant occupation on a warm sunny day. The highest, Uruguay Island, rises only to 65 m (213 ft).

Most of the islands are part-covered with ice or persistent snow. On snow-free areas there seems to be plenty of groundwater, enough to support a remarkably rich vegetation, including meadows of moss, grass and algae, which is quite anomalous for the high latitude. Bird life too is abundant, every island having a complement of gulls, skuas and terns, though there is a curious dearth of penguins.

An old British station, dating from 1947, stands on the south-eastern end of Winter Island. Here stood the BGLE (The British Graham Land Expedition) base

## Box 7.7    The British connexion

*The British Graham Land Expedition of 1934–37 was a small expedition, funded on a shoestring by scientific societies and private subscriptions, with limited government support. Led by Australian John Rymill, the 16 members included some who had worked on similar expeditions in the Arctic. Using an ancient Brittany schooner Penola (named for Rymill's family sheep station), a small, single-engined Gipsy Moth aircraft fitted alternately with floats and skis, and traditional dog sledging, they explored the west coast of the peninsula thoroughly from the Argentine Islands south to Marguerite Bay, Alexander Island and beyond.*

*The expedition wintered first on the Argentine Islands in 1935, from there sledging south to Beascochea Bay, and extending their survey with flights to Adelaide Island. In the following summer they moved to the Debenham Islands, Marguerite Bay, sledging to King George VI Sound, an ice-filled rift between Alexander Island and the mainland. From the Sound they sledged east to a range of mountains that were subsequently identified as Lincoln Ellsworth's Eternity Range, spotted on his overflight just 1 year earlier. The ship and aircraft extended their survey round the northern end of Alexander Island and into Bellingshausen Sea.*

*For its size and budget the BGLE was a remarkably successful venture, rationalizing and placing in context the aerial observations of Wilkins and Ellsworth, and providing a foundation for future exploration. British explorers who worked in Antarctica during and immediately following World War II drew heavily on the experience of this expedition, living in bases similar to theirs, first following and later developing their techniques of sledging, camping, surveying and flying.*

until 1946 (Box 7.7), when it appears to have been carried away by a tidal wave. A newer, larger station, Faraday, was built in 1954 on Galindez Island. After several refurbishments and extensions it has recently (1994) passed to the Ukrainian Republic, becoming Vernadsky, their first Antarctic station. Visitors are welcome by prior arrangement.

### Crystal Sound

South of the Argentine Islands stretches a long extent of coast, much like the Danco Coast we saw lining Gerlache Strait, but icier and more rugged. Here it is called the Graham Coast; farther south it becomes the Loubet Coast, and before it lies a maze of islands, archipelagos and channels, including Crystal Sound. Despite scenic attractions, cruise ships tend to avoid this area. There is little to see that has not already been seen farther north. Pack ice is often a hazard, particularly because it hides the many known shoals and reefs, and the many more that are doubtless still to be found. Ships heading south simply to cross the Antarctic Circle (66° 32′ S) take the long, rather dull run down Penola Strait to Crystal Sound.

## Prospect Point

En route they may pass or stop at Prospect Point, a headland emerging from the mainland ice cliff, ringed by a cluster of small islands. In this pleasing setting stands an abandoned British station, Base J of the Falkland Islands Dependencies Survey. Built in 1956, almost immediately it was found to have been sited in a place from which little survey work could be done. Two years later it was closed, and assigned the status of 'refuge hut'.

In 1959, only 1 year after closure, inspection showed this expensive and well-founded timber hut already to be 'in poor condition'. Subsequent years, and possibly thoughtless visitors, have reduced Base J to a shambles of debris, scattered in and around the hut. In Antarctic cold, it rots only slowly away: it will remain a mess until someone cleans it up. Unless you are curious to visit such a site, keep away, and hope that neither you nor anyone else need ever seek refuge at Prospect Point.

## The Antarctic Circle

The Antarctic Circle crosses Crystal Sound some 56 km (35 miles) farther south, just short of Cape Rey. It is usually after midnight when you get there. Though there is nothing in particular to see, and nothing to hear but the ship's hooter and perhaps the popping of corks, crossing the circle for the first time can still be a memorable event. You have come a long way, perhaps paid a lot of money. You are in a magical setting of sea and mountains, sky and ice, probably in good company, and you have achieved an Antarctic milestone. Smart alecs who say they feel nothing at the crossing, equally with humorists who claim to have felt a bump or a draught of especially cold air, should not be encouraged. Give them to have a drink and tell them to go to bed.

## Detaille Island

Another possible landing just a few miles beyond the circle is Detaille Island, one of a group of snow-covered islands in Hanusse Bay, that again bears a British station hut. Built in 1956 as Base W, a centre for survey operations in this little-known area, the station was found to be almost as ill-sited as Prospect Point. Though sledging was possible, unreliable sea ice made it risky even to reach the mainland, and access to the interior and plateau were difficult. So Base W, like Base J, closed down after only two seasons' operations.

However, it stands within a superb bay, in an incredible setting, and remains in far better shape than Prospect Point. On my last two visits to Detaille Island, landing has been prevented by swell. Instead we made wonderful Zodiac runs around the islands, meeting killer and minke whales, having humpbacks approach close enough to touch (Figure 7.21), and drifting through mile-long flocks of feeding, chattering petrels. So who needs scruffy old huts?

**Figure 7.21** *An inquisitive humpback whale investigates our Zodiac. Slow-moving and richly endowed with blubber, humpbacks were a prime target of whalers, all but disappearing during the 1930s. Now the whalers have gone, and the chances of encounters like this increase every year.*

## Marguerite Bay

This final destination along the peninsula coast fills the huge area, 150 km long and 100 km wide (90 × 60 miles), between Adelaide Island, Alexander Island and the mainland. From Hanusse Bay there is a highly scenic back entrance through The Gullet, a narrow channel between Adelaide Island and the mainland. Strong currents keep this unfrozen in winter, though seldom free of pack ice and bergs in summer. The few cruise ships that get as far south as this usually take the longer, front-door route around Adelaide Island.

Immediately inside the northern end of Marguerite Bay stand the Dion Islands, the site of a small emperor penguin colony. By the time that cruise ships arrive in summer the colony has usually dispersed, but you may be lucky enough to see chicks on their floating nurseries of pack ice, or moulting adults. Further round, beyond the Leonie Islands, lies Rothera Station, Britain's largest scientific base with a recently extended airstrip, from which much of the current work of British Antarctic Survey is conducted. Visits are possible, but have to be arranged beforehand.

Some 65 km to the east, under the lee of the land, stand the Debenham Islands, the site of General San Martín, an Argentine research station built in 1951. Sadly, this was put up on the site of the old BGLE hut (Box 7.7) which was destroyed and all traces obliterated.

A few miles to the south is Stonington Island, site of the West Base of the US Antarctic Service Expedition of 1940–41, which most US visitors find the main attraction to this area. This island was chosen as a base site because of an ice causeway that linked it to the glacier immediately behind. Using this ramp, dog sledges and tractors could run up from sea level to Northeast Glacier, and from thence to the plateau. For the same reason Base E of the Falkland Islands Dependencies Survey was built on the island in 1946, and the US Ronne Antarctic Research Expedition (1947–48) based itself in the old US huts in the following year. That expedition, incidentally, included the first two women to overwinter: (Jennie Darlington, Jackie Ronne). All three expeditions, working with aircraft and dog teams, contributed substantially to exploration of the southern peninsula from this small, insignificant island.

Now the glacier has retreated and the causeway gone. The surviving US huts, of tough Oregon pine, have recently been stabilized and refurbished, creating a mini-museum. Base E (a 1960 replacement, not the original) remains in good condition on a neat and tidy site. Sit quietly on the ridge of Stonington Island and imagine if you can the roar of aircraft, the howling of a hundred sledge dogs, and the bustle of busy research stations—where now all is silent.

## Further reading

Charcot, J. B. 1906. *Le 'Français' au Pôle Sud. Journal de l'Expedition Antarctique Français 1903–1905.* Paris, Flammarion.

Charcot, J. B. 1911. *The Voyage of the 'Why Not' in the Antarctic.* London, Hodder and Stoughton.

Cook, F. A. 1900. *Through the First Antarctic Night.* London, Heinemann.

de Gerlache, Adrian. 1902. *Voyage de la Belgica. Quinze Mois Dans l'Antarctique.* Bruxelles, Ch. Bulens.

Darlington, J. 1947. *My Antarctic Honeymoon: A Year at the Bottom of the World.* London, Frederick Mueller Ltd.

Fuchs, Sir V. E. 1982. *Of Ice and Men: The Story of the British Antarctic Survey 1943–72.* London, Anthony Nelson.

Murphy, R. C. 1936. *Oceanic Birds of South America.* New York, Macmillan.

Nordenskjöld, N. O. G. and others. 1905. *Antarctica, or Two Years Amongst the Ice of the South Pole.* London, Hurst and Blackett.

Ronne, F. 1949. *Antarctic Conquest: The Story of the Ronne Expedition 1946–48.* New York, G. P. Putnam's sons.

Rymill, J. R. and others. 1938. *Southern Lights.* London, Chatto and Windus.

Walton, E. W. K. 1955. *Two Years in the Antarctic.* London, Lutterworth Press.

Walton, E. W. K. and Atkinson, R. 1996. *Of Dogs and Men.* Malvern, Images Publishing.

# Chapter Eight

# The Ross Sea sector

## Introduction: the Ross Dependency

The sector of Antarctica south of New Zealand is named for Captain James Clark Ross RN, who discovered it during a voyage of exploration in the summers of 1840–41 and 1841–42 (Box 8.1). Already a veteran explorer of the Arctic (and, for what it is worth, reputedly the handsomest officer in the Royal Navy), Ross was investigating the area south of New Zealand in the hope of finding both the southern continent and the South Magnetic Pole. Encountering the edge of the pack ice on 3 January 1841, he pressed southward through it, relying on the strength of his two well-founded ships. After almost a week of pushing through loose pack, to his surprise he found himself in open water, running parallel with a coastline of spectacular mountains and glaciers (Map 11).

Though frustrated in attempts to reach the South Magnetic Pole (which lay behind the mountains), Ross pressed southward to the astonishing latitude of 78° 4′ S—only 1320 km (823 miles) from the South Geographic Pole, a feat that he repeated the following year.

## Geology and ice

The Transantarctic Mountains, which form a constant backdrop in the coastal scenery of Victoria Land, are mainly sedimentary and of Jurassic to Carboniferous age (100–350 million years ago). They include sandstones, shales and coal measures, testifying to the very much warmer climate of Mesozoic Antarctica. Effectively a barrier or dam, they hold back the ice of the high plateau behind, letting it through only in the huge glaciers that pour down between individual blocks of mountains, often along fault lines.

Many of the glaciers combine to form broad ice shelves that line the piedmont coast. However, this is an area of very little precipitation, especially in the south. Several major ice streams—for example the Taylor and Ferrar glaciers—have shrivelled and retreated for want of snow, leaving 'dry' valleys and extensive ice-free or 'oasis' areas (Map 11).

Rifts or lines of weakness in the floor of the Ross Sea basin, aligned roughly north-to-south, have made this a region of intermittent volcanic activity, which has added considerable variety to the coastal scenery. In the north, activity along the line of the coast produced dark volcanic massifs extending from Cape Adare, through the Possession Islands and Cape Hallett to Coulman Island. Farther south

### Box 8.1   Discovering the Ross Sea sector

In November 1840 Captain James Clark Ross RN sailed from Hobart, Tasmania in HMS Erebus. Leader of a 3-year naval expedition to investigate terrestrial magnetism, his orders for this leg of the journey included a search for the unknown southern continent, and for the South Magnetic Pole, which was known to lie in a high latitude south of New Zealand or Australia.

Well experienced in ice work, Ross was accompanied by Commander Rawdon Crozier, another Arctic veteran, in HMS Terror. The two ships were wooden monitors, strongly built as platforms for heavy guns, and now strengthened further for icebreaking. On 17 December Erebus and Terror left Campbell Island. By then some 15 months out from England, Ross felt himself starting on that part of their long voyage that would yield the most remarkable and important results. Of his loyal and long-suffering crew, his diary recorded, not altogether probably, that '. . . joy and satisfaction beamed on every face . . .'

Christmas Day was celebrated in a strong gale with constant snow and rain. On 28 December the ships were surrounded by large tabular bergs. On 30 and 31 December they found themselves sailing through loose pack ice. On 1 January 1841 at 10.00 a.m. they crossed the Antarctic Circle in a longitude close to 170° W. Very much to his surprise Ross found himself able to continue south with relative ease. Even more to his surprise, on 10 January, after several hours of easterly gales, his ships lay in open sea with not a particle of ice to be seen in any direction from the masthead.

Nine years earlier, in a voyage to the Arctic, Ross had planted the British flag on the North Magnetic Pole. He wanted above all to be first to reach its southern counterpart. Measurements during the preceding few days confirmed that magnetic dip had increased to 85°, indicating that the pole was close at hand, and Ross steered toward it with confidence. 'Our hopes and expectations of attaining that interesting point were now raised to the highest pitch,' he wrote—'. . . soon, however, to suffer as severe a disappointment.' What dashed his hopes was an appearance of land, which '. . . rose in lofty peaks, entirely covered with perennial snow . . .' at a distance of about 160 km (100 miles).

Ross had discovered a whole new sector of Antarctica, including one of the continent's more spectacular mountain ranges. However, it lay between him and the magnetic pole, and completely spoiled his morning. Sadly he named his mountains Admiralty Range, and their peaks after members of the Board of Admiralty and others who had sponsored and equipped the expedition. Ross landed on a near-shore island (see Possession Islands, p. 191), claimed the coast for Britain and named it Victoria Land after his young queen.

Continuing south, the expedition ran into several days of gales and poor visibility. Then came clear weather, revealing an even more spectacular mountain range. By this time Ross could appreciate more cheerfully his splendid discoveries. On the morning of 15 January he and his crew '. . . gazed with feelings of indescribable delight upon a scene of grandeur and magnificence far beyond anything we had before seen or could have conceived.' These mountains, rising to over 4200 m

*(14 000 ft) he called the Royal Society Range, naming the peaks after prominent Victorian scientists.*

*Ross pressed southward through relatively light pack ice to the record latitude of 78°S, discovering in turn an island of two ice-mantled volcanic peaks, a deep embayment close by, and an unbroken ice cliff averaging over 50 m (160 ft) high, some 700 km (450 miles) long. The sea in which he sailed, the volcanic island and the ice front or barrier, all now bear his name. On 18 February, now heading northward, he reached a point within 20 km (12 miles) of land and 256 km (160 miles) from the magnetic pole. Naming the nearest point of land Cape Gauss, after the Göttingen mathematician who currently led the science of terrestrial magnetism, he continued toward Cape North, the Balleny Islands and the open ocean.*

*Ross's discoveries of January 1841, though remarkable in themselves, were more significant than he could then have guessed. The deep bay between Ross Island and the mainland, named McMurdo Bay (later McMurdo Sound) after the senior lieutenant of HMS Terror, turned out to be the southernmost point of ocean—the closest to the geographical pole that explorers in expedition ships could ever reach. So the Ross Sea, relatively ice free in summer despite its high latitude, became the route of choice for successive polar expeditions. The Ross Barrier became the highway later used by Scott, Shackleton and Amundsen to reach the South Pole.*

*Byrd used the eastern end of the Barrier, where Amundsen had built his base, as the starting point for a flight to the pole, and later for more extensive continental exploration. Later still McMurdo Sound became the site of Antarctica's largest settlement, McMurdo Station, from which is serviced Amundsen-Scott, the permanent scientific station at the South Pole.*

lie Mount Melbourne (probably active as little as 200 years ago, and still warm from its exertions) and the dark lavas of Cape Washington. South again, lack of ice cover has revealed over 50 volcanic vents in the Royal Society Range, and more in the neighbouring dry valleys. Ross Island is a complex of at least three volcanoes, of which one, Mount Erebus, is still active. Beyond lie White Island, Black Islands, Minna Bluff, Mount Discovery and Mount Morning, also volcanic in origin. Beaufort and Franklin Islands, far out in the Ross Sea, are ice-capped fragments of isolated volcanoes that were probably active 4–5 million years ago.

## Sea ice

Explorers who followed Ross confirmed that, despite its high latitude, the southern Ross Sea becomes relatively clear of sea ice every summer, affording an easy route to the southernmost point of Antarctica's coast, and the shortest land journey to the South Pole. Hence this sector's historical interest, and its continuing use as the most reliable approach to the continental interior. Cruise ships today follow the route that Ross pioneered into McMurdo Sound.

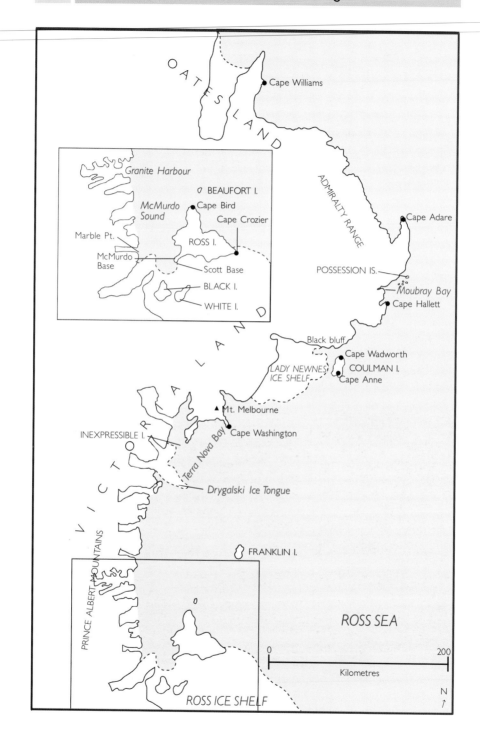

**Map 11** *The Ross Dependency.*

## Climate

This is among the colder sectors of Antarctica's coasts. Mean July (midwinter) temperatures fall to −25.8°C at McMurdo, −26.4°C at Cape Hallet. Mean January temperatures are comparatively mild, respectively −3.1°C and −1.1°C. None of these temperatures will dismay visitors from the North American Midwest, who know far more about cold than most Antarctic explorers. The southern Ross Sea has also one of the driest climates: hence the dry valleys and open ground at many points along the coast. Remember this when you are standing in a summer blizzard at McMurdo, with cold sleet trickling down your neck.

## Vegetation and wildlife

Over much of this sector we are in a cold, dry desert, with vegetation restricted to algae, mosses and lichens, and meagre even by Antarctic standards. Marine birds and mammals are relatively unaffected: they breed as far south as they can, while remaining within reach of the sea. Hence there are colonies of Adelie penguins in McMurdo Sound (Figure 8.1), emperors just round the corner at Cape Crozier, and breeding seabirds on many of the seabound cliffs of Victoria Land. Weddell seals have managed to penetrate under the Ross Ice Shelf: some 20 individuals breed successfully in a self-contained colony close to White Island.

**Figure 8.1** *Both Franklin Island and Beaufort Island, in the southern Ross Sea, support large colonies of Adelie penguins. The nests occupy ridges, formed by accumulations of nest pebbles, resting on raised beaches that mark successive stages in uplift of the islands.*

## Politics

James Clark Ross claimed Victoria Land for Britain in 1841. When over 80 years later, in 1923, Norwegian whalers began to investigate possibilities of whaling in the Ross Sea area, Britain issued an Order in Council defining the sector between longitudes 160°E and 150°W as the Ross Dependency, and placing it under New Zealand administration. New Zealand made little of its Dependency until 1956–57, when it opened a station, Scott Base, at Pram Point on Hut Point Peninsula, Ross Island, and shared responsibility with the USA for a station at Cape Hallett. Scott Base has continued in operation ever since, and the New Zealand Heritage Trust has taken responsibility for the several historic huts in the Ross Sea area.

## Visiting the Ross Dependency

The Ross Dependency has become a much appreciated venue for shipborne tourists. A glance at Map 11 confirms that it lies many degrees farther south than Antarctic Peninsula. That makes it colder, with a shorter season for ships to visit. There is more and heavier sea ice to negotiate, and the shores—when they can be reached through persistent belts of inshore pack ice—are wilder and more remote. There is scenic splendour on a much grander scale, with correspondingly less of the intimate beauty of the Peninsula's channels, islands and fjords.

In more practical terms, the main disadvantage of this sector is time spent at sea, making for longer and more expensive cruises. The northernmost landing points on Antarctica lie 5 or 6 days' sailing from the usual ports of departure—The Bluff, Dunedin or Lyttelton in New Zealand's South Island, or Hobart in Tasmania, Australia. The long days of sea time, which many find tedious and uncomfortable, may be broken by calls at one or more of the fascinating 'sub-Antarctic' (actually cold-temperate) islands that lie along the way. However, time is money: hence voyages to the Ross Dependency sector have to be more expensive than the shorter runs to and from the South American sector.

There are many compensations. The southern islands are rich in wildlife, as is the ocean surrounding them. Victoria Land is just as majestic as Ross described: the panorama of the Admiralty and Royal Society Ranges, the grandeur of McMurdo Sound, dominated by the still-active volcano Mount Erebus (Figure 8.2), and the fascination of the ice barrier, are still well worth at least one visit in every lifetime.

To those brought up on tales of the 'heroic age' of Antarctic exploration, this is undoubtedly the sector to visit. Eleven expeditions that visited the area between 1840 and 1935, several with confusingly similar names, are listed in Box 8.2. Cape Adare is the point where the first fully documented landing on Antarctica was made. There we can visit the first-ever living huts erected on the continent, and see on the hilltop the earliest explorer's grave. Farther south, in McMurdo Sound, are Scott's and Shackleton's huts, more or less as the explorers left them. Beyond lies the start of the route to the South Pole, clearly visible when the weather allows. All the historic huts in this sector are in the care of the wholly admirable New Zealand Heritage Trust, and can be visited by authorized parties under supervision. Anyone who is even remotely moved by tales from this period of exploration will find a visit

**Figure 8.2** *Emperor penguins parade the sea ice of McMurdo Sound, posing before a background of Cape Royds and volcanic Mount Erebus. They are probably from the breeding colony at Cape Crozier (Figure 8.9), some 65 km (40 miles) away on the far side of Ross Island.*

to any of the huts a never-to-be-forgotten experience. Contributions to the Trust are always welcome.

For those who relish time spent at sea, the Ross Dependency may also be visited by circumnavigating cruises from South America. Circumnavigations—usually only halfway round the continent—are the means by which cruise operators get a ship profitably from the South American sector to New Zealand or Australia. Thus the ship leaves South America or the Falkland Islands late in the season, makes landings on the South Shetlands, Antarctic Peninsula and possibly Peter I Øy (p. 247), then continues through the Bellingshausen and Amundsen Seas to the Ross Sea.

These are voyages for hearty folk who like sea time. In a fast ship the run from the southern Peninsula to McMurdo takes 9 days, in a slower ship 2 to 3 days longer. That is more than enough for people who want to see Antarctica as well as ocean. The land (far to the south and unseen) is a region of high snowfall, so the icebergs tend to be softer and the pack ice thicker. There are plenty of seabirds, though this is not an especially rich or exciting patch of ocean. Bring your knitting, and prepare for a programme of long and frequent shipboard lectures.

## Ports of departure

### Hobart, Tasmania

Hobart is a starting point for cruises both to the Australian sector and to the Ross Sea sector: for details of the city and its environs see p. 212.

Box 8.2 Historic expeditions in the Ross Sea region

1839–43     *British Naval Expedition. Leader: Captain James Clark Ross. Ships HMSs Erebus and Terror. Explored the Ross Sea region in two successive summers: charted the Victoria Land coast, discovered McMurdo Sound and the Ross Ice Shelf.*

1893–95     *Norwegian sealing and whaling expedition. Leader: Henrik J. Bull. Ship: Antarctic. Landed at Cape Adare and Possession Island.*

1898–1900  *British Antarctic (Southern Cross) Expedition. Leader: Carsten E. Borchgrevink. Ship: Southern Cross. Built huts and wintered at Cape Adare: explored Robertson Bay.*

1901–04     *British National Antarctic Expedition. Leader: Commander Robert F. Scott. Ship: Discovery. Built hut at Hut Point: wintered ship nearby. Extensive sledging in Victoria Land and on Ross Ice Shelf.*

1907–09     *British Antarctic (Nimrod) Expedition. Leader: Ernest H. Shackleton. Ship: Nimrod. Built hut at Cape Royds. Discovered Bay of Whales. First ascent of Mount Erebus; sledged to South Magnetic Pole; sledged across Ross Ice Shelf, up Beardmore Glacier and across the polar plateau almost to the South Pole.*

1910–12     *Japanese Antarctic Expedition. Leader: Lt. Nobu Shirase. Ship: Kainan-Maru. Visited Bay of Whales: sledged 250 km inland.*

1910–13     *British Antarctic (Terra Nova) Expedition. Leader: Captain Robert F. Scott. Ship: Terra Nova. Built huts at Cape Evans and Cape Adare. Sledging party reached the South Pole on 17 January 1912; died on return journey. Northern Party wintered at Cape Adare and Inexpressible Island.*

1910–12     *Norwegian Antarctic Expedition. Leader: Captain Roald E. G. Amundsen. Ship: Fram. Built hut at Bay of Whales. A sledging party crossed Ross Ice Shelf, climbed Axel Heiberg Glacier and reached the South Pole on 14 December 1911. A second party explored King Edward VII Land.*

1914–17     *Imperial Trans-Antarctic Expedition (Ross Sea Party). Leader: Aeneas L. A. Mackintosh. Ship: Aurora. Party of 10 wintered at Cape Evans: sledging parties laid depots on Ross Ice Shelf for trans-Antarctic party that did not appear.*

1928–30     *United States Antarctic Expedition. Leader: Commander Richard E. Byrd. Ships: City of New York, Eleanor Bolling. Built huts at Bay of Whales (Little America): made flights to King Edward VII Land and South Pole, discovered Rockefeller Mountains, Marie Byrd Land.*

1933–35     *United States Antarctic Expedition. Leader: Admiral Richard E. Byrd. Ships: Bear of Oakland, Jacob Ruppert. Built huts at Bay of Whales (Little America 2): sledged to Ford Ranges, Rockefeller and Queen Maud Mountains: extensive flying programmes.*

## Lyttelton and Christchurch

Banks Peninsula, New Zealand, was discovered by Captain James Cook RN and named for Sir Joseph Banks, who was his senior naturalist. Remnants of twin volcanic cones form a fine landlocked harbour, occupied by Lyttelton, a small port that has recently been modernized and appears to be growing. So it should, for it is the port of Christchurch, capital of Canterbury Province and New Zealand's second-largest city.

Lyttelton has many Antarctic connections. Captain Scott's *Discovery* was here in 1901 and again homeward bound in 1904. Ernest Shackleton's ship *Nimrod* berthed here in 1907-08, Scott's *Terra Nova* in 1910. Quail Island, in the middle of the harbour, was the quarantine station where the unfortunate ponies of both expeditions enjoyed their last grazing, before crossing the Southern Ocean to their cold death in Antarctica. Transient visitors are unlikely to spend time in Lyttelton or about the peninsula: most will want to visit the big city. More's the pity, for Banks Peninsula has several hamlets of great charm and historic interest. If you have time visit Akaroa, a delightful old port and settlement with historic French connections, just a few miles along the road. If you find yourself along the shore at dusk, watch out for white-flippered penguins, a local variant of the little blue or fairy penguin. They burrow under beach cottages and bray like donkeys.

Christchurch is separated from its port by a high ridge, forming part of the rim of one of the interlocking volcanoes that make up the Peninsula. Early Canterbury settlers from Britain had to trudge over from port to city with their baggage: more than one blacksmith is said to have carried his anvil over. Today there are two good roads, one a quick run through a tunnel, the other a longer and more picturesque route winding back into the hills, traversing the rim and descending more scenically into the city.

Generally considered the most attractive of New Zealand's four main cities, Christchurch was founded in 1843 on the small winding river Avon. The city fathers laid out a large central park, museum, university, main square and cathedral, a complex that still forms the heart of the modern city. The university, vastly expanded, has moved to an outlying campus, but its old buildings provide a centre for crafts and social activities. There are lively shops, cafes, restaurants and theatres.

Visit the old Canterbury Museum, which has outstanding exhibits of provincial history, natural history and Antarctic connections. It is one of the few places in the world where you can drink your mid-morning coffee in the company of a complete blue-whale skeleton. Take a bus or taxi to the airport and visit the new Antarctic Centre, which houses several Antarctic research bureaux and an excellent display showing New Zealand's current involvement in Antarctica. Many young and not-so-young New Zealanders have worked in Antarctica, and all take their responsibilities toward the Ross Dependency very seriously.

## Dunedin

Founded in 1848 by Scottish Free Church immigrants and endowed with the ancient Gaelic name for Edinburgh, Dunedin stands at the head of a fine harbour, ringed by rich farmland and the remnants of forests, some of which are preserved in the green Town Belt. The main port of the southern province of Otago, it became a city in 1865, quickly acquiring a university noted for medicine and natural history. There is a well-laid-out botanic garden, and an interesting art gallery with good modern New Zealand art and ceramics.

If you are a Scot, you'll feel very much at home, for this is still very much a Scottish city. If you have time, visit the Otago Museum and the Early Settlers' Museum. Grab any opportunity on offer to visit the Taiaroa Head bird observatory on the north end of Otago Peninsula, where you may see nesting yellow-eyed penguins and royal albatrosses. Take in the Portobello marine research station on the way. Keep your cold-weather kit handy. Remember that Dunedin stands at the colder end of New Zealand: southerly winds blow straight up from Antarctica, with not much between to temper them.

### Invercargill and Bluff

These far southern ports serve the fertile plains of Southland, a major dairy-farming and meat-producing area of New Zealand. Invercargill is the country's southern-most city (though not the world's: that honour goes to Ushuaia, p. 68). Settled in 1855, mostly by Scots, it stands on the sheltered estuary of Waihopai River, becoming a town in 1861 and a city in 1930. Local industries include inshore fishing (excellent oysters and crayfish) and sawmilling.

On a cold, wet day Invercargill may well seem close to the end of the world. You will probably not stay long enough to discover the pleasant little community, still inherently Scottish, that has developed an engaging self-sufficiency far from the rest of the world. As a port, Invercargill is rapidly being challenged by Bluff, a growing township with more modern harbour facilities.

Ferries connect Invercargill with Oban, the main settlement of Stewart Island, some 56 km (35 miles) away across Foveux Strait. If you have time, visit a travel agency and arrange to take a break there, to enjoy the natural bush, sheltered bays, forest and coastal birds, seals, and out-of-this-world isolation. You may even see a kiwi, though they are nocturnal and shy: you could well see the beak marks they make in probing the mud for earthworms. An old lady I met in Oban swore that her garden was visited regularly by moas—large New Zealand flightless birds that the rest of the world deems long extinct. Keep an eye open for them too: they would be good ones to add to your life list.

## Southern islands

For islands in the Pacific sector and Southern Ocean (Antipodes, Auckland and Bounty Islands, Campbell Island, Scott Island, Balleny Islands) see Chapter 10.

## The Victoria Land coast

### Cape Adare and Ridley Beach

A prominent massif of dark volcanic rock, Cape Adare forms the northern extremity of Victoria Land and often the first landfall after the Balleny Islands. The highest point, Cape Hanson, rises to 1256 m (4121 ft). Immediately south of the cape lies Ridley Beach, a triangle of cobbles and shingle facing westward into Robertson Bay. This is the site of man's first recorded landing in this sector of Antarctica—possibly, though doubtfully, the first-ever landing on the continent. It is also the home of some 270 000 pairs of Adelie penguins, and the site of three historic huts of great interest.

The first landing was made in the early morning of 24 January 1895, when a party of four—expedition leader Henrik Johan Bull, Captain Leonard Kristensen, second mate Bernhard Jensen and naturalist Carsten Borchgrevink—stepped ashore after an hour's rowing through loose ice. Their ship was the steam whaling vessel *Antarctic*, their expedition a singularly disorganized sealing and whaling venture financed by Captain Svend Foyn, the pioneering Norwegian whaler. 'The sensation of being the first men who had set foot on the real Antarctic Mainland was both strange and pleasurable', wrote Bull. Having caught not a single whale, and being an honest man, he had to admit that Foyn '... would no doubt have preferred to exchange this pleasing sensation on our part for a Right whale even of small dimensions'.

Four years later Carsten Borchgrevink (like Bull, a Norwegian living in Australia), returned to Cape Adare with his own expedition. His ship was the converted whaler *Southern Cross*, with his old shipmate Bernhard Jensen now in command. Financed this time by the British newspaper magnate Sir George Newnes, Borchgrevink landed in April 1895 and built two sturdy log cabins, prefabricated in Norway, that became the living quarters and store. His was the first-ever expedit-ion to overwinter on land in Antarctica. One member of the party, zoologist Nicolai Hanson, died on 14 October 1899, probably of scurvy. His grave can be seen on the heights above the camp. The New Zealand Antarctic Heritage Trust has refurbished Borchgrevink's living hut and stabilized the now-roofless stores hut.

Close by stands a third hut, built in February 1911 to house the six-man Northern Party of the British Antarctic (*Terra Nova*) Expedition (Box 8.3). It held them comfortably for almost a year but, less sturdy in fabric and construction than the Norwegian huts, eventually collapsed. Today little remains but the porch and fallen-in walls and roof.

### Possession Islands

On the morning of 12 January 1841 Captain James Clark Ross braved a strong current and shifting ice floes to land on the western flank of the largest and northernmost of these islands. Finding himself on '... a beach of large loose stones and stranded masses of ice', with the weather rapidly deteriorating, he hastily ran up the flag of his country and drank to the health, long life and happiness of Queen

## Box 8.3   Scott's Northern Party

*The more dramatic exploits of the main party of Scott's* Terra Nova *expedition at Cape Evans (p. 198), culminating in the tragic polar journey, eclipsed the work of the small but lively Northern Party of the same expedition. Lt. Victor Campbell, naval officer and mate of* Terra Nova, *led the party, which included naval surgeon George Murray Levick, geologist Raymond Priestley, petty officers George P. Abbot and Frank V. Browning, and seaman Harry Dickason. They lived in reasonable comfort on Ridley Beach for almost a year, exploring and surveying the Robertson Bay area, studying the Adelie penguins, recording weather, tides and aurora, and making extensive geological and biological collections.*

*Their troubles began in early January 1912, when* Terra Nova *transferred the party to Inexpressible Island, Terra Nova Bay, for a 6-week summer sledging programme among the mountains and glaciers of the hinterland. This they completed but, returning to the shore, they found that pack ice had drifted in, making it impossible for the ship to pick them up. After living for a few days longer in their tents, the six dug their way into a snowdrift, hollowing out a cave which they lined with ration boxes and seal skins. There they wintered from early March to September.*

*They fed mainly on penguin and seal meat, fortified by 4 oz of biscuit on Mondays, Tuesdays, Thursdays and Fridays, 2 oz of biscuit with an ounce of chocolate on Wednesdays, Saturdays and Sundays, 12 lumps of sugar on Sundays, and a dozen raisins apiece once per month. Despite ill health and appalling conditions they survived until spring. In October they marshalled their scant remaining rations and began a man-hauling journey of more than 350 km (230 miles) over sea ice, shelf ice and glaciers, that brought them back to the main base at Cape Evans.*

Victoria and Prince Albert. He reported '... not the smallest appearance of vegetation': however, '... inconceivable myriads of penguins completely and densely covered the whole surface of the island, along the ledges of the precipices and even to the summit of the hills'.

The penguins disputed possession of the islands, attacking the landing party vigorously with sharp beaks and 'loud coarse notes'. Ross recorded '... the insupportable stench from the deep bed of guano ... which may at some period be valuable to the agriculturists of our Australasian colonies ...', and found difficulty in negotiating the strong tide running in the channel between the islands and the mainland. The Possession Islands form part of the volcanic complex that lines the coast of Victoria Land. Scott, who sailed through the group on his way home in 1904, counted nine islands, some of very curious shapes, one an almost perfect column over 300 ft (90 m) tall, another pierced with huge arches, the larger 150 ft (46 m) high. Very little has changed since Ross's time. The islands lie in a sea area rich in summer nutrients, supporting a huge penguin population. On Possession Island itself more than 140 000 pairs of Adelie penguins crowd into the limited space ashore: Svend Foyn Island, another of the larger islands, hosts a further 40 000 pairs, and all continue to dispute possession with beaks no less sharp than before, and notes no less raucous. If you land on the Possession Islands, take care to wear your gumboots: those Australasian agriculturists never got around to collecting their guano.

## Cape Hallett

Similar to Cape Adare in appearance and structure, Cape Hallett presents a steep, dark eastern face to the sea, and gentler, ice-clad slopes to Edisto Inlet, Moubray Bay and the mainland. The cliffs of Hallett Peninsula rise to about 1200 m (3900 ft), the highest point to about 1770 m (5800 ft). Seabee Hook, the landing on the north-western corner of the cape, is a beach of boulders and shingle similar to Ridley Beach. The huts, however, are much younger: here are the remains of Hallett Station, a research station of the International Geophysical Year erected by US SeaBees (military engineers) in 1957 and run jointly by New Zealand and the US for many years. About 60 000 pairs of Adelies nest on the Hook. An area inland from the base of the hook, between Willet Cove and the margin of permanent ice, includes a small patch of particularly rich and diverse vegetation, and is designated a Specially Protected Area.

## Coulman Island

Lying 16 km (10 miles) off the north-eastern corner of Lady Newnes Bay, Coulman Island is the steep remnant of a complex shield volcano, heavily ice capped, and rising to almost 2000 m (3200 ft) with a caldera toward the southern end. Ross, who discovered and first charted the island, named it after his wife's family. The northernmost point became Cape Wadworth after her family home in Yorkshire: the prominent south-eastern point he named Cape Anne, after the lady herself.

Precipitous on all sides, Coulman Island is flanked by piedmont glaciers and narrow raised beaches. Beaches along the eastern shore provide rather difficult landings, and support four colonies of Adelie penguins totalling 20 000–30 000 pairs. Borchgrevink made the first landing in February 1900, under the towering cliffs of Cape Wadworth. Scott in *Discovery*, sheltering under the lee of the island in January 1902, put down a net and trawled a rich catch of 'mud, stones and animals', to the delight of his biologists. He too landed at Cape Wadworth, erecting a staff with a tin cylinder and a message to inform others of his whereabouts. Each winter the fast ice close to the cape shelters a colony of over 20 000 pairs of emperor penguins: the colony disperses with the ice in summer, but adults, juveniles and chicks may still be seen on nearby floes throughout spring and early summer.

## Inexpressible Island

This dreary spot was named by the members of Scott's Northern Party (Box 8.3), who lived there between February and late September 1912, for much of the time in an igloo dug from a snowdrift. Some 5 km (3 miles) long, the island is little more than a ridge of granite and gneiss, part-covered in moraine from retreated glaciers.

Shingle beaches show it to have recently risen from the seabed, due to loss of overlying ice.

The igloo was dug in the island's only deep snowdrift, close to a bay toward the western end of the island. The drift still forms each year and lasts well into the summer: only late-season visitors are likely to find the site, with its remnants of boxes and skins, now marked by a plaque. Some 25 000 pairs of Adelies nest on Inexpressible Island, they and Weddell seals providing much of the food that kept the party going.

## Marble Point

One of several prominent capes along the western shore of McMurdo Sound, this was named after a visit by geologists of Shackleton's British Antarctic (*Nimrod*) Expedition of 1907–09, who discovered a hard white marble there. The headland overlooks a wide expanse of moraine, backed by the starved glaciers that have retreated from it. In December 1957, as part of US Operation Deepfreeze III, the moraine became the site of North Camp, a collection of temporary huts, which for two seasons housed parties of naval and civilian engineers. Their task was to survey the area as a possible site for the United States' main logistic base—indeed as a possible major airfield that might have served some of the needs of commercial aviation in the far south. There were plans for a 3000 m paved runway, a deep-water jetty and a township powered by a nuclear generator. The engineers bulldozed, blasted and graded extensive areas, raising berms (embankments) to create freshwater reservoirs, levelling sites for buildings, testing different kinds of surfacing and creating a network of roads.

This effort came to nothing: the plan was abandoned on grounds of cost, and McMurdo Station, some 70 km (42 miles) away across the Sound, was chosen instead. North Camp was abandoned, part-buried and left to rot. Some of the debris has recently been removed, and efforts to restore the site continue. Marble Point is occasionally visited by cruise ships for its historic interest, and is the site of a helicopter refuelling station.

## McMurdo Sound

Flanked to the east by Ross Island, to the west by piedmont ice shelf along the Scott Coast of Victoria Land (Figure 8.3), this is one of Antarctica's southernmost embayments. When the sea ice clears completely in late summer, ships can reach almost to 78°S: hence the popularity of the Sound for expeditions to the interior of Antarctica, both historic and recent. Annual fast ice starts to clear usually in late November or early December, but has been known to survive into January or February. At the southern end of the Sound in some years it fails to clear at all, requiring icebreakers to cut a passage for ships servicing McMurdo and Scott stations.

Ross Island is famed for its twin volcanic peaks Erebus (3795 m, 12 451 ft) and Terror (3230 m, 10 597 ft), named after Ross's two sturdy ships. Only Mount Erebus is currently active. In Ross's time it belched flames and lava; now it burps a

**Figure 8.3** *Early spring view from Ross Island across the sea ice of McMurdo Sound to the mountains of Victoria Land. Despite its high latitude (78° S), the Sound is open for 1 or 2 months every year, and regularly visited by cruise ships. Photograph by Guy Mannering.*

gentle but constant plume of steam and gases, which provides pilots and meteorologists with a useful indication of upper winds. A splendid landmark, in clear weather it has been seen from over 320 km (200 miles) away (Figure 8.2, p. 187).

The flanks of the volcanoes are composed of lava and scoria, largely covered with ice. At sea level shelf ice alternates with glaciers and stretchers of bare rock and moraine. On 28 November 1979 a DC10 aircraft of New Zealand Airlines, carrying 257 overflying passengers and crew, crashed in broad daylight into the side of Mount Erebus, killing all on board. Much of the wreckage remains, now entombed in ice.

Once the sea ice has dispersed in the Sound, winds keep the eastern side clearer than the west. Ships heading south tend to move close to the Ross Island coast, a course that brings them past successive landing sites of unique historic interest. Chronologically the story starts in the far south, at Hut Point, so that is where we shall start our descriptions of landings.

## Hut Point

On a rocky headland close to Cape Armitage, in the far south-east corner of the Sound, stands the small wooden hut that Robert Falcon Scott erected for his first expedition, the British National Antarctic Expedition (1901–04). Following the tradition of the 19th-century Arctic naval expeditions, Scott allowed his ship

**Figure 8.4**  *Hut Point, Ross Island, McMurdo Sound. Captain Robert Scott wintered his ship RRS* Discovery *off this point in 1902 and 1903, building the hut ashore as a store house. Today the hut stands at the edge of McMurdo Station (Figure 8.5), overshadowed by fuel tanks.*

*Discovery* to be frozen in, with all hands wintering aboard. The hut, just 9 m (30 ft) square, was prefabricated in Australia, with insulated double walls and a verandah on three sides (Figure 8.4). Mainly for emergency, it was there in case land parties were stranded by bad weather, or the ship suffered damage by fire or pressure from the ice. From time to time it became a store, theatre, laboratory, drying room and workshop.

    Later expeditions were unable to reach so far south, and did not overwinter their ships. Working from bases at Cape Royds and Cape Evans, respectively 36 km (23 miles) and 24 km (15 miles) to the north, sledging parties found more reason to camp in the *Discovery* hut, which accordingly contains relics from several generations of usage. It has been cleared, refurbished, and set out as a mini-museum, run by the New Zealand Heritage Trust. The wooden cross 100 m from the hut commemorates Able Seaman George Vince, who fell into the sea while crossing shelf ice during a blizzard in March 1902.

## McMurdo Station

When first erected in February 1902 the *Discovery* hut stood alone on its peninsula, apart from tiny magnetic and seismological huts set up nearby. Today it stands close to the busy dockyard area of McMurdo Station, essentially a small American township from which most of the US research and logistic operations in the interior of Antarctica are managed (Figure 8.5). The station includes laboratories,

**Figure 8.5** *Downtown McMurdo Station, Ross Island. Antarctica's largest station, McMurdo is a township with permanent hostel accommodation for several hundred technicians, administrators and scientists. From its airstrips, transport aircraft service Amundsen-Scott, the US south polar station.*

stores depots, repair shops, fuel dumps, garages, a supermarket selling T-shirts and trinkets, a church, a cinema, hostels, offices and administration centres. Two airfields lie peripheral to it, one on sea ice and the other on land, with a convenient town helipad for commuters. The population of scientists, technicians and service personnel fluctuates from a few hundred in winter to several thousand in summer.

By far the largest Antarctic station, McMurdo was established during the International Geophysical Year (IGY) as a research station in its own right, and to service US stations at the South Pole (Amundsen-Scott) and elsewhere on the polar plateau. Over 40 years of existence it has grown and spread. Transport aircraft fly in from Christchurch throughout the summer and occasionally in winter: tankers and cargo bring in fuel and stores by sea. Shipborne visitors are offered tours of the station and facilities. Surprising numbers end up in the supermarket buying souvenirs.

## Observation Hill

The reddish hill overlooking McMurdo is Observation Hill, a volcanic cone 230 m (755 ft) high, that successive expeditions have used as a lookout point. On clear days anxious observers could scan the length of the Sound for relief ships, or the route south for returning sledge parties. There is a well-worn track to the top. The cross that appears on the skyline was built by Frank Davis, ship's carpenter of *Terra Nova*, to commemorate the polar party (Robert Scott, 'Birdie' Bowers, Edgar

Evans, Edward Wilson and Lawrence Oates) who reached the South Pole but failed
to return. Made of Australian jarrah, it has twice blown down and been replaced,
most recently in 1994.

## Scott Base

Take the main highway south out of McMurdo, bear right at the crossroads, and
follow the road signs to Scott Base. This is New Zealand's Antarctic research
station at Pram Point, on the east side of Hut Point Peninsula, also set up for the
IGY and occupied continuously ever since. In size and layout more typical of
national Antarctic stations than McMurdo, it accommodates up to 20 in winter, up
to 40 in summer. One of the original IGY huts is still extant, but the station has
changed and developed since then, generally for the better. Visitors may be shown
around by previous arrangement: most find it very comfortable, practical, pleasing,
and altogether more homely than the township of McMurdo.

## Cape Evans

North from Hut Point along the Ross Island coast lies the dark promontory of
Cape Evans. Here Robert Scott based his British Antarctic (*Terra Nova*)
Expedition of 1910–13. Like Shackleton before him, Scott was unable to reach
the southern end of the Sound, so built his hut as far south as the ice would allow
him to penetrate, naming the cape for Lt. Edward Evans RN, his second in
command. Scott's expedition hut, built close to the shore, is a rather formidable,
barn-like building with built-on stores and pony stables. From it in June 1911
Edward Wilson, 'Birdie' Bowers and Apsley Cherry-Garrard left on their
extraordinary 5-week journey to visit the emperor penguins at Cape Crozier, on
the far eastern side of Ross Island. In the following spring the main sledging
parties—a cavalcade of ponies, tractors and dog teams—left southward on the
polar journey that was the main purpose of the expedition. Those that reached the
pole did not return.

A visit to Scott's hut authenticates many details of expedition life: the crowded
bunks, pony and dog harnesses, Edwardian calendars, darned woollen socks and
comforters, and everyday expedition litter. Photographer Ponting's darkroom has
been tidied, and surgeon Atkinson's laboratory reassembled. In the porch are worn
spades, picks, boots and skis, in the stable roughly stitched canvas nosebags and
shoes for the stumbling ponies, in the workshop cans of oil for the motor tractors.
Sadly, visitors from cruise ships seldom have time to linger and savour.

The gloom of the interior is accentuated by grime, almost certainly due to a later
expedition, the Ross Sea Party of the Imperial Trans-Antarctic Expedition, that
lived at Cape Evans in 1914–17. Stranded when their ship *Aurora* was blown out
to sea (her mooring anchor is still on the beach) the party of 10 was left with
minimal food, clothing and fuel. The grime in the hut is due to their burning lamps
of seal blubber, to save kerosene for a vital sledging programme. Their over-riding
responsibility was to lay depots toward the Beardmore Glacier. On these depots
would depend the safety of a sledging party led by Sir Ernest Shackleton, that was
supposed to be crossing Antarctica from the Weddell Sea.

How they laid their depots is another splendid story. That three of the party died on the return journey is attested by the wooden cross on Windvane Hill, near the point of Cape Evans. Arnold Spencer-Smith died of scurvy on the ice shelf, not far from Hut Point. Aeneas Mackintosh and Victor Hayward recovered from scurvy, but disappeared when walking over thin sea ice between Hut Point and Cape Evans.

## Cape Royds

Moving northward again, Cape Royds is a low prominence of dark rock forming the western corner of Ross Island, named for Lt. Charles Royds of Scott's *Discovery*. In February 1908 Ernest Shackleton, unable to penetrate farther down McMurdo Sound, chose the cape as the home for his British Antarctic (*Nimrod*) Expedition. He built his timber hut by a freshwater tarn, surrounding it with bales of fodder for the ponies and boxes of canned food for the 14 men who overwintered (Figure 8.6).

From Cape Royds Australian geologist William Edgeworth David led a late-summer sledging party up Mount Erebus, to examine the crater. In the following spring he led a second party across the sea ice of the Sound to Victoria Land, successfully locating the elusive South Magnetic Pole. Meanwhile Shackleton himself led the main sledging journey south toward the South Geographical Pole. Extending a route that he and Scott had already pioneered across the Ross

**Figure 8.6** *Ernest Shackleton chose Cape Royds for his 1907–09 expedition base. His hut still stands and has become a tourist attraction (Figure 8.7). His party exercised the expedition ponies on the frozen lake, and slaughtered many penguins from the nearby colony as a food reserve.*

**Figure 8.7**  *The interior of Shackleton's hut, painstakingly restored by members of New Zealand's Antarctic Society. The hut remains much as he left it, preserved by intense winter cold. Recently, it has undergone changes to restore it to a more historically accurate layout. It is now in the charge of New Zealand's Antarctic Heritage Trust, and can be visited only by special arrangement.*

Ice Shelf in 1902, he discovered and climbed the Beardmore Glacier (named after a leading Scottish engineer who helped finance the expedition), and crossed the polar plateau to a point within 180 km (113 miles) of the pole itself.

Shackleton's hut stands much as the expedition left it, complete with kitchen range, table, magazines, sledges, boots, surplus stores (including mummified hams, cans of mustard and boxes of Price's Edible Candles), and pictures of King Edward VII and Queen Alexandra on the walls (Figure 8.7). Shackleton, whose background was the Merchant Marine rather than the Royal Navy, was an inspired leader who saw no reason to maintain distance between officers and other ranks. In contrast to Scott's, his hut is a cheerful, homely place, redolent of high spirits, good humour and success.

Outside the hut are remnants of the stables and dog lines, and the weather-station screen. Close by is Pony Lake, frozen for much of the year, where the expedition exercised their ponies. Beyond the lake lies the rubbish heap, and surrounding all is the small colony of Adelie penguins, currently numbering some 4000 pairs (Figure 8.8). That it is the world's southernmost penguin colony did not protect it from the early explorers: both Scott and Shackleton regarded the Cape Royds penguins as an emergency source of food. Today only the hut can be visited, and only by permit, with an approach up the crumbling lava cliffs of Backdoor Bay. The area south and west of the lake, including much of the colony, is a rigorously protected Site of Special Scientific Interest.

**Figure 8.8** *Adelie penguins nesting at Cape Royds, Ross Island, Antarctica's south-ernmost colony. The box, in which this pair raised two chicks annually during the 1960s, is a packing case abandoned by Ernest Shackleton's* Nimrod *expedition of 1907–09.*

## Cape Bird

Cape Bird owes its name to Lt. Edward J. Bird RN, an officer of HMS *Erebus*. The cape forms the north-western corner of Ross Island: in bad weather its ice-covered slopes are often the first land to be sighted by ships approaching from the north. Only the western side has bare rocky slopes and beaches, over which are scattered some 40 000–50 000 pairs of Adelie penguins. On fine sunny days this is an agreeable place for watching skuas and penguins going about their business: indeed a small hut between the nesting areas was for several summers the home of biologists who were so employed. An ill-demarcated area named 'New College Valley', between the beach and the ice cap, includes both a Specially Protected Area and a Site of Special Scientific Interest.

## Cape Crozier and the Ross Barrier

The easternmost point of Ross Island is Cape Crozier, a high, prominent cape, much of it ice covered, that abuts onto the cliffs of the Ross Ice Shelf. On the north-eastern side ice gives way to gravel-covered slopes, where live over 175 000 pairs of Adelie penguins, breeding in two extensive colonies. Most breed on the lower slopes close to the landing beaches, but nests in the larger western colony extend to heights above 120 m (400 ft) and distances of more than 1 km inland—a long way for birds with short legs.

**Figure 8.9** *Cape Crozier and the Ross Ice Shelf. Within enclaves of the ice shelf, emperor penguins gather to breed each autumn. This was the first emperor colony to be discovered (1902), and the first to be visited in winter (1910), during the 'Worst Journey in the World' (see Further reading).*

At one point on the beach is a message post—a timber joist that once bore a metal cylinder, set upright in a stone cairn. This is a relic of the *Discovery* expedition; in the cylinder were left messages telling relief ships where the expedition would be found.

The sea ice alongside Cape Crozier supports a celebrated colony of emperor penguins, which forms each winter in enclaves of the nearby ice shelf (Figure 8.9). Numbers breeding vary from several thousand to fewer than a hundred pairs. Discovered during Scott's first expedition, this colony was visited on a winter journey of the second (*Terra Nova*) expedition. Wilson, Bowers and Cherry-Garrard man-hauled to the colony around the south end of Ross Island, to confirm the species' winter breeding and obtain early embryos from the eggs. In his book of the expedition Cherry-Garrard termed it 'the worst journey in the world'.

Though breeding ends and the colony disperses by November or December, there are usually a few of these magnificent birds to be seen in the area when the cruise ships arrive in January and February. Larger colonies are found farther north on Franklin and Beaufort Islands.

Eastward from Cape Crozier extends one of Antarctica's most remarkable features—an ice cliff over 780 km (480 miles) long, of mean height 45 m (150 ft), called the Ross Barrier. The Barrier is the front of the vast, triangular Ross Ice Shelf that extends a similar distance inland, flanked to the east by the Transantarctic Mountains, to the west by the gentler slopes of the polar ice cap. Much of the ice shelf is afloat, moving northward at rates of several hundred metres per year: the Barrier retains its position by calving to form tabular icebergs.

Toward the eastern end of the Barrier the level of ice drops and a deep bay forms. Persisting despite the constant turnover of ice, this feature was discovered by Shackleton and named Bay of Whales. Amundsen, who had read every available source of information, perceived that it lay closer to the Pole than McMurdo Sound, and provided a better point of departure. Byrd, who backed winners rather than losers, followed Amundsen to the same site.

The Barrier's southernmost point lies usually between 170 and 180°W. By nosing in toward it a cruise ship can cross the magic parallel of 78°S and reach the world's southernmost limit of navigation—usually an excuse for issuing certificates and opening the champagne (well, the sparkling German wine that passes for champagne on these occasions). Whatever you may think of the wine, the scenery is magnificent, the weather often sunny, and there are usually whales, snow petrels and chequered cape petrels to share the celebration.

## Further reading

Bernacchi, L. 1901. *To the South Polar Regions: Expedition of 1898–1901*. London, Hurst and Blackett.

Bull, H. J. 1896. *The Cruise of the 'Antarctic' to the South Polar Regions*. London, Edward Arnold.

Borchgrevink, C. E. 1901. *First on the Antarctic Continent: Being an Account of the British Antarctic Expedition 1898–1900*. London, George Newnes.

Cherry-Garrard, A. 1923. *Worst Journey in the World*. London, Constable.

Harrowfield, D. L. 1981. *Sledging into History*. Auckland, Macmillan.

Harrowfield, D. L. 1995. *Icy Heritage: The Historic Sites of the Ross Sea Region, Antarctica*. Christchurch, Antarctic Heritage Trust.

Hatherton, T. (editor). 1990. *Antarctica: The Ross Sea Region*. Wellington, DSIR Publishing

Huxley, L. 1914. *Scott's Last Expedition*. London, Smith Elder.

King, H. G. R. (editor). 1988. *The Wicked Mate: The Antarctic Diary of Victor Campbell*. Alburgh, Bluntisham Books and the Erskine Press.

Levick, G. M. 1914. *Antarctic Penguins: A Study of their Social Life*. London, William Heinemann.

Priestley, R. E. 1914. *Antarctic Adventure: Scott's Northern Party*. London, T. Fisher Unwin.

Ross, J. C. 1847. *A Voyage of Discovery and Research in the Southern and Antarctic Regions, During the Years 1839–43*. London, John Murray.

Scott, R. F. 1905. *The Voyage of the 'Discovery'*. London, Smith, Elder.

Shackleton, E. H. 1909. *The Heart of the Antarctic*. London, William Heinemann.

Shackleton, E. H. 1919. *South—the Story of the 1914–1917 Expedition*. London, William Heinemann.

# Chapter Nine

# The continental coasts and interior

## Introduction: the ice coasts

We have dealt in Chapters 7 and 8 with 96% or thereabouts of Antarctica's coast that is made up of mountains and islands. This chapter covers the remaining 3–4% that lies scattered along the continental mainland coast of East Antarctica (see Map 1, pp. 8–9). There is little to be said about the coast of mainland West Antarctica, which is virtually inaccessible by sea. I add a short note on air travel to the interior of Antarctica, which is by contrast entirely open—but only to those who can afford it.

## Geology and ice

Ice coasts are icy because of heavy snowfall, originating from cyclonic storms (depressions) that spiral eastward over the Southern Ocean and track in toward the continent. Depressions follow each other at intervals of a few days. Relatively few get far inland: most drop their load of snow on or close to the coast. Strong winds grind the snowflakes to powder and pack it down into layers, and the weight of successive layers converts snow to solid ice. Some is lost as vapour, and some melts and pours off in summer torrents; however, the bulk of accumulated ice flows slowly downhill to the coast, there to form ice shelves that extend over the shore and out to sea.

How far the ice spreads beyond the coast depends on precipitation, underlying topography and other factors. Much of the ice cliff of mainland Antarctica lies well beyond the actual shoreline, and is afloat in deep water. In early 1840 Lt. Charles Wilkes sailed for over a month along the ice cliffs of the coast that now bears his name. Almost every day he saw ice-covered mountains inland, up to heights that he estimated at 3000 ft (900 m). Often he stood within soundings, on one occasion reaching bottom at 30 fathoms (55 m, 180 ft). Quite clearly he lay close to a very large landmass. Yet the shore, when he could get near it, was almost entirely ice covered: the only rocks he saw were basalt and sandstone boulders frozen into an iceberg.

This is not pleasing to geologists, who like to have good, solid rocks to hammer. However, there is some consolation for them in 'oases'—ice-free patches, in areas that the depressions seem to skirt around or avoid. Like the dry valleys of Victoria Land (Chapter 8), these provide welcome windows where geologists can examine coastal rocks. Most oases were found by air, rather than from the sea. Several that were discovered during overflights from US operations Highjump and Windmill (p. 252), have since provided sites for research stations.

### Sea ice

Fast ice forms around much of this coast in winter, breaking out in spring to form pack ice, that drifts westward under prevailing easterly winds (Figure 9.1). Incorporated among it are fleets of icebergs and bergy bits that have calved from the cliffs. Around much of the coast this floating ice gradually disperses northward, allowing ice-strengthened ships with experienced masters to approach, usually in mid- to late summer.

Off some stretches of coast, however, winds, currents and topography consolidated the ice into hard, congested pack, that persists from year to year. Much of the southern and western Weddell Sea is covered with persistent ice of this kind. So are long stretches of the Bellingshausen, Amundsen and eastern Ross Sea coasts, which are unapproachable by any but the most powerful icebreakers. Other stretches of the East Antarctica coast provide very difficult ice navigation, to be tackled only in emergency or for compelling scientific reasons. Cruise ships sensibly keep clear of them.

**Figure 9.1**   *In a polynya (wind-formed stretch of open water) in the Weddell Sea pack ice, the German icebreaker* Polarstern *cuts a harbour for an overnight stopover. Icebreakers use polynyas as much as possible, cutting ice only when necessary, and relying on their power mainly as a safety margin.*

## Box 9.1   *Katabatic winds*

At Commonwealth Bay, on the Adélie coast of Wilkes Land, Douglas Mawson's Australian expedition recorded a mean annual wind speed of 19.4 m/sec (43.4 miles per hour)—well over gale force for the whole period of the expedition. The mean for February, the quietest month, was 11.7 m/sec (26.2 miles per hour), and for July, the windiest month, 24.8 m/sec (55.5 miles per hour). There were very few days of complete calm. Extreme gusts exceeded 62 m/sec (140 miles per hour), and usually broke the anemometer.

Practically all these winds were katabatic or downslope winds, which are experienced at many other coastal stations. Cold air rolls under its own weight down the long, smooth slopes of Antarctica, in a layer only a few metres thick. The cataract reaches top speed near the coast, and may maintain enough momentum to clear the fast ice locally, but then slows and disappears. Mawson was attracted into Commonwealth Bay by relatively ice-free water, on a fine day of comparative calm. The first winds hit as the expedition began to offload its stores.

Winds of any strength pick up recently fallen snow and whirl it around, creating the very uncomfortable conditions called 'blizzard'. In Terre Adélie Mawson had unwittingly found what he was later to call 'The home of the blizzard' (Mawson 1915).

## Climate

Scientific stations along the ice coasts experience mean temperatures intermediate between those of the peninsula and the northern Ross Sea—slightly below freezing point in summer, well below in winter. Snowfall is predictably heavy on the icy sections, where single falls of 2–3 m are not uncommon: the oases get away with relatively little.

Wind, rather than cold, plagues many coastal stations—both the strong easterlies and westerlies that accompany depressions, and more persistent southerlies that pour down the slopes of the continent and sweep out to sea (Box 9.1). Winds are often slightly warmer than the still air they replace, due to compression and other factors. However, moving air feels colder than still air, because it drives away the boundary layer or 'skin' of warmth that we build around ourselves. It also increases danger of frostbite to exposed skin. Not every coastal station experiences the constant gales of Commonwealth Bay, but all get a taste of them from time to time.

## Vegetation and wildlife

Not much grows on the ice of the ice cliffs: snowfalls are too heavy and persistent for snow algae to survive. Oases, as we have seen elsewhere, have nothing in common with green patches in deserts: they are dry-desert patches in ice, with only the most meagre polar desert vegetation. Inshore fast ice provides a platform for Weddell seals to breed in early spring. Pack ice supports crabeater seals in immense numbers: look out for pale silver-grey seals, often with prominent scars on their flanks. You may also see Ross seals—much rarer, dark silver grey, with curiously inflated throat and huge eyes.

Adelie penguins are the sole representation of the pygoscelid penguins, and they nest only in the few places where rock outcrops lie close to the sea. Emperor penguins, which nest mainly on fast ice, have more sites to choose from: still, only about 40 colonies are known, about half of them on the ice coast. A few are accessible by helicopter from icebreakers. Whales were formerly abundant within the pack ice: this was indeed where most of the rorquals—blue, fin and sei whales especially—were caught by the offshore hunters from 1923 onward. Today minke and fin whales are the species most often around.

## History of discovery

The ice coast was discovered piecemeal over more than a century. Following the naval expeditions of James Cook and Thaddeus von Bellingshausen, hardy sealing captains, in ships no bigger than modern lifeboats (Figure 9.2), were the next to penetrate the pack ice, making several positive landfalls along the continental coast. Three outstanding naval expeditions—French, American and British—of the early 1840s charted in further stretches of coast: by the mid-century it was becoming clear that a land of continental size surrounded the South Pole, though there were still more gaps than certainties in the coastline, and the interior remained totally blank.

**Figure 9.2**  *'Sea smoke', composed of fine ice crystals, rising like steam over open water in the Weddell Sea. This indicates that air and sea are cold enough for sea ice to form, and a warning for less powerful ships to go home before they are frozen in.*

The 1895 declaration of the Sixth International Geographical Congress was a timely call for action. Public opinion was stimulated by current exploration in the Arctic, particularly by Robert Peary's attempts to reach the North Pole, which newspapers represented as heroic ventures against the unknown. Costs lay well beyond the means of most individuals, requiring cooperation between governments, public benefactors and the public itself. Finding charismatic leadership for Antarctic ventures was no problem: prestige and personal honours would accrue to whoever first planted his country's flag on any part of Antarctica, especially on the South Pole.

So the geographers of Britain, Belgium, France, Germany and several other countries stimulated public opinion, prodded governments into action, planned programmes of research, found the field leaders, and ultimately acquired the funds for a new round of Antarctic exploration (Box 9.2). Expeditions varied in detail, some emphasizing scientific research, others geographical exploration. All involved a strong element of political chauvinism—the desire to see the flag of their own own country fluttering above the new continent. A few included plans to reach the South Pole.

## Politics

Politically continental Antarctica is divided into British, Norwegian, Australian, French and New Zealand sectors, and an additional sector, most of it in West Antarctica, that nobody seems to want (Map 1, pp. 8–9). These claims are still meaningful to those who make them, and invalid to those who do not. There are no overlaps, boundary quarrels or confusions: Australia, for example, accommodates happily to a sector split by French Terre Adélie.

All claims extend to the South Pole except that of Norway, which of all nations might be thought to have a particular interest there. However, claims were vested during the whaling period, and related more to the coasts than to the interior. This chapter deals with the Norwegian, French and Australian sectors, and with the small British segment of East Antarctica on the eastern flank of the Weddell Sea. The rest of the British sector is covered in Chapters 6 and 7, the New Zealand sector in Chapter 8.

## Ports of departure

### Cape Town

Said to be among the world's most beautiful cities, Cape Town is certainly one of the best known and most interesting. It began in 1652 as a market-garden settlement, providing fresh fruit and vegetables for ships of the East India Company. Growing quickly into a port, it developed as a major southern centre for maritime trade. Now the capital of a province blessed with magnificent scenery and wildlife, fertile soils, and a healthy, stimulating climate, Cape Town has become

Box 9.2   *Expeditions that explored the coasts*

1822–24     British sealers James Weddell and Matthew Brisbane penetrated to 74°S in the Weddell Sea, reporting very little pack ice.

1830–33     British sealers John Biscoe and George Avery circumnavigated the Southern Ocean, discovering Enderby Land in February 1831.

1833–34     British mariner Peter Kemp discovered an island since identified as Heard Island on 27 November 1833, and Kemp Land 1 month later.

1837–40     César Dumont d'Urville in Astrolabe and Charles-Hector Jacquinot in Zélée led a French naval scientific expedition which discovered and took possession of Terre Adélie in January 1840.

1838–39     British sealers John Balleny in Eliza Scott and Thomas Freeman in Sabrina discovered Balleny Islands in February 1839 and described an appearance of land (Sabrina Coast, East Antarctica) to the south.

1838–42     The US Exploring Expedition, a naval scientific expedition led by Lt. Charles Wilkes in Vincennes, made a world cruise that included Antarctica and the Southern Ocean. Wilkes reported many appearances of land along the coast of what is now Wilkes Land.

1839–43     Captain James Clark Ross in HMS Erebus and Commander Rawdon Crozier in HMS Terror discovered the Ross Sea and Victoria Land in January 1841.

1851–55     US sealer Mercator Cooper in Levant passed through pack ice to an extensive coast, near the present Oates Coast, claiming to have landed on 26 January 1853.

1901–03     The German South Polar Expedition, led by scientist Erich von Drygalski, wintered on board their ship Gauss in pack ice some 80 km (50 miles) from the East Antarctica coast.

1902–04     The Scottish National Antarctic Expedition, led by William Bruce in Scotia, discovered Coats Land on the eastern Weddell Sea coast.

1911–14     The Australian Antarctic Expedition, led by Douglas Mawson in Aurora, discovered and explored King George V Land and Queen Mary Land,

East Antarctica: parties overwintered at Cape Dennison and Shackleton Ice Shelf.

1923–24    Norwegian Captain Carl A. Larsen began Antarctic pelagic whaling in the Ross Sea.

1927–34    Lars Christensen's seven Norwegian research expeditions surveyed in the Norwegian sector of Antarctica and on Bouvetøya and Peter I Øy, identifying and charting Dronning Maud Land, King Leopold and Queen Astrid Land and Ingrid Christensen Land.

1928–30    Richard Byrd wintered at Bay of Whales, flying to the South Pole and exploring Edward VII Peninsula by air and sledge.

1929–31    British, Australian and New Zealand Antarctic Research Expedition, led by Sir Douglas Mawson in Discovery, explored the coast of the Australian sector of Antarctica with ship and aircraft.

1938–39    The German Schwabenland expedition overflew and photographed the coasts and interior of western Dronning Maud Land.

1939–41    The United States Antarctic Service Expedition, led by Rear-Admiral Richard Byrd, established stations in the Bay of Whales and at Stonington Island, exploring widely from both by sledge and aircraft.

1946–47    Operation Highjump. Three US shipborne task forces, commanded by Richard Byrd, made scientific studies and aerial surveys of wide expanses of Antarctic coast and interior.

1947–48    Operation Windmill. A US naval task force (two icebreakers with helicopters) made scientific studies and aerial surveys of coastal areas.

1949–52    The Norwegian-British-Swedish Expedition, led by John Giaever, explored western Dronning Maud Land with aircraft and sledge teams.

1955–58    The Commonwealth Trans-Antarctic Expedition, led by Dr V. E. Fuchs, crossed Antarctica from Filchner Ice Shelf, Weddell Sea, to McMurdo Sound, Ross Sea, using dog teams and motorized transport with air support.

an exciting modern city, with plenty of diversions for the traveller passing through to Antarctica.

In its time the port served sealers and whalers en route for the south, and some of their legacy can be found in the museums, particularly the South African Museum. There are several connexions with more recent Antarctic expeditions, but this is not what Cape Town is about. Enjoy it rather for its wonderful setting. Take the cable car up Table Mountain on a fine morning. Sample the Victoria and Alfred waterfront, now a lively centre of boutiques, restaurants and exhibitions. Visit the colonial British and Dutch buildings, superb botanical gardens, fish and vegetable markets, flea markets, art galleries, and excellent shops and restaurants.

Should you tire of the city, there is a wide choice of half-day, 1-day and longer excursions to coastal fishing villages, vineyards, small country towns, beaches, game parks, penguin reserves and ostrich farms. There are also easy-to-reach wilderness areas of forest, semi-desert, mountains and spectacular coastal scenery. Especially recommended are the West Coast National Park, with its spectacular spring flowers, the Cape of Good Hope Nature Reserve, historic towns Stellenbosch and Worcester, Boulder Bay, home of jackass penguins, and False Bay—with its many inshore havens for calving right whales from September to November.

## Hobart

The capital city of Tasmania, Hobart began in the late 18th century as one of several settlements along the sheltered Derwent River. In 1803 Lt. John Bowen RN in HMS *Lady Nelson* took possession of Tasmania (then Van Diemen's Land), establishing Hobart Town as its seat of government. The little port developed quickly into a market for local farm produce, a centre for ship building and repairing, and a focal point for the sealing and whaling industries that were already well established in the area.

In 1837 Captain Sir John Franklin RN, a prominent Arctic explorer, was appointed Lieutenant Governor of the colony, and Hobart became a port of departure for scientific expeditions to the Southern Ocean. The French explorer Dumont D'Urville visited in 1839, and 2 years later Sir James Clark Ross spent several weeks there. His ships' companies contributed to the festivities when they laid the foundation stone of the new Government House in May 1841. Franklin left Tasmania 2 years later, returned to the Arctic, and died in 1847 seeking the North-west Passage. Hobart's main wharf is named for him, and his statue stands in Franklin Square.

Ross's discovery of the sea route to high-latitude Antarctica led many subsequent explorers to sail from Hobart, including Henryk Bull (1894), Carsten Borchgrevink (1898), Robert Falcon Scott (1901), Roald Amundsen (1910), Douglas Mawson (1911), and the factory ships and catchers of the later whaling fleets. The tradition continues: today Hobart is the point of departure for national Antarctic expeditions of several nations, including Australia's own: look out for her bright-orange icebreaker *Aurora Australis* at Prince's Wharf.

Antarctic visitors waiting for their ship in Hobart will find themselves in a small but lively southern city (population about 140 000), still centred around its historic port, Sullivan's Cove. An hour or two's walking in the dock area and Battery Point gives the feel of the old town. A good starting point is the interpretation centre on Waterman's Dock. Wander along Salamanca Place with its warehouses and flea market, paying your respects to the statue of Abel Tasman, the 17th-century Dutch explorer who discovered Australia, and for whom Tasmania is named. Visit the old wharf buildings lining Victoria Dock in Hunter Street: spend time in the Tasmanian Museum and Art Gallery on Macquarie Street, with its collection of Antarctic whaling and expedition artefacts.

Hobart retains many Antarctic connections, including an active university Institute of Antarctic and Southern Ocean Studies, and several government departments concerned with Antarctica, the Southern Ocean and its islands. In 1974 the headquarters of Australia's Antarctic Division was transferred from Melbourne to Hobart, and in 1981 the new headquarters for Australian Antarctic operations opened in the suburb of Kingston. Easy half-day excursions take you to very delightful surrounding countryside: visit the old colonial gaol at Port Arthur, out-of-town nature centres that feature wombats, wallabies and other marsupials, or take sailing excursions on the River Derwent.


## Visiting the southern islands

The Falkland Islands and South Georgia are dealt with in Chapter 5, the southern South Orkney, South Shetland and South Sandwich Islands in Chapter 6, and the rest of the southern islands in Chapter 10.


## Visiting the continental coast

Cruising the continental coasts feels different from cruising Antarctic Peninsula and the Scotia Arc islands. Once you have reached them, the peninsula and islands present a succession of immediate stimuli—this cape, that mountain, these islands, ice shelves and glaciers—all follow each other in quick succession. If you are not recovering from the last landing, you are preparing for the next: Where are my dry socks? what happened to my binoculars? Is my camera loaded and ready to go?

Cruising the coast is a more leisurely business: the distances are greater, the landings farther apart. There is more time to appreciate the travelling, the ship, the staff and crew, the lectures, colleagues and fellow-passengers: there is often more time to read and talk, and indeed more time to be bored. While landings on the peninsula favour sites of scenic or wildlife interest, coastal landings are usually on the sea ice, or at scientific stations. Scientists along the continental coast receive far fewer visitors than those on the peninsula and islands. This does not mean inevitably that they are more glad to see you. Like monks in monasteries, they have their own round of things to do, and may or may not welcome diversions.

How do we find our way around the continent? I personally still think in terms of British, Norwegian, Australian and French sectors (Map 1). However, for those who do not favour political claims, I divide the continent into named 'lands', and the coastline into named 'coasts'. In fact these are as politically loaded as the sectors, though perhaps less blatantly so. This survey starts in the Weddell Sea, works clockwise around the continent, and finally deals briefly with the interior.

## Coats Land

Coats Land is a narrow sector forming the eastern coast of the Weddell Sea, inland as far as longitude 20°E, and south to 82°S. The Scottish explorer William Bruce was first to explore it, naming it for two brothers from the Glasgow cotton-spinning firm, who supported his expedition. Like Ross on the far side of the continent, Bruce discovered an unexpected polynya or stretch of open water, caused by strong offshore winds, that allowed him to penetrate far to the south (Figure 9.2). Others who tried it later were less fortunate: William Filchner in *Deutschland* was trapped in the pack ice for 9 months: Shackleton drifted in *Endurance* for 10 months, then lost his ship. This is an ice coast, fronted all along by ice cliffs. Underlying rocks are visible only in the far south by Vahsel Bay, and in the Theron and Shackleton Mountains.

### Luitpold Coast

The southern half of the coast, named by Filchner for a Bavarian prince, extends south to the Filchner Ice Shelf. Here ice-covered mountains come close to the shore, and General Belgrano II, an Argentine research station, stands on the only rocky enclave to be found in the area. Built in 1985, Belgrano II replaced an earlier station built on the shelf ice in the late 1950s, that disappeared completely under accumulated snow. Indeed the shelf itself broke away in 1985, so Belgrano is entombed and adrift somewhere in the southern Weddell Sea. This is a coast where icebreakers are needed: the Argentine icebreaker *Almirante Irizar* maintains Belgrano II each year.

### Caird Coast

The sub-glacial mountains of Coats Land curve eastward in 76°S, so the northern half of the coast, called the Caird Coast, is fronted by the wide Brunt Ice Shelf. This section was explored by Shackleton, who named the coast for one of his supporters—James Caird, a Dundee jute manufacturer. Caird's name was borne also by one of *Endurance*'s lifeboats, the one in which Shackleton and his companions sailed from Elephant Island to South Georgia.

Far south on the ice shelf stands Halley Station, a British station founded in 1956 for the IGY, and named for the astronomer who is celebrated also for his comet. Four former versions of the station have disappeared under the snow: the current station, completed in 1992, stands on extendable stilts that allow it to be jacked up as the snow level rises. On the sea ice below the station some 15 000 pairs of emperor penguins breed each year (Box 9.3).

There is a slightly smaller emperor-penguin colony of about 12 000 pairs at the Dawson Lambton Ice Stream 80 km (50 miles) south of Halley, and one of 6600 pairs at the Stancombe-Wills Ice Stream (Figure 9.3), 160 km (100 miles) to the north. (An ice stream, incidentally, is a glacier flowing between walls of ice, rather

## Box 9.3 At home with emperor penguins

*Largest of all living penguins, emperors stand about 1 m (3 ft) tall and weigh up to 40 kg (90 lb) in full fat. Up to 1947 only two breeding colonies were known in the whole of Antarctica, at Cape Crozier (p. 202) and Haswell Islands (p. 221). A third was discovered at the Dion Islands, Marguerite Bay (p. 179), and since then about 40 more have been found in widely scattered locations around the continental coast.*

*Emperors breed in winter, assembling in May on newly formed sea ice. Courtship and laying take 3 to 4 weeks. There are no nests: males take the single egg on their feet, and hold it there for the full incubation period of about 60 days. During incubation they live only on the food reserves in their bodies, huddling tightly together to conserve energy. This is usually the coldest period of the year, with temperatures down to −40°C or lower.*

*Females spend the same period at the ice edge, which by this time may be many miles away. They return to the colonies around hatching time, find their mates, and take over the care of the hatching egg or chick.*

*Males return to the sea, feed, and bring back food in their crops for the chicks. Thereafter both parents forage, at first alternately, then simultaneously as the chicks gain in size and strength. As the ice edge retreats their foraging journeys shorten. Chicks grow slowly at first, then rapidly, shedding their grey woolly down by November or December. When the fast ice that has been their nursery breaks up, chicks drift away with parents still in attendance: chicks seem able to swim, and possibly to forage at least partly for themselves, while still in down. In late summer adults undergo a complete moult, and fatten ready for their autumn breeding.*

**Figure 9.3** *In spring sunshine, under the shelter of towering ice cliffs, emperor penguins tend the chicks that they incubated and brooded through the winter. Winter incubation ensures that chicks will be ready for the sea in November or December, when their sea-ice nursery disintegrates.*

than of rock.) ~~All three colonies form on sea ice at the foot of ice cliffs, where the~~ birds are protected during their winter breeding, but the sea ice is certain to break away by mid-summer.

Both the Dawson-Lambton and the Stancomb-Wills colonies assemble in spectacular settings of ice cliffs, glaciers and tumbled bergs. Huge concentrations of Weddell seals also breed along this coast. An area that seems at first glance to be almost empty of life is in fact very rich, due to the polynya, which provides a wealth of food from early spring onward (Figure 9.1).

Cruise ships with ice-breaking capacity, carrying helicopters to view the way ahead, can usually come and go as they please along this coast, at least as far as Halley. Icebreakers are needed, not so they can barge about breaking ice (which spoils them, and ruins their captain's digestion), but so they can be sure of being able to break out if necessary, and not be trapped like the unfortunate *Endurance*.

## Dronning Maud Land

Dronning Maud Land is the wide sector of East Antarctica between 20°W and 45°E (Map 1). The name means 'Queen Maud Land', and using the Norwegian form follows the modern geographical convention of adopting native names. So here we are back into politics—or are we? The name was given by the Norwegian whaler and explorer Lars Christensen to honour his Norwegian queen, and it seems to me churlish to anglicize it.

### Kronprinsesse Märtha Kyst

Here again the mountains of Antarctica lie far behind the coast, which is lined by a broad ice shelf. On a clear day from a helicopter you can just see the Heimefront Fjella (would you prefer 'Home-front Range'?) 320 km (200 miles) inland. The ice shelf is Riiser-Larsenisen, named for a Norwegian pilot of the Christensen expeditions who overflew and photographed the area in 1933–34.

This corner of Dronning Maud Land and a substantial area of mountains to the east were overflown again in February 1939 by German aircraft operating from *Schwabenland*, an offshore seaplane tender. Thousands of aerial photographs were taken, though without ground control, and cylinders containing claims to the area were dropped at several points. News of the impending expedition led Norway to make its own pre-emptive claim in January 1939. Records of the expedition were destroyed in World War II, and any possible German claim to 'Neu-Schwabenland' was forfeited in the post-war peace settlement. However, the name New Schwabenland has been given by some authorities to mountains close to the Greenwich meridian, to honour a hard-working expedition.

There is a colony of 6000 pairs of emperor penguins at Drescher Inlet, a deep nick in the ice cliff, where German biologists have a small research station for studying penguins and Weddell seals. Under the cliffs of this inlet I once found a tiny colony of Adelie penguins—two nests with eggs and one without. The nests were no more than hollows in the snow: the birds sat on them uneasily, as though certain that something was wrong, but not sure what. A second colony of

**Figure 9.4** *A line of ventilators and hatches: all that can be seen of a scientific station beneath the snow. In areas of heavy snowfall, a station built on the surface may disappear within 3 or 4 years, and be destroyed within a few more years by the weight of overlying snow.*

emperors, again of about 6000 pairs, gathers a few miles farther north along the sea ice.

On the north-western corner of Dronning Maud Land stands Kapp Norvegia, an ice promontory and landmark along an otherwise confusing coast. Immediately beyond it is Norselbukta, an ice bay named for *Norsel*, the ship of the Norwegian-Swedish-British Antarctic Expedition of 1949–52. This was a small but highly successful international expedition that explored extensively inland, making topographic, geological and biological surveys, and pioneering a technique of measuring ice thickness by seismic sounding. Their station Maudheim, built a short distance inland from Norselbukta, disappeared under the snow within a couple of seasons, and has not been seen since.

About 140 km (80 miles) north-east is another large bay, Atka Ice Port, which is the landing point for Georg von Neumeyer, a German research station. Built originally at the surface in 1980, the station consisted of a container-like building in an H-shaped steel tube, designed to resist the weight of overlying snow. It soon disappeared (Figure 9.4), but the scientists continued to work as troglodytes, climbing an ever-growing spiral staircase to reach the surface. A new station has recently replaced the original—the old staircase grew too long even for the fittest. Atka Ice Port is the site of two small and easily visited emperor-penguin colonies.

Some 400 km (250 miles) east, on Vesleskarvet Nunatak in the Fimbulisen Ice Shelf, stands Sanae, South Africa's research station. Built on the side of a nunatak (rock outcrop surrounded by ice) about 16 km (10 miles) from the sea, this is the fourth station to bear its name: the three earlier ones, all built on ice shelves, each disappeared under snow and became untenable after 8–10 years of use. Like most modern stations, Sanae IV is a series of box-like buildings, created from insulated plastic panels, and raised on metal stilts to prevent drifts building up around it.

## Prinsesse Astrid Kyst

To reach this coast we head eastward again, crossing the 0° Greenwich meridian and entering the eastern hemisphere. Physically there is little change: sea ice drifting westward before the prevailing easterly winds may open to yield a highway, or cluster, to form a barrier that can only be circumnavigated. A few miles inland, across a barrier of shelf ice, is sited Dakshin Gangotri, India's first Antarctic research station. About 100 km (60 miles) farther inland stand the Schirmacher Hills, the first Antarctic oasis area ever to be identified, named for a pilot of the Schwabenland expedition who spotted them. In the oasis stand Maitri, Novolazarevskaya and Georg Forster—respectively Indian, Russian and German stations. All have to be serviced by tractor train or helicopter from the coast.

## Kronprins Olav Kyst

Toward the eastern end of Dronning Maud Land the coast turns sharply northward. Here in an oasis area of islands and low, ice-scoured rocks stands Syowa, the main Japanese research station. Opened originally in 1956 for the IGY, Syowa had to be abandoned in February 1958 because of bad sea-ice conditions. It was reopened in the following summer and has run ever since. Of 15 sledge dogs left behind when the station was evacuated, two survived to greet the incomers. Pack ice in Lützow-Holmbukta make this a difficult station to manage and visit, but the setting is delightful.

## Enderby Land, Kemp Land

Crossing meridian 45°E brings us to Australian Antarctic Territory (you don't like that? go argue with the Australians). Enderby Land and neighbouring Kemp Land too have ice-fringed coasts, but with high, ice-draped mountains forming a dramatic shoreline. Several peaks close to the coast rise to 600 m (2000 ft), and the Tula and Scott mountains rise above 1500 m (5000 ft), all within sight of passing ships. These are the mountains that the Enderby Company sealers saw during their extraordinary voyages of the early 1830s (Box 9.2), making them certain they were seeing a substantial new country. The coast is fringed with islets and bays, many of them ice free when winter snows have melted.

## Molodezhnaya

In the corner of Alashayev Bight, just east of the border, stands this Russian station opened in 1961–62 in an oasis setting of lakes, islands and hills. With its relatively mild climate and pleasing aspect, Molodezhnaya is the favourite station of many Russian polar biologists and geologists. Easier to reach than Mirny, from 1969 it became the main headquarters of Soviet expeditions in Antarctica, and in 1977 it acquired a landing ground for enhancement of air operations.

East of this point the coast bears northward, crossing the Antarctic Circle in a wide bulge that accommodates the Napier Mountains, and recrossing in Edward VIII Gulf—named in 1936 for a newcomer to the British throne, who abdicated shortly afterwards to marry an American lady named Mrs Simpson.

## Proclamation Island

Off the northern tip of the Enderby Land bulge, this tiny island was one of five points where Sir Douglas Mawson, leading the British, Australian and New Zealand Antarctic Research Expedition (BANZARE) of 1929–31, stepped ashore to make formal proclamations that claimed this sector of Antarctica for the British crown. It has no further distinction but a colony of about 5000 pairs of Adelie penguins, whose forebears were the only natives to witness the proclamation.

## Mac. Robertson Land

Continuing eastward we move along the island-studded Mawson Coast of Mac. Robertson Land. The full stop is not a misprint: this area was named for Australian industrialist Sir MacPherson Robertson, who backed BANZARE financially. His full name is generally deemed too full for small maps. Here again is a steep coast, with ice-covered mountains rising to 1200 m (4000 ft) less than 50 km (30 miles) inland.

### Mawson Station

Mawson Station stands midway along the coast, in the sheltered inlet of Horseshoe Harbour. The main station of Australia's national Antarctic research operations, Mawson has operated since 1954, though few of the original buildings remain. The station was rebuilt completely in time for its 40th anniversary, with new scientific laboratories and workshops, excellent living quarters, and recreational facilities unimaginable even a generation earlier. Over the years Mawson has maintained a steady record of scientific achievement, both in the immediate area and in the Prince Charles Mountains 250 km (150 miles) inland.

### Scullin Monolith

About 160 km (100 miles) east of Mawson, in lonely splendour on the Lars Christensen Coast, stands this huge block of dark gneiss some 430 m (1420 ft) high. Its nearest companion some 8 km (5 miles) beyond is Murray Monolith, similar but only 240 m (790 ft) high. Providing the only bare rock for miles around, these are well populated with Adelie penguins, shags and petrels, and carry a rich vegetation of lichens and moss.

## Princess Elizabeth Land

Just east of ice-covered Cape Darnley the coast swings far southward into Mackenzie Bay, occupied by the Amery Ice Shelf. Beyond lies Prydz Bay, where the rocks re-emerge as the steep, spectacular Ingrid Christensen Coast of Princess Elizabeth Land. Ingrid, the wife of Lars Christensen, and Karoline, the wife of Captain Klarius Mikkelsen (master of the whale factory ship *Thorshavn*), both accompanied their husbands to Antarctica. They were probably the first women ever to see the continent, and Karoline, who made a landing with Klarius on this coast in January 1935, was probably the first woman to step ashore in Antarctica.

### Progress, Zhongshan and Davis

The coast, relatively ice free, is one of islands, lakes and low hills, backed by steep ice-covered mountains. In the Larsemann Hills are sited the Russian station Progress and the Chinese station Zhongshan, both relatively recent. In the more complex and scenic Vestfold Hills, farther east, stands the Australian station Davis, first opened in 1957. The most recent round of rebuilding was completed in 1994. Like Mawson, this is a strikingly modern and efficient station, with a high standard of comfort for its occupants.

## Wilhelm II Land

### Gaussberg

East of an extensive ice shelf, close to the meridian of 90°W, stands a prominent ice-free mountain on an ice-bound coast. Gaussberg is a solitary heap of lava, almost conical, rising to 370 m (12 000 ft) and ringed by spectacular ice falls. The structure and composition of the lava suggests that it erupted some 50 000–60 000 years ago under a massive ice sheet—a sheet far more extensive than currently provides its backdrop. There is no vent: the surface is covered with weathered debris, with bedrock emerging at the summit and in ridges down the side.

Gaussberg was discovered by the German South Polar Expedition of 1901–03, led by Erich von Drygalski. Trying to approach it, their ship *Gauss* was caught and held by the ice, eventually freezing-in some 80 km (50 miles) from the shore. The Germans spent a limited but profitable winter sledging to the mountain and studying the biology of the sea around them. Sea ice seldom breaks completely from around this coast, so few ships manage to approach closer than *Gauss*.

## Queen Mary Land

This area was discovered by Douglas Mawson's Australasian Antarctic Expedition of 1911–14, and named after the contemporary British queen. It was explored by the expedition's Western Party, led by Frank Wild and based on the Shackleton Ice Shelf. Their story, one of Antarctica's most interesting, has been eclipsed by accounts from the main base at Cape Denison (p. 222). They found themselves in an area of high snowfall, strong winds, turbulent glaciers, crevasses, avalanches and icefalls, but managed significant exploration eastward across the ice shelf and westward as far as Gaussberg. Their hut, built on the ice shelf, has long since disappeared.

Three of the Western Party, sledging in January 1912 along the ice cliffs toward Gaussberg, dropped to a small rocky point at sea level and walked over the sea ice to examine a small group of islands 8 km (5 miles) from the coast. Their reward was discovery of the second-known breeding colony of emperor penguins, and an area, later to be named the Haswell Islands, containing in the words of one of its discoverers, 'the most wonderful abundance of bird life' and a parallel wealth of vegetation. Now read on.

### Mirny Station

In 1956 the USSR chose the rocky point behind the Haswell Islands for the site of Mirny, one of their IGY stations. A scientific station in its own right, Mirny became also the main operational base from which stations on the interior ice cap were serviced, using massive tractor trains and aircraft. After more than 40 years of these activities, Mirny has become a repository—somewhere between an industrial museum and used-car lot—of worn heavy equipment, none of which seems to find its way back to Russia.

Fortunately this has had little direct effect on the islands: despite wind-blown debris from the shore, this continues to be an area of great biological interest. The main island of the group, nominally a Site of Special Scientific Interest, maintains its superb avifauna and rich vegetation, and the emperor penguins continue to assemble each autumn as soon as the sea ice allows.

### Wilkes Land

#### Casey Station

Named for the leader of the US Exploring Expedition of 1838–42, Wilkes Land is a broad sector including the Knox, Budd, Sabrina, Banzare and Wilkes coasts. On the Windmill Islands of the Budd Coast stands the remains of an old US station, Wilkes, that was built for the IGY in 1956 and transferred to Australian management 3 years later. After some years it became unserviceable, and in 1968 Casey, a completely new station, was opened close by.

This is the current station, set in an attractive and biologically rich area. Ardery and Odbert Islands 12 km (7 miles) to the south form a Specially Protected Area, designated particularly for their breeding petrels. However, their biological characteristics are shared by many other islands in the Windmill group.

### Terre Adélie

Between 136° and 142°E we leave the Australian sector and enter French territory. Terre Adélie, a mere 260 km (163 miles) wide along the coast, marks the area where César Dumont d'Urville made his landfall in January 1840. Faced by a continuous wall of ice cliffs he was unable to land on the mainland. He landed instead on a small islet, already well occupied by penguins, and claimed the territory for France. France took very little note of the matter until 1924, when—prompted perhaps by Britain's renewed interest in the territory on either side—her government issued a series of decrees controlling mining, hunting and fishing in Terre Adélie.

### Dumont d'Urville Station

Again spurred to action by restless neighbours, France in January 1950 established a research station at Port-Martin. Two years later this was destroyed by fire, and a reduced party wintered on Ile des Pétrels, off Point Geólogie, 100 km (60 miles) to the west. In 1956 this became the site of an IGY station, Dumont d'Urville, which has remained in operation ever since. Situated in a biologically rich area, this station became an important centre of long-term marine bird and mammal studies, based on local populations of penguins, petrels and seals.

During the late 1980s France sought to increase the value of the station for geophysical studies by installing an air strip. This involved major alterations to several islands in the Pointe Géologie archipelago, with consequent disruption to wildlife. Work proceeded for several summers, but was eventually halted by irreparable storm damage. Visitors to Pointe Géologie may view the devastated islands, the abandoned runway, and the philosophical acceptance of the penguins and petrels that continue to live there.

## George V Land

Crossing back in Australian territory at Point Alden, the coast retreats southward to form Commonwealth Bay. On a raised beach by Cape Denison stand the lonely, weather-beaten huts of the Australasian Antarctic Expedition, erected by Mawson in 1911 and occupied for three winters. Living and working under extraordinarily difficult conditions, Mawson and his party undertook a full programme of sledging and scientific investigations, exploring along the coast and inland to the South Magnetic Pole. The living hut, battered but still sound, has recently been excavated and stabilized. Australian authorities control as best they can the number of visitors who examine it each year.

## Oates Land

This sector of Antarctica was first surveyed from Scott's expedition ship *Terra Nova* in February 1912, and later named for Captain Lawrence Oates, who died with Scott on returning from the South Pole in the same year. Rather confusingly, Oates Land is divided by the border (meridian 160°E) between Australian and New Zealand claims, but neither country perceives serious problems in the matter.

## Leningradskaya Station

Within the Australian sector, at the head of a deep bay, stands Leningradskaya, a Soviet station opened in 1969. Persistent pack ice in this corner by the Balleny Islands makes it an unlikely venue for casual visitors.

## Marie Byrd Land

Named for the wife of Admiral Byrd, this is the 'mainland' sector of West Antarctica, and by far the most difficult corner of Antarctica to reach by sea. Perhaps that is why nobody has bothered to stake a claim. It is an area both of congested sea ice, making maritime operations hazardous, and also of high precipitiation, with many active ice shelves and ice streams producing bergs at a phenomenal rate. Only one research station, Russkaya, has operated there, under constant difficulties and uncertainties of annual resupply.

## The continental interior

Less than 90 years ago Robert Falcon Scott, determined to explore the interior of Antarctica, set to it with manpower and pony-drawn sledges. Roald Amundsen, using polar techniques that were superior in almost every respect, relied entirely on dogs. Less than 70 years ago Wilkins, Ellsworth and Byrd made the first tentative flights over Antarctica, concerned as much with keeping in the air as with exploration. Less than 50 years ago heavy tracked vehicles were first used to bring stations, stores and equipment to previously inaccessible places.

From these early starting points came the technical developments that have now brought virtually every corner of Antarctica within reach of visitors. Ships and land transport still take many of the loads, but if you cannot get in by sea, if the icy terrain is too tough to cross, in one way or another you can fly. Helicopters and fixed-wing aircraft alike have become more reliable: improved design has extended their ranges and increased their payloads. The South Pole? The Pole of Inaccessibility, far out on the empty plateau? Neither presents problems that cannot be solved with thought, intelligent forward planning, and a great deal of money.

One important development has been the discovery, from satellite imagery, of patches of snow-free 'blue ice' all over the interior of Antarctica. These make serviceable runways for wheeled aircraft, eliminating the use of drag-inducing skis. Aircraft can thus take off from hard runways in civilization, and land substantial payloads—including passengers—in a wide choice of venues all over Antarctica.

Among those interested in the possibilities opened by these developments are private adventurers alone or with small expeditions, climbers, nature photographers, and scientists who seek to work where nobody has worked before. A popular venue is the Ellsworth Mountains, which includes Antarctica's highest peak and seems to experience some of its sunniest and most stable weather. If you are interested, decide where you want to go, scan the list of operators in Chapter 3, and make enquiries. But do not be surprised at the cost. Setting up such an operation safely requires first-rate equipment, good planning, and high levels of skill, knowledge and experience. Those are what you will be paying for. Wrap up well and have a good trip.

## Further reading

Christensen, L. 1935. *Such is the Antarctic*. London, Hodder and Stoughton.
Mawson, D. 1915. *The Home of the Blizzard: Being the Story of the Australasian Antarctic Expedition, 1911–1914*. London, William Heinemann.
Price, A. G. 1963. *The Winning of the Australian Antarctic: Mawson's BANZARE Voyages 1929–31*. Sydney, Angus and Robertson.

# Chapter Ten

# Southern islands

## Introduction

The Southern Ocean beyond the Convergence, and southern reaches of the Atlantic, Indian and Pacific Oceans, are dotted with tiny, isolated islands and island groups (see inside front cover). Once the world's remotest places, several are now visited by cruise ships travelling to and from Antarctica. You have never heard of Campbell Island? Heard Island? Iles Kerguelen? And you don't want to know about them? Then skip this chapter.

There is magic and mystery in every island, and these southern islands pack their share of both. In the 19th century they were milestones for sailing ships running the Great Circle routes (the shortest possible) from Europe to the Antipodes. The trick was to sail close enough for the master to check his position, but not so close as to risk foundering on them, or on uncharted reefs close by. The trick did not always work: every island claimed its toll of wrecks, its tally of castaways and lonely graves. There is even a tale of unrecovered gold. You still don't want to know?

Practically all the islands stand within the Roaring Forties and the Howling Fifties—that broad belt of westerly winds and ocean currents that dominates the southern hemisphere. Traditionally they are called 'subantarctic islands', which is fine if you think of them only as islands on Antarctica's doorstep. However, it is a very wide doorstep. Far-southern islands are heavily iced, far-northern ones ice free; some grow trees, others nothing bigger than moss clumps; some are snow covered for 6 months each year, others virtually snow free. I prefer to forget 'subantarctic' and group them in ecological zones that help to explain their differences (see below).

By no means all bitterly cold, they tend rather to be cloudy, gloomy, storm wracked and rainy. If you are looking for an oceanic island to be cast away on, think twice about these: there are thousands with better climates. On the other hand, if you are water resistant and enjoy seabirds, you could hardly do better: on most of them you can count on a sound pecking from petrels, penguins, gulls, skuas and shags.

Almost all have been altered by man, mostly by sealers and penguin hunters, some by castaways, a few by settlers. Some have been devastated by burning or farming, others more subtly spoiled by the introduction of alien mammals. Rats and mice came in accidentally from wrecks or landed stores. Cats were introduced to catch the rats and mice—only they didn't: catching birds was more fun. Dogs were brought in presumably to chase the cats, and pigs, rabbits, goats, sheep and cattle, to keep the dogs and castaways happy and well fed. Some of the drier islands were burnt accidentally, or to provide better pasture for the introduced grazing animals . . . and so it went on.

Today all the islands north of 60°S come under the sovereignty of one nation or another, and are to some degree protected by conservation legislation. You can land on some but not all: the more exposed ones are protected more effectively by wind and swell than by legislation.

Ecologically it makes sense to think of them in their natural zones—those north of the Antarctic Convergence as warm temperate or cool temperate, and those south of the Convergence as periantarctic or Antarctic. In practice they are easier to identify within their ocean sectors—Atlantic, Indian, Pacific. Then if you are heading south down, say, the Atlantic Ocean, you know which islands to look out for on the way. Here I present them both ways: the rest of the chapter deals first with the ecological zones, then with the islands ocean by ocean, and this is all summarized in Box 10.1.

Some islands we have already met: I include them here just to show where they fit into the scheme. You will find details of the Falkland Islands and South Georgia in Chapter 5, the southern Scotia Arc islands in Chapter 6.


# The ecological zones

## Warm temperate islands

On these islands mean temperatures for the warmest month (usually January or February) lie above 10°C. Originally the islands were forested at sea level with tall shrubs or trees, wind sculptured and growing from peaty soils, but few remain pristine. Nightingale, Inaccessible and Gough Islands retain their cover, while Tristan has been modified by almost two centuries of occupation. Iles Amsterdam and St Paul have lost their forest cover by burning. The Auckland Islands, south of New Zealand, represent the zone fairly: the neighbouring Bounty Islands are exceptional in being almost bare of soil and vegetation, and colonized only by seabirds and seals.


## Cool temperate islands

Here mean temperatures for the warmest month lie within the range 6 to 10°C. Snow may fall in any month, but lies around only in winter. Iles Kerguelen and Macquarie Island are the coldest, standing very close to the Antarctic Convergence: only Kerguelen has a small, permanent ice cap.

Cool temperate islands are treeless: natural coastal vegetation is usually tall shrubs or tussock grasses, rising to grassland or fellfield inland. Iles Kerguelen and Campbell Island have been farmed: the Falklands currently support a population of over 2000 people and many times that number of sheep. On the Falklands, trees have been planted as windbreaks: visit Stanley or any farming settlement in the group, and you will see introduced pines and cedars doing their best to stand up to searing, salt-laden winds.

Box 10.1   *Islands and zonation of the Southern Ocean*

| tlantic sector | Indian sector | Pacific sector | Characteristic vegetation |
|---|---|---|---|

**oundary: Subtropical Convergence**

*Varm temperate zone: mean summer temperatures above 10°C*

| | | | |
|---|---|---|---|
| ristan da Cunha group | Ile Amsterdam | Snares Islands | Trees, shrubs, bushes and |
| ough Island | Ile St Paul | Bounty Islands | tussock meadows on |
| | Prince Edward Islands | Antipodes Islands | coasts: shrubs and |
| | | Auckland Islands | fellfield on uplands. Soils |
| | | | mature, fertile, with |
| | | | thick peat deposits. |

**oundary: 10°C isotherm for the warmest month**

*ool temperate zone: mean summer temperature 6–10°C*

| | | | |
|---|---|---|---|
| alkland Islands | Iles Crozet | Campbell Island | Grasses and herbs form |
| | Iles Kerguelen | | meadows on coasts and |
| | Macquarie Island | | uplands: small shrubs |
| | | | prominent. Soils mature, |
| | | | fertile, with peat |
| | | | deposits. |

**oundary: Antarctic Convergence**

*eriantarctic zone: mean summer temperature 2–6°*

| | | | |
|---|---|---|---|
| outh Georgia | Heard Island | | Several species of flowering |
| ouvetøya | McDonald Islands | | plants prominent at sea |
| | | | level: tussock grasses |
| | | | and fellfields pre- |
| | | | dominant, with mature |
| | | | soils patchy. |

**oundary: northern limit of pack ice**

*ntarctic zone: mean summer temperature from −1 to +2°C*

| | | | |
|---|---|---|---|
| outh Orkney Islands | | Balleny Islands | Snow-free ground mostly |
| outh Shetland Islands | | Scott Island | bare. Algae, lichens and |
| outh Sandwich Islands | | Peter I Øy | mosses predominant: |
| | | | two species of flowering |
| | | | plants only in the |
| | | | Atlantic sector: little soil. |

## Periantarctic islands

These islands stand south of the Antarctic Convergence (and hence within the Southern Ocean), but north of the northern limit of pack ice. Mean summer temperatures lie within the range 2 to 6°C. Both summers and winters are cooler than those on islands to the north, but winters are milder than on southern islands invested by winter sea ice. All are snow covered for several months each year: all but the McDonald Islands carry a capping of permanent ice.

Tussock grass, if present, is limited to a narrow coastal zone: fellfield, bare rock and permanent snow replace it a few metres inland. Heard Island and several of the South Sandwich islands are active volcanoes. Bouvetøya is probably in the right climatic zone to grow tussock sward, but too small, steep and lashed with spray to grow anything more substantial than mosses and lichens. South Georgia is the largest and most alpine of all the southern ocean islands. It is a popular tourist attraction with several tricky but worthwhile landing areas (Chapter 5).

## Antarctic islands

These are surrounded for part of each year by sea ice. Mean summer temperatures lie within the range −1 to 2°C. Summer temperatures are slightly lower than on the periantarctic islands: winter temperatures dip 5 to 10°C lower, because sea ice isolates them from the warming effects of the sea. They have more permanent ice and snow than periantarctic islands, and keep their seasonal snows longer. Growing seasons are shorter, and there is far less vegetation and soil. Most of these islands appear in the Atlantic sector, and are dealt with in Chapter 6.

## Atlantic sector islands

### Tristan da Cunha group (warm temperate)

Tristan da Cunha and neighbouring Nightingale and Inaccessible Islands form a cluster 4000 km (2500 miles) east of South America and 2700 km (1700 miles) west of South Africa. Standing where two submarine ridges meet, they result from intermittent volcanic activity that began at least 18 million years ago: Nightingale Island has the oldest rocks, Tristan da Cunha some of the youngest.

Tristan da Cunha is roughly circular, 12 km (7.5 miles) in diameter, and is the tip of a submarine cone that rose above the waves about 1 million years ago. It rises in steps of interbedded lava and scoria to a central cone (called simply 'The Peak') 2060 m (6760 ft) high. In 1961 its northern flank erupted, providing a small platform of fresh lava close to Edinburgh, the settlement. The climate is mild and damp, with rainfall 170 cm per year. The peak is usually shrouded in cloud, and snow covered in winter.

Over 70 native species of flowering plants and ferns have been recorded. Close to sea level stand remnants of a wind-sculptured forest of trees and ferns: above rise tussock meadows, moorland and fellfield. Seabirds are abundant, including breeding rockhopper penguins, yellow-nosed and sooty albatrosses, several species of smaller petrels, and terns, noddies and skuas. Land birds include an endemic thrush and two endemic species of bunting.

Tristan was discovered in 1506 by the Portuguese navigator whose name it bears. It was settled initially by an American seaman in 1811, and annexed in 1816 by a British garrison, sent there to forestall possible efforts by the French to rescue Napoleon Bonaparte from St Helena. The military soon withdrew, but the settlement continued under British sovereignty, maintaining a fluctuating population of 50–100 that supported itself by fishing, farming and barter with passing ships.

As steam replaced sail, fewer ships visited Tristan, but the community survived and grew to about 300. During World War II the island acquired a garrison and meteorological station, and later a cray fishery. After the eruption of 1961 the whole population of 290 was moved to the United Kingdom: 250 returned in 1963, relieved to be able to resume their old way of life. The Tristan da Cunha Islands, together with their nearest neighbour Gough Island, are administered by Britain as a dependency of St Helena.

Edinburgh provides the only safe landing point (Figures 10.1 and 10.2). Visit the small settlement with its traditional cottages, church and shop. See the lava flow that in 1961 threatened to engulf them, but resulted ultimately in a new wave of prosperity for the islanders. Visit the potato patches, a short drive or walk out of town. It does not sound an exciting excursion, but the walk is pleasant and the huts reflect the ingenuity of a lively, inventive community that, for a long time, made do with very little.

**Figure 10.1**  *Edinburgh, the capital and only settlement of Tristan da Cunha, housing a population of around 300. The ridge in the foreground is part of the lava flow that, in 1961, threatened to engulf the settlement, and caused the islanders to be evacuated.*

**Figure 10.2**  *The 'new' harbour of Tristan da Cunha, completed in 1967 after the islanders had returned to their homes, which vastly increases chances for safe landing of passengers and stores. Previously, generations of islanders launched their boats from the open beach, often through heavy surf.*

Lying 35 km (22 miles) south-west of Tristan da Cunha, Inaccessible Island is a rectangular slab of lava and scoria 4 km (2.5 miles) long and almost as wide. Rimmed on all sides by steep cliffs and narrow beaches, it rises to a dissected plateau up to 600 m (1970 ft) high: access is possible only by scrambling up steep water-cut ravines. The climate is similar to that of Tristan, possibly wetter. The dominant vegetation is a tall tussock grass, giving way to shrubs in the sheltered gullies, and moorland and bog on the uplands.

Millions of seabirds, notably rockhopper penguins and burrowing petrels, nest on the island, which also supports an endemic species of rail. Elephant seals and Amsterdam Island fur seals breed on the beaches. Sealing gangs and castaways have lived on the island, and Tristan islanders visit to collect seabird eggs, but there is no human settlement. The island is a nature reserve, and landings are unlikely.

Nightingale Island and its close companions Stoltenhoff and Middle Islands, together with many stacks and isolated rocks, form a compact group some 38 km (24 miles) south-south-west of Tristan da Cunha. The main island, 2.5 km (1.6 miles) long and 1.5 km (just less than 1 mile) wide, rises to 400 m (1312 ft). Oldest and most eroded of the Tristan group, Nightingale is composed of lava and trachyte, rugged and rimmed by cliffs and narrow beaches.

Climate and vegetation are similar to those of Inaccessible Island. Seabirds including rockhopper penguins and two species of albatross nest in abundance: the main island has a breeding population of great shearwaters estimated at several millions. Amsterdam fur seals breed on some of the beaches. There is no permanent human habitation. The islands are nature reserves, though Tristan islanders by tradition are allowed several visits per year to collect eggs, young birds and guano.

## Gough Island (warm temperate)

Standing in isolation 350 km (219 miles) south-south-east of Tristan da Cunha, Gough Island is a layer cake of lava and scoria 14 km (8.7 miles) long and 5 km (3.1 miles) wide. It rises to a plateau at 300 m (984 ft) from which emerge a cluster of higher peaks exceeding 800 m (2625 ft): the highest, Edinburgh Peak, stands central at 910 m (2986 m). Some 6 million years old, the island is ringed by steep cliffs and narrow beaches, with few landing points providing access to the interior.

The climate is both cooler and wetter than Tristan's. Tall tussock grass grows in exposed coastal areas, scrub and forest in the steep-sided coastal valleys, giving way to wet heath and moorland on the heights: over 60 species of flowering plants and ferns have been recorded. Snow lies on high ground in winter. Rockhopper penguins breed in abundance, together with yellow-nosed, sooty and wandering albatrosses, 10 species of lesser petrels, skuas, terns and noddies, and an endemic rail and bunting. Elephant seals and Amsterdam Island fur seals breed on the beaches.

Probably first sighted by Portuguese navigators in 1505, Gough Island was rediscovered, charted and named by Captain Charles Gough in March 1732. Throughout the 19th century it was a profitable hunting ground for sealing gangs. House mice, probably introduced by sealers, are the only alien. The island was investigated by a scientific survey in 1955–56, and from then onward occupied permanently by a South African meteorological station. It is a wildlife reserve. When conditions permit, landing is possible close to the weather station, allowing brief walks along the beach and a little way inland.

## Bouvetøya (periantarctic)

Standing 4800 km (3000 miles) east of Cape Horn, 3000 km (1875 miles) southwest of Cape Town, this speck of an island is roughly 8 km (5 miles) in diameter, and rises to 780 m (2560 ft), with a liberal topping of permanent ice (Figure 10.3). A relatively young volcano, marking the southern end of the mid-Atlantic sea-floor ridge, it is composed of flows of black basalt lava, on a broad submarine base: its caldera, now partly eroded and ice filled, can be seen in the north-western cliffs. Steam rises from the caldera rim, often obscured by mist and cloud.

Discovered in January 1739 by the French navigator Jean-Baptiste-Charles de Lozier Bouvet, the island was frequently lost and rediscovered. Its position was finally fixed by Norwegian expeditions of 1927–29 that mapped it and studied its meagre flora of algae, lichens and mosses. Scientists visiting during the 1950s discovered a new beach and raised platform on the north-western flank, initially interpreted as a lava flow, later identified as a landslide. In 1977 Norwegian scientists installed on the platform an automatic weather station. Fur seals were even quicker to discover it, making the platform and a new beach that developed

**Figure 10.3** *The wild southern shore of Bouvetøya, the tiny, ice-capped island in the southern Atlantic Ocean that marks the southern end of the Mid-Oceanic Ridge. This flank of the island suffers rapid erosion from heavy swells and surf. Fur seals and seabirds are its main inhabitants.*

alongside into a breeding ground. Erosion has reduced it to half its original size: the weather station has toppled, but the fur seals continue to breed on the remnant.

Norway annexed Bouvetøya in 1930 and has made it a nature reserve. Special permission is required even for scientists to land there, and good weather essential. Cruise ships en route from Cape Town occasionally drop by when fog and pack ice allow. Passengers cannot usually land on it, but it is something to have seen and appreciated what is said to be the world's most isolated fragment of land.

## Indian sector islands

### Ile Amsterdam (warm temperate)

Iles Amsterdam and St Paul are a closely neighbouring pair of islands some 80 km (50 miles) apart. They stand 4500 km (2800 miles) from southeastern Africa and 3500 km (2200 miles) from south-western Australia, on a submarine ridge that they share with Iles Kerguelen. Ile Amsterdam is oval, roughly 10 km (6.2 miles) long and almost as wide, rising to a central plateau at 600 m (1968 ft) and a complex of cones up to 880 m (2900 ft) high. Composed of interbedded lavas and tuffs, this is the eastern remnant of a larger island, most of which has disappeared under the sea. Lying close to the Subtropical Convergence, it has a mild and windy climate, with a little over 100 cm of rain per year.

**Figure 10.4**  *Amsterdam Island fur seal, a grey and white species that breeds on the warmer southern islands of the Indian Ocean. Like the Antarctic fur seal, its pelt was much in demand during the 18th and 19th centuries, and stocks have only recently shown signs of recovery.*

Originally forested close to sea level, with tussock grassland and bog above, Ile Amsterdam has been devastated repeatedly by fire and also by the grazing of introduced mammals. Currently its forest is confined to small remnant stands and its grasslands, contaminated by thistles and other alien species, are grazed by feral cattle. Norway rats, house mice and feral cats are abundant. The island supports breeding rockhopper penguins, an endemic species of great albatross, yellow-nosed and sooty albatrosses, smaller petrels, terns and skuas. Land birds include pintails and waxbills.

Sighted in March 1522 by Juan Sebastian de Elcano, Ile Amsterdam was first charted and named by the Dutch navigator Willem de Vlamingh in 1696–97, and subsequently visited by sealers from the late 18th century onward. France claimed it in 1843, and French entrepreneurs released cattle in 1871. The island has supported a permanent scientific station, La Roche Godon, since 1949, and has the protected status of a French national park. Landings are made on a beach within easy walking distance of the settlement. Watch out for Amsterdam Island fur seals (Figure 10.4), a silver-grey species with grey and white face: the males have an Apache-style quiff of hair. You will know when they are around—they bark like overwrought Alsatians.

## Ile St Paul (warm temperate)

Within sight of its larger neighbour, Ile St Paul is the crescentic remnant of a volcanic cone 5 km (3.1 miles) in diameter and up to 270 m (860 ft) high—an

**Figure 10.5**  *Steep scoria cliffs of Ile St Paul, a tiny, cratered volcanic island of the southern Indian Ocean. The stack marks the entrance, via a narrow channel, to the inner harbour. The island, currently unpopulated, was formerly occupied by cray fishermen from Reunion.*

island of interbedded tuffs and lava that has lost its north-eastern half (Figure 10.5). There is a central caldera, flooded to make a tiny yacht harbour less than 1 km across. Fresh-looking scoria cones and active hot springs enhance a record of eruptions and natural fires in historic times.

Ile St Paul's climate is similar to that of Ile Amsterdam. Little remains of the original vegetation. The exposed western slopes carry a sparse covering of tussock, scrub and sedge: the more sheltered crater is lined with tall tussocks. Rabbits and house mice abound. Together with its outlying stacks the island supports rockhopper penguins (a northern subspecies with very long crests, Figure 10.6), yellow-nosed and sooty albatrosses, five species of smaller petrels, and small stocks of terns and skuas. Amsterdam Island fur seals breed on the crater beach.

Long used as a summer base for fishing boats, the harbour contains the ruins of a canning factory that was active in the 1920s. The island has the protected status of a French national park.

### Prince Edward Islands (warm temperate)

Some 1800 km (1125 miles) south-east of South Africa, this group includes Marion Island and the slightly smaller Prince Edward Island. Marion Island is roughly circular and about 20 km (12 miles) in diameter: Prince Edward Island is a rectangle 9 km (5.6 miles) long and about half as wide. Each is a low, irregular dome, composed of lavas and tuffs. Marion rises to 1230 m (4035 ft) and, though

**Figure 10.6** *Rockhopper penguin of the southern species* Eudyptes crestata moseleyi, *distinguished by long yellow and black crests (compare with Figure 2.16). These breed on southern warm temperate islands including Iles Amsterdam and St Paul, Tristan da Cunha and Gough Island.*

currently ice-free, shows evidence of former glaciation. Prince Edward rises only to 672 m (2200 ft) and appears never to have borne an ice-cap. Both volcanic, they stand 22 km (14 miles) apart on a submarine platform that marks the western edge of the Prince Edward—Crozet Ridge.

Steep cliffs and rocky beaches line the coasts: inland are rolling plains crossed by steep lava ridges, covered with moorland and scrub vegetation. The islands are damp and humid, persistently overcast with 250 cm of rain per year. Though they were probably known to 17th-century Dutch navigators, discovery is usually credited to the French explorer Marion du Fresne, who in January 1772 named them Terre d'Espérance—Land of Hope. Captain James Cook gave them their present names in 1775. Both islands were frequented by sealers from the early 19th century onward. In 1948 the group was annexed by South Africa, which in the following year established a scientific station at Transvaal Cove, Marion Island. South African scientists have worked there ever since, visiting Prince Edward Island occasionally.

Marion Island has 24 native species of flowering plants and over a dozen introduced species. Prince Edward shares many of the native species, and both are well endowed with algae, lichens and mosses. Both islands support breeding fur seals, elephant seals, and seabirds including penguins, albatrosses and lesser petrels, and both are managed as nature reserves. Visitors are occasionally allowed ashore close to the station on Marion Island, but not on Prince Edward Island, which is kept strictly as a reserve.

## Iles Crozet (cool temperate)

This group comprises a chain of three small volcanic islands extending over 160 km (100 miles) of the southwestern Indian Ocean, with a scattering of outliers. Ile de la Possession, the central island, is 18 km (11 miles) long and 11 km (6.9 miles) wide, rising to a peak 934 m (3064 ft) above sea level (Map 12). Ile de l'Est, a close neighbour 15 km (9.4 miles) away, is of similar area with a central ridge rising to 1090 m (3576 ft). About 100 km (63 miles) west lies Ile aux Cochons, a round island 9–10 km (6 miles) in diameter with a central cone 775 m (2543 ft) high. Outlying Ile des Pingouins and Ilots des Apôtres are relatively tiny. The group shares a submarine platform with the Prince Edward Islands. Though they are

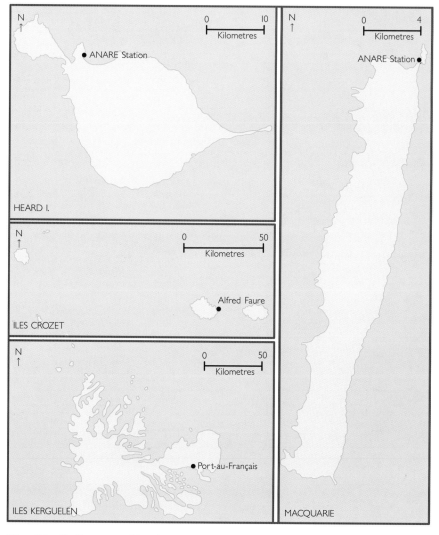

**Map 12**   *Indian sector islands.*

**Figure 10.7** *Iles Crozet, a group of three large and two smaller cool temperate islands in the southern Indian Ocean, claimed and administered by France. Of volcanic origin, they are remarkable for equable temperatures, strong winds, and an almost constant pall of cloud with persistent rainfall.*

clearly of volcanic origin, with scoria cones and lava reefs and ridges (Figure 10.7), none of the islands has been active recently.

Damp, cloudy and windy, Iles Crozets are currently without glaciers, though small patches of ice remain year-round on the peaks of the eastern islands. Predominantly green at sea level, they have a rich flora of grasses, shrubs and mosses, including tussock meadows close to sea level and fellfield above. Vegetation is fertilized by the droppings of seabirds, which breed at all levels. The islands support huge colonies of king penguins, macaronis and rockhoppers (Figure 10.8), several species of albatrosses and lesser petrels, and breeding seals.

Discovered in 1772 by Marion du Fresne, the islands were of interest particularly to 19th-century sealers, who stripped them of fur seals and elephant seals. Both have now returned. Formally claimed by France, since 1938 they have held the protected status of a national park. A scientific station was established on Ile de la Possession in 1962, and since then the group has been thoroughly studied by French scientists. Biologically and geologically they are perhaps the best known of all the southern islands. Landing is often possible close to the research station, on a beach shared by thousands of king penguins. Look out for Kerguelen cabbage growing in the cliffs by the landing (Figure 10.9). This was known to seamen as an antiscorbutic: leaves from the inner whorls have a pleasantly sharp flavour.

## Iles Kerguelen (cool temperate)

Over 4000 km (2500 miles) east-south-east of South Africa and slightly further west-south-west from Australia, this archipelago stands on a submarine platform

**Figure 10.8**    *King penguins line a freshwater stream: part of a massive colony on Ile de la Possession, Iles Crozet. A nearby research station provides facilities that make these islands an important centre for scientific research on seabirds of the southern ocean.*

**Figure 10.9**    *Kerguelen cabbage. Widespread on Iles Crozet and Kerguelen, similar in form and related to the common cabbage, this little plant was valued by 18th-century navigator Captain James Cook as a remedy for scurvy. The property is reflected in its Latin name,* Pringlea antiscorbutica.

shared with Heard Island. One large, deeply indented island is surrounded by 200–300 smaller ones: all are volcanic, composed of lavas and tuffs representing outpourings over a period of at least 40 million years (Map 12). Fumaroles still steam in the south-western corner.

Grande Terre, the main island, is roughly triangular, 120 km (75 miles) east to west and 110 km (70 miles) north to south, terminating in extensive peninsulas and rising to a cordillera of peaks in the west and south. The highest peak, Mont Ross (1850 m, 6070 ft), stands on the southern seaboard. Separate and westward from it rises Calotte Glaciaire Cook (1049 m, 3442 ft), a broad, ice-covered plateau. Deep valleys and fjords indicate that ice formerly extended over most of the island. The lesser islands cluster about Grande Terre, mainly to north and east.

First seen in 1772 by the French explorer Yves Joseph de Kerguelen-Tremarec, the islands appeared green and fertile, offering opportunities for settlement and farming. A shipload of potential settlers, arriving from France the following year, took one look and returned home in disgust. Iles Kerguelen are green indeed, with 36 species of flowering plants and ferns, and an unusual wealth of cushion-forming mosses. Meadows of tussock and other grasses predominate at sea level: cliffs hang with mosses and Kerguelen cabbage, and the higher ground supports green moorland of shrubs, herbs and moss.

However, the islands stand on or just south of the Antarctic Convergence, washed by cold southern waters: they are wet, windy, cold, often fogbound, with rainfall exceeding 110 cm per year. The growing season is short, and soils are thin and acid. Down-to-earth James Cook, who visited in 1776, at first called them the Islands of Desolation, only later renaming them after their discoverer.

Sealers visited frequently during the 19th century, hunting for fur seals and elephant seals. Visiting scientists also called, and from 1908 to 1932 the sheltered harbour of Port Jeanne d'Arc provided a base for commercial whaling, fishing and sheep farming. France claimed the islands formally in 1924, designating them a national park and refuge. In 1949 a scientific station was established at Port-aux-Français, on the north coast of Golfe du Morbihan, which has operated continuously since then.

Sealers, scientists and settlers introduced a menagerie of mammals including black rats, mice, rabbits, cats, dogs, sheep, mouflon and reindeer. Stocks of these survive on many of the islands, presenting a range of problems for conservation. Char and salmon have been introduced more recently into some of the rivers, where they feed on freshwater invertebrates. However, the islands are best known for their huge stocks of seabirds, including king, macaroni and rockhopper penguins, lesser sheathbills, wandering albatrosses, black-browed and light-mantled sooty albatrosses (Figure 10.10) and many species of smaller petrels. Look out for the particularly elegant Kerguelen cormorant (Figure 10.11). Elephant seals are plentiful: fur seals are returning after a long absence to some of the northern islands and beaches.

There are many possible landing sites in the sheltered harbours of Iles Kerguelen, providing walks along beaches and clifftops, over moorland and fell. Wherever you land, take care not to move out of sight of your party. It is easy to get lost, particularly when fog, low cloud or drizzle move in to obscure vision. If you are

**Figure 10.10**  *Delicately shaded light-mantled sooty albatrosses nest on cool temperate and periantarctic southern islands. Sailors called them 'Pee-orrs', from their haunting call: you hear pairs calling to each other on their cliff nests long before you see them.*

not used to walking, or are out of practice, be warned: this is a very unstable climate—warm one moment and dangerously cold the next—in which it is easy to get tired, wet and thoroughly chilled.

## Macquarie Island (cool temperate)

Macquarie Island stands 1760 km (1100 miles) south-east of Tasmania and 850 km (531 miles) south-west of Stewart Island, New Zealand (Map 12). At the junction of the Indian, Pacific and Southern Oceans, formed mainly of oceanic crustal rocks, it is an isolated ridge 34 km (21 miles) long, up to 6 km (3.7 miles) wide, and rising to 430 m (1411 ft) above sea level. This is the small visible section of a much longer ridge that extends under the sea in a north-to-south arc between New Zealand and the Balleny Islands. The top is an elongate plateau dotted with lakes and low, unspectacular peaks. Steep cliffs and small, boulder-lined bays form the coastline.

Macquarie Island has a cold wet climate, with annual rainfall exceeding 90 cm. The flora includes 45 species of shrubs, herbs and ferns and over 50 species of mosses. A green sward of tussock grass covers the cliff tops and spreads into the valleys, growing from mature loams. The moorlands above, poorly drained and acid, support fellfield and bog. There is evidence of recent glacial activity, but no permanent ice.

King, gentoo, rockhopper and royal penguins, four species of albatrosses and many smaller petrels breed on the island, together with shags, skuas, terns and

**Figure 10.11**   *Kerguelen cormorants. At first glance similar to other Southern Ocean forms, these are remarkable for the brilliant blues and greens of their mantle. The colours are brightest during and immediately after breeding, quickly dulling as the season wears on.*

gulls. Elephant seals and two species of fur seals breed on the beaches. Black rats, house mice, domestic cats and rabbits are abundant.

The British sealing captain Frederick Hasselburg discovered the island in 1810, naming it after the current governor of New South Wales. From 1825 it was administered as part of Van Dieman's Land, now Tasmania. Sealing gangs stripped it repeatedly of fur seals and elephant seals, later making inroads into the stocks of penguins for oil. Douglas Mawson established a station in Hasselburg Bay on the northern end in 1911–14, and a permanent station has occupied the site since 1948. The island is currently a nature reserve administered by the Wildlife and Heritage Department, Tasmania. Small numbers of tourists visit each year under permit: they are allowed ashore only close to the station, and remain under supervision until they leave.

## Heard Island (periantarctic)

Roughly circular, some 25 km (16 miles) across (Map 12), Heard Island lies south of the Indian Ocean almost equidistant (4550 km, 2844 miles) from Africa and Australia. An eastern spit and western peninsular extension combine to give it an overall length of 42 km (26 miles). Dominated by the 2745 m (9006 ft) massif of Big Ben, it stands on a platform that accommodates also the McDonald Islands and Iles Kerguelen.

Heard Island consists of laval outpourings and scoria arising from a basement of limestone. About 90% ice covered, it has a coastline of alternating glaciers, rocky headlands and beaches. Big Ben is volcanically active, frequently producing lava flows and vapour from its ice-covered flanks.

The climate is cold, with strong, persistent westerly winds. The flora of eight species of flowering plants includes tussock grasses, the antiscorbutic Kerguelen cabbage, and a dwarf shrub that grows in sheltered areas. Fur seals and elephant seals dominate the beaches in spring and summer, and there are large colonies of breeding birds. Sealers probably discovered Heard Island as early as 1833, but it remained uncharted until rediscovered by the US merchant captain John J. Heard in November 1853. It was repeatedly stripped of fur seals and elephant seals throughout the 19th century.

The island was occupied by Australian scientists from 1947 to 1954, working from a station in Atlas Cove. In 1953 it was designated part of Australian External Territory, and summer-only expeditions have since visited it sporadically to study its many interesting biological and geological features. Permission is needed for landing, which in good weather is usually possible in Atlas Cove, close to the old station site.

## McDonald Islands (periantarctic)

Some 40 km (25 miles) west of Heard Island, the McDonald Islands form a tiny group 2 km (just over a mile) long and half as wide, with a total area of about 260 ha. McDonald Island, largest of the group, consists of two steep-sided platforms rising to about 230 m (755 ft), joined by a narrow isthmus: the rocks are volcanic tuffs intruded by veins of harder phonolite. Two smaller islets flank the main island. Standing on the Kerguelen submarine platform, the group is probably a remnant of a once-larger volcanic mass.

Though discovered in 1854 by a British captain, William McDonald, the islands were too steep to accommodate many fur seals, and seem to have remained relatively untouched by man for over a century. Australia assumed sovereignty in 1947. The first recorded landing was a brief visit by helicopter from the French research ship *Galliéni* in January 1971, and in 1980 an Australian party worked for 4 days on and around the islands. Five species of flowering plants were recorded, including tussock grass, Kerguelen cabbage and small shrubs: macaroni penguins and several species of petrels were noted, together with breeding fur seals and elephant seals. This is a strict reserve: no visits are allowed.

## Pacific sector islands

### Snares Islands (warm temperate)

This scattering of small granitic islands lies 100 km (63 miles) south-west of Stewart Island, the southernmost point of New Zealand (Map 13). The largest island, central to the main cluster, is 3.5 km (2 miles) long and rises to about 50 m (164 ft): the group as a whole extends over about 16 km$^2$ (6 square miles) of turbulent sea. The larger islands wear a forest of twisted, contorted olearia trees, growing from a carpet of black peaty soil. Steep slopes carry tussock grass and rushes. There is only one anchorage, in Ho Ho Bay on the eastern side of the main island, where a small research station is from time to time occupied by biologists.

Landing is not allowed, but much can be seen from Zodiac tours. Endemic crested Snares penguins breed in large colonies in the forest edge, entering and leaving the water in Ho Ho Bay. Giant petrels float offshore, waiting to catch unwary young penguins. Fur seals and Hooker's sea lions loaf along the shore and play in the water. Buller's mollymawks breed in colonies among the tussock: along the shore you may see the endemic snipe, black tits and fern birds, all remarkably tame. Brown skuas and both red-billed and Dominican gulls fossick in the intertidal zone, paddling among writhing strands of kelp.

Late evening brings in hordes of sooty shearwaters and smaller petrels, that drop through the forest canopy and nest in their thousands in burrows among the tree roots. At first light they leave the islands in streams from the cliff tops, forming huge flocks that feed well out to sea.

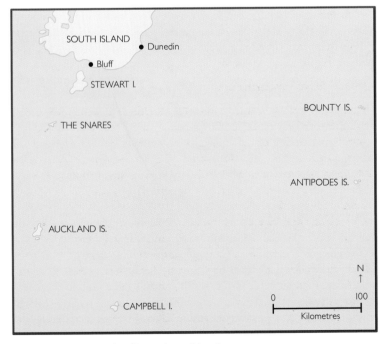

**Map 13**  *New Zealand's southern islands.*

## Bounty Islands (warm temperate)

The Bounty Islands form an archipelago of low islands and stacks 700 km (440 miles) east-south-east of New Zealand's South Island (Map 13). Clustering in three groups on the eastern flank of the Campbell submarine plateau, they are the eroded, sea-washed remnants of a once-larger granitic landmass: the highest rises to 90 m (295 ft). There is no soil, and vegetation is limited to salt-loving algae and lichens. There are no climatic records, but the mean annual temperature is 9 to 10°C.

Breeding seabirds include erect-crested penguins, Salvin's mollymawk, endemic prions and shags, and cape petrels, terns and southern black-backed gulls. The islands are the main breeding ground of New Zealand fur seals.

The Bounty Islands were discovered in 1788 by Captain William Bligh during his ill-fated voyage in HMS *Bounty*. Sealers were frequent visitors during the 19th century. A refuge hut was established in the 1880s, but no castaways are known to have used it, and no human settlement has ever been attempted. The islands are a New Zealand National Nature Reserve, with limited access for visitors. It is usually too rough to land anyway, but they provide exhilarating Zodiac runs.

## Antipodes Islands (warm temperate)

Antipodes Island and the off-lying Windward Islands, Bollons Islands and Leeward Island, form a small grass-covered archipelago on the eastern edge of the Campbell submarine plateau, 800 km (500 miles) east-south-east of New Zealand's South Island (Map 13). Remnants of volcanic action within the last million years, they consist of lava and scoria which is rapidly eroding to form precipitous cliffs and stacks. The main island, some 6–7 km (4 miles) across, rises to a central plateau 300 m (984 ft) above sea level: the highest peak, Mount Galloway, rises to 402 m (1,320 ft). There are no long-term meteorological records, but the climate is cool and windy, with estimated rainfall 150 cm per year.

Over 60 species of flowering plants and ferns have been recorded, forming rich tussock meadows with patches of shrubs and upland bog. Erect-crested and rockhopper penguins nest on the cliffs and in gullies; other breeding seabirds include three species of albatrosses, giant petrels, several species of smaller petrels and brown skuas. Endemic land birds include snipe, pipits and two species of parakeets: this is one of a very few places in the world where penguins and parrots nest close together. Redpolls, dunnocks and starlings also breed there, presumably having crossed from New Zealand.

The islands were discovered in 1800 by Captain Henry Waterhouse RN, on a voyage from Australia to England. Though often visited by sealers, and the site of several wrecks, they appear never to have suffered occupation and remain relatively pristine. The only introduced mammals are house mice. Now protected as a New Zealand National Nature Reserve, they may be visited only by authorized scientific parties.

## Auckland Islands (warm temperate)

Standing 400 km (250 miles) south of New Zealand on the Campbell submarine plateau, this is a close-knit archipelago of two large islands and several smaller islets and stacks (Map 13). Auckland Island, the largest, is 30 km (19 miles) long, up to 20 km (12.5 miles) across, and rises to over 600 m (1969 ft), with precipitous western cliffs and a deeply indented eastern seabord. Adams Island immediately to the south is 22 km (14 miles) long and up to 8 km (5 miles) wide, rising to 667 m (2188 ft) in Mount Dick, the archipelago's highest peak. Enderby, Rose, Ewing and Dundas Islands to the north and Disappointment Island to the west are much smaller.

All are volcanic islands, the product of two main centres of activity which flowed some 15–20 million years ago. Prolonged marine erosion and glaciation followed. Basement granites appear on Musgrave Peninsula in the south of Auckland Island. There is no current volcanic activity or permanent ice. The climate is mild and damp, with rainfall of 150–200 cm. The islands support a rich flora including over 200 species of flowering plants and ferns. Sheltered eastern flanks of the main island feature a forest of flowering southern-rata trees, that burst into crimson flower in early summer: Ewing Island is forested with more prosaic olearia. Uplands carry scrub, tussock meadows, moors and bogs.

There is a rich seabird fauna including rockhopper, erect-crested and yellow-eyed penguins, wandering, royal, shy and light-mantled sooty albatrosses, many species of petrels, terns, skuas and shags. Endemic pipits, teal, rail, banded dotterel, tomtits and snipe breed on the larger islands. Fur seals and elephant seals are abundant, and these islands are the main breeding area for Hooker's sea lions.

The group was discovered in 1806 by the British sealer Abraham Bristow, and for long became a haunt of sealers and whalers. Maoris from New Zealand formed small settlements during the 1840s, and from 1849 to 1852 a whaling and farming settlement with population of up to 300 was established at Port Ross, Enderby Island. There were later attempts at sheep farming. Rabbits, house mice, domestic cats, cattle, sheep, pigs and goats have been introduced at different times with varying levels of success.

Many ships were wrecked on the islands. Most noteworthy was *General Grant*, a US merchantman out of Melbourne with 83 passengers and crew, and a cargo of wool, hides and gold bullion. She ran ashore in May 1866, in a cave under steep cliffs on the weather side of Enderby Island. Of 15 survivors who sailed and rowed to the safety of Port Ross, only 10 remained to be rescued some 18 months later. Several attempts have been made to recover the *General Grant*'s gold: if any succeeded, they succeeded also in keeping quiet about their good fortune.

Coast-watching stations were maintained in Port Ross and Carnley Harbour from 1941 to 1945, to report on possible enemy activities. Since then, New Zealand scientists have worked intensively over the islands, which are administered as a National Nature Reserve. They may be visited only under supervision, but a visit is well worth while. On the fringes of the Enderby Island forest may be seen a unique combination of species—tiny flightless teals, bellbirds, tomtits, colourful parakeets, ginger, blue and black rabbits, and an abundance of Hooker's sea lions.

## Campbell Island (cool temperate)

Campbell Island stands on an extensive submarine platform 620 km (388 miles) south of New Zealand's South Island (Map 13). Raised by volcanic activity 6 to 8 million years ago, it has since been eroded by sea and glaciers into a rough, deeply indented dome 16–18 km (10–12 miles) across: the highest point, Mount Honey, rises to 569 m (1867 ft). There are several small off-lying islets. No recent volcanic activity has been reported. The climate is cool and damp, with 140 cm of rain per year.

The flora includes over 200 species of flowering plants and ferns, including many alien species from New Zealand. Woody shrubs and ferns dominate coastal areas, forming miniature forests in gullies sheltered from the winds. Uplands support tussock meadows, bogs and peat-based moors. Yellow-eyed, rockhopper and erect-crested penguins breed among the coastal vegetation, together with pipits, dunnocks, redpolls and an endemic teal. Royal, black-browed and grey-headed albatrosses, giant petrels, many smaller petrels, shags, skuas and terns also breed in abundance, especially on offshore islands. Elephant seals, fur seals and sea lions are seasonally abundant on the beaches.

Discovered by sealing captain Frederick Hasselburg in January 1910, the island was visited irregularly by sealers throughout the 19th century, and by whalers hunting its inshore waters up to 1916. From 1895 to 1931 it was farmed for sheep. In 1941 a coast-watching and meteorological station was set up in Tucker Cove, Perseverance Harbour: in 1953 the station was moved to Beeman Cove, closer to the harbour shore, where it operated continuously until closure in 1996.

Bird populations on the main island have been severely affected by introduced Norway rats and cats, and feral sheep have altered the tussock meadows; however, many of the small off-lying islands remain relatively pristine. Campbell Island is a New Zealand National Nature Reserve, with access for visitors strictly limited.

## Balleny Islands (Antarctic)

Lying almost due south of New Zealand, some 500 km (300 miles) north-west of Cape Adare, these are often the first Antarctic landfall for tour ships from New Zealand. Three large and several smaller islands form a north-west–south-east chain 200 km (125 miles) long. They were discovered in 1839 by John Balleny, enterprising captain of *Eliza Scott*, a tiny sealing vessel belonging to the Enderby Brothers, whalers and sealers of Dundee. Sturge and Young, the largest islands, form the ends of the chain, Sturge Island rising to over 2000 m (6500 ft). Buckle Island is slightly smaller, and Borradaile, Rowe and Sabrina Islands are relatively tiny. Volcanic islands made up of lava flows, scoria and tuffs, they are ice capped, steep, ringed by ice cliffs, and often surrounded by pack ice that keeps intruders at bay.

Captain Balleny reported Buckle Island to be in eruption. Similar activity was reported in 1899, but none has been seen since; the islands appear quiescent. There is little vegetation or wildlife to be seen, apart from Adelie-penguin colonies on Buckle and Sabrina Islands. A few pairs of chinstrap penguins have been reported on an islet within this group. They must be very confused or very adventurous birds, because this species breeds almost exclusively in the South American sector. Sabrina Island, immediately south of Buckle Island, is a Specially Protected Area.

## Scott Island (Antarctic)

Standing in isolation 700 km (438 miles) east of the Balleny Islands, Scott Island is a steep-sided cone of dense phonolitic rock 3 km (1.9 miles) across and about 100 m (330 ft) tall. It stands on a much broader submarine plateau, and is probably the remnant of a volcano that erupted within the past 5–10 million years. Discovered in December 1902 by Captain W. Colbeck, who commanded *Morning*, a relief ship of the British National Antarctic Expedition, it was named for the expedition leader, Captain Robert Falcon Scott. The island is usually surrounded by pack ice and difficult to reach, except by the many seabirds that nest on it. Passengers from a tour ship are said to have landed, but it is hard to see where. Scott Island is claimed by New Zealand as part of the Ross Dependency.

## Peter I Øy (Antarctic)

In the far-south-eastern corner of the Pacific sector stands Peter-the-First Øy, alone in a wide expanse of semi-permanent pack ice in the Bellingshausen Sea. Thaddeus von Bellingshausen discovered it in 1821, naming it after the czar who had ordered his expedition. Roughly 19 km (12 miles) long and 11 km (7 miles) across, the island is heavily ice capped and ringed by ice cliffs. The summit is a single peak rising to about 1640 m (5380 ft), and topped by an ice-filled crater 100 m (330 ft) across. This is the tip of a single huge volcano, formed of successive flows of basaltic lava accumulating from a seabed some 3600 m (12 000 ft) below.

Very few people have seen the Peter I Øy, and even fewer landed on it. Norway claims the island, and Norwegian scientists have made efforts to survey it. Some of its rocks have been dated at about 13 million years, others are thought to be much younger, though no recent volcanic activity has been reported. There is little vegetation, or wildlife other than a few dozen pairs of Adelie penguins, skuas and probably other breeding seabirds. Currently the most frequent visitors are passing cruise ships, attracted by the island's remoteness.

## Further reading

Frazer, C. 1986. *Beyond the Roaring Forties: New Zealand's Subantarctic Islands.* Wellington, Government Printing Office Publications.

Selkirk, P. M., Seppelt, R. D. and Selkirk, D. R. 1990. *Subantarctic Macquarie Island: Environment and Biology.* Cambridge, Cambridge University Press.

van Zinderen Bakker, E. M., Winterbottom, J. M. and Dyer, R. A. 1971. *Marion and Prince Edward Islands: Report on the South African Biological and Geological Expedition 1965–66.* Cape Town, A. A. Balkema.

# Chapter Eleven

# Return from Antarctica

## Introduction: homeward bound

Well, we've visited Antarctica—in reality or in spirit—and now we're rolling back to civilization. This is the time when thoughtful travellers sit down (or maybe lie down if the ship is rolling) and think. On the way south we were too excited; in Antarctic waters we were too busy. Now there is time for reflection. What have 1, 2 or 3 weeks in the wilderness taught us? What are we taking home from Antarctica? Has it all been worth while?

Most passengers I've met, on dozens of cruise-ship voyages, are at this stage exhausted but pleased with life. They have had a wonderful experience. There have been things to complain about on board—the cabins, the plumbing, the food, the stuffy lecture room—all matters that good cruise operators want to hear about and take seriously. There are seldom complaints about Antarctica itself. People have loved it: in sunshine, sleet or rain, in howling gales or flat calm, with three landings a day or none—Antarctica has met and far exceeded their expectations.

Underlying the euphoria is often a sense of unease, perhaps even of guilt. We have put down money and bought Wonderland: Is it really as easy as that? Have we harmed Antarctica? Do visitors like us really leave no traces? Are there no lasting effects on the environment? Don't we owe Antarctica something in return? Then come the practical questions. Who owns Antarctica? Who manages it? Who controls its exploitation? Who left all that rubbish, and why are they allowed to get away with it? How many people like us visit each year? Who keeps an eye on tour operators, to see that they stay up to the mark, and who sets the mark anyway?

Cruise operators issue all kinds of handouts containing information on the politics and management of Antarctica, and staff may lecture on these topics early in the voyage. However, the homeward run is usually the best moment to raise the issues again. Some cruise leaders organize workshops and discussions in the last couple of days, to allow everyone to express their concerns, and discover what can be done to keep Antarctica the way it is.

This chapter provides background for some of the issues that come up at those meetings. If I seem to raise more questions than I answer, it is probably because many answers have not yet been thought up. You may feel, as I do, that those who claim to manage Antarctica need to think both harder and faster, to keep up with a new industry that, though by no means malign, is expanding and diversifying as we watch.

## Who owns Antarctica?

It is a simple enough question, but don't look for a simple answer. Seven countries (see next section) claim to own bits of Antarctica (Map 1, pp. 8–9). Some of these recognize each others' claims: others recognize some claims but not all. Other countries do not recognize any claims: others again—the majority—cannot be bothered to say whether they recognize claims in Antarctica or not. While all claims have temporarily been shelved (some like to say 'put on ice') under the Antarctic Treaty, none has been dropped. So for seven countries at least, claims still exist.

The Treaty originated as an effort to secure cooperation between 12 countries with interests in Antarctica, avoiding the question of ownership. Those nations, plus others that have since joined the Treaty, have become the de facto managers of the continent. So, while the question 'Who owns Antarctica?' has no simple answer, the question 'Who runs Antarctica?' is easier to deal with. The answer is the countries—currently 26 of them—that are consultative parties to the Antarctic Treaty System. Now read on.

## Claims to Antarctica

Why is there doubt about ownership? Elsewhere in the world it is generally accepted that patches of land are owned by the people who live there: the owners have rights to organize themselves into states and govern both themselves and their land as they think fit. If nobody lives there, the land is *terra nullius*—empty, and up for grabs.

Antarctica has no native population, so it has no natural owners. It was discovered during the 19th century when colonialism was rife. Colonially minded powers had no qualms about claiming empty tracts of land that might eventually show strategic or economic value. Based on exploration and discovery, Britain and France laid claims to bits of Antarctica during the 18th and 19th centuries. No one—not even themselves—felt it necessary either to spell out their claims in detail, or to substantiate them with further exploration.

Claims remained vague until the early 20th century, when land-based whaling offered promise of revenues. Britain was first off the mark: prompted by a courteous enquiry from Norway, in 1908 it filed a formal claim to a wide swathe of the Antarctic region in the South American sector, extending from the Scotia Arc to the South Pole. In 1923 for a similar reason Britain claimed a further swathe, this time of East Antarctica including Victoria Land and the Ross Ice Shelf, passing responsibility for it to the Dominion of New Zealand.

In 1924 France dusted off and formally lodged its claim to Terre Adélie. In 1933 Britain claimed a further vast stretch of East Antarctica on either side of the narrow French sector, which became Australian Antarctic Territory. Norway, that in 1928 had claimed Bouvetøya and in 1929 Peter I Øy, 10 years later claimed the one remaining stretch of East Antarctica, heading off a possible German claim. In 1940 Chile and in 1943 Argentina resurrected their claims, based on historic rights and contiguity or closeness, to parts of the South American sector that Britain had specified as its own.

These claims were valid in the sense that they were notified to the international community in the proper way, though three of them—Argentine, British and Chilean—overlapped seriously. Between them they account for some 85% of the continent, leaving unclaimed only a virtually inaccessible sector of West Antarctica.

## Non-claimants: US attitudes

That seven nations claimed bits of Antarctica mattered little to most other nations, who didn't want any of it anyway. However, the United States was one country that took a great interest. Traditionally it was anti-colonial, and wary of European colonial incursions into the western hemisphere, which includes West Antarctica. On the other hand, here was a huge area that Richard Byrd and fellow-Americans were exploring, that might have all kinds of natural resources awaiting development: Hadn't they better at least reserve rights to claim, if nothing more?

US attitudes during the 1920s and 30s were guided by the 'Hughes doctrine' (named for Charles E. Hughes, Secretary of State 1921–25)—which was essentially a refusal to respect claims of sovereignty if the territories claimed were not actually settled and under administration. The US might reasonably have claimed Wilkes Land, discovered during the US Exploring Expedition in 1840. It might have supported claims made by its own more recent explorers, Ellsworth and Byrd, to lands that they had discovered during overflights and sledging journeys. However, seeing no reason to settle and administer these remote, ice-bound territories, the US made no claims of its own to Antarctica. Seeing no attempts by others to settle and administer, it recognized no claims advanced by other countries.

Instead it maintained toward Antarctica the 'open door' policy that it adopted worldwide, as a counter to 'neo-colonialism'—the tendency among European powers to make deals, excluding outsiders, with undeveloped countries. In the rest of the world the open door allowed US citizens and government agencies freedom to walk in and negotiate trade wherever they could. In Antarctica it left them free to explore as, when and where they wished. They incurred no immediate responsibilities of ownership, but reserved for the future the possibility of US claims.

## Occupation and administration

The United States Antarctic Service (USAS) Expedition of 1939–41 marked a turning point in Antarctic political history. Its two bases, one in the Bay of Whales and the other in Marguerite Bay, were intended to be 'permanent'—the first ever to be occupied by successions of scientists who would be relieved annually. This came close to the US's own criteria of settlement and administration, required for claims to be taken seriously. Was the USAS Expedition a first US move toward a definitive American claim in Antarctica? Quite possibly it was: but Pearl Harbour put an end to the experiment. Both bases closed in 1941 and the expedition was disbanded.

When Britain decided, in 1943, to reinforce its own claims in the South American sector, it took no chances over settlement and administration. Scientists and handymen of Operation Tabarin, who manned the new bases, found themselves sworn in as magistrates or justices of the peace, furnished with copies of *Stone's Justices' Manual* and the contents of a small post office, and solemnly told that, among more down-to-earth duties (like feeding the sledge dogs and emptying the rubbish), they represented a civil administration.

Argentine and Chilean stations established soon afterwards were military rather than civil, but again took pains to represent occupation and administration: French, Australian and New Zealand expeditions later followed the civil pattern. Issuing postage stamps became a further hallmark of occupation. This delighted philatelists, enriched stamp dealers, and brought revenue to the governments concerned. It profoundly irritated base personnel, who had to spend hours in Antarctica franking stamped envelopes when – even during the long winter night – there were far better things to do.

## Post-war initiatives

During the post-war years the US mounted large-scale naval expeditions around Antarctica. Operation Highjump in 1946–47 and Operation Windmill in the following year brought icebreakers and long-range aircraft to bear on the continent, leaving very little of it unexplored. These efforts strengthened US claims, if not for a piece of Antarctica, at least for a moral right to be involved in determining its future. Simultaneously the US government became concerned at growing tensions between the UK, Chile and Argentina over their rival claims to the South American sector, and proposed to all claimant nations that some form of international regime was needed to govern the continent as a whole.

The claimants rejected any concept of international control, though Chile proposed a 5-year suspension of sovereignty issues in the interests of cooperation and scientific research. However, the US initiative triggered a response from the USSR, which until then had shown little interest in post-war Antarctica. In 1950, recalling Russia's historic interests based on the voyages of Thaddeus von Bellingshausen, the Soviet government declared that it could not recognize as lawful '. . . any decision on the Antarctic regime taken without its participation'. What the US had hoped might prove a cosy agreement between itself and immediate allies must now involve the USSR, and bring in unwelcome overtones of the cold war.

## International Geophysical Year

During the International Geophysical Year (IGY) expeditions of 1957–58, the US, the Soviet Union, the seven claimant nations, plus Belgium, Japan and South Africa cooperated effectively in scientific research. Between them they manned a total of 55 stations in the Antarctic and Southern Ocean areas, in what everyone agreed was a splendid year's research. Around the planning tables, even more so in Antarctica, there was genuine cooperation between nations that elsewhere were barely on speaking terms. Scientists demonstrated a unity of purpose that ignored political differences and divergences.

Even before the start of the IGY, plans had been mooted for continued research on a long-term basis. This was partly to rationalize the scientific effort—it seemed a long way to go and a lot of expense for a single year's results. However, no less important were the political implications. Under cover of the IGY, whispered the politically minded, the USSR had established a strong foothold in Australian Antarctic Territory. Its stations could well become military bases, and strategic threats to Australian interests. Similarly, the political conflicts in the South American sector remained unresolved, and might escalate dangerously (and expensively) once IGY constraints were removed.

There were therefore strong political reasons to continue the cooperation under a formal agreement between nations. So arose the Antarctic Treaty, negotiated between June 1958 and May 1959, signed in Washington by representatives of the 12 IGY nations on 1 December 1959, and brought into force on 23 June 1961.

Did the scientists find it distasteful to be used as pawns in a political game? Not so you would notice. Scientific research became the credential for nations to join the Treaty. That implied, for the first time ever, long-term government funding for Antarctic research. Scientists of many nations quickly developed a lifelong interest in Antarctica, and a wholesome respect for the Antarctic Treaty that maintained the peace and kept the funds flowing.

In 1958 the International Council of Scientific Unions (ICSU, the driving force behind IGY) set up a Special Committee on Antarctic Research, charged with initiating, promoting and coordinating scientific efforts in the Antarctic region. This quickly became the permanent Scientific Committee on Antarctic Research (SCAR), which maintains those functions today.

## The Antarctic Treaty

The Antarctic Treaty itself is a simple document (Box 11.1), including a preamble and 14 articles, each making one or more points. The preamble lists the original 12 signatories and outlines the context in which the Treaty was framed. The first three articles are straightforward: Antarctica shall be used for peaceful purposes only; the freedom of scientists to pursue research, enjoyed during the IGY, shall continue; and scientific cooperation will be encouraged. Article 4 deals neatly with the issue of sovereignty or ownership: claimant nations are not required to renounce their claims, but they will not seek to enhance them while the Treaty is in force. Article 5 prevents any possibility of using Antarctica as a nuclear testing ground or dump: both possibilities were being seriously considered at the time.

Article 6 clarifies the area in which the Treaty is effective, specifically excluding the high seas: trying to include them would have complicated negotiations very considerably. Article 7 provides for mutual inspections of operations and stations (though not of ships), to see that the terms of the Treaty are being observed. Article 8 ensures that officials remain under the laws of their own country while visiting other stations. Article 9 provides for meetings to review the progress of the

Box 11.1   Text of the Antarctic Treaty (1961)

*The Governments of Argentina, Australia, Belgium, Chile, the French Republic, Japan, New Zealand, Norway, the Union of South Africa, the Union of Soviet Socialist Republics, the United Kingdom of Great Britain and Northern Ireland, and the United States of America,*

*Recognizing that it is in the interest of all mankind that Antarctica shall continue for ever to be used exclusively for peaceful purposes and shall not become the scene or object of international discord;*

*Acknowledging the substantial contributions to scientific knowledge resulting from international cooperation in scientific investigation in Antarctica;*

*Convinced that the establishment of a firm foundation for the continuation and development of such cooperation on the basis of freedom of scientific investigation in Antarctica as applied during the International Geophysical Year accords with the interests of science and the progress of all mankind;*

*Convinced also that a treaty ensuring the use of Antarctica for peaceful purposes only and the continuance of international harmony in Antarctica will further the purposes and principles embodied in the Charter of the United Nations;*

*Have agreed as follows:*

**Article I**

*Antarctica shall be used for peaceful purposes only. There shall be prohibited, inter alia, any measure of a military nature, such as the establishment of military bases and fortifications, the carrying out of military manoeuvres, as well as the testing of any type of weapon.*

*The present Treaty shall not prevent the use of military personnel or equipment for scientific research or for any other peaceful purpose.*

**Article II**

*Freedom of scientific investigation in Antarctica and cooperation toward that end, as applied during the International Geophysical Year, shall continue, subject to the provisions of the present Treaty.*

**Article III**

*In order to promote international cooperation in scientific investigation in Antarctica, as provided for in Article II of the present Treaty, the Contracting Parties agree that, to the greatest extent feasible and practicable:*

a.   *information regarding plans for scientific programs in Antarctica shall be exchanged to permit maximum economy of and efficiency of operations;*

b.  scientific personnel shall be exchanged in Antarctica between expeditions and stations;
c.  scientific observations and results from Antarctica shall be exchanged and made freely available.

In implementing this article, every encouragement shall be given to the establishment of cooperative working relations with those Specialized Agencies of the United Nations and other international organizations having a scientific or technical interest in Antarctica.

## Article IV

Nothing contained in the present Treaty shall be interpreted as:

1.  a.  a renunciation by any Contracting Party of previously asserted rights of or claims to territorial sovereignty in Antarctica;
    b.  a renunciation or diminution by any Contracting Party of any basis of claim to territorial sovereignty in Antarctica which it may have whether as a result of its activities or those of its nationals in Antarctica, or otherwise;
    c.  prejudicing the position of any Contracting Party as regards its recognition or non-recognition of any other State's rights of or claim or basis of claim to territorial sovereignty in Antarctica.
2.  No acts or activities taking place while the present Treaty is in force shall constitute a basis for asserting, supporting or denying a claim to territorial sovereignty in Antarctica or create any rights of sovereignty in Antarctica. No new claim, or enlargement of an existing claim, to territorial sovereignty in Antarctica shall be asserted while the present Treaty is in force.

## Article V

Any nuclear explosions in Antarctica and the disposal there of radioactive waste material shall be prohibited.

In the event of the conclusion of international agreements concerning the use of nuclear energy, including nuclear explosions and the disposal of radioactive waste material, to which all of the Contracting Parties whose representatives are entitled to participate in the meetings provided for under Article IX are parties, the rules established under such agreements shall apply in Antarctica.

## Article VI

The provisions of the present Treaty shall apply to the area south of 60° South Latitude, including all ice shelves, but nothing in the present Treaty shall prejudice or in any way affect the rights, or the exercise of the rights, of any State under international law with regard to the high seas within that area.

## Article VII

In order to promote the objectives and ensure the observance of the provisions of the present Treaty, each Contracting Party whose representatives are entitled to participate in the meetings referred to in Article IX of the Treaty shall have the right to designate observers to carry out any inspection provided for by the present Article. Observers shall be nationals of the Contracting Parties which designate them. The names of observers shall be communicated to every other Contracting Party having the right to designate observers, and like notice shall be given of the termination of their appointment.

Each observer designated in accordance with the provisions of paragraph 1 of this Article shall have complete freedom of access at any time to any or all areas of Antarctica.

All areas of Antarctica, including all stations, installations and equipment within those areas, and all ships and aircraft at points of discharging or embarking cargoes or personnel in Antarctica, shall be open at all times to inspection by any observers designated in accordance with paragraph 1 of this Article.

Aerial observation may be carried out at any time over any or all areas of Antarctica by any of the Contracting Parties having the right to designate observers.

Each Contracting Party shall, at the time when the present Treaty enters into force for it, inform the other Contracting Parties, and thereafter shall give them notice in advance, of

a.    all expeditions to and within Antarctica, on the part of its ships or nationals, and all expeditions to Antarctica organized in or proceeding from its territory;
b.    all stations in Antarctica occupied by its nationals; and
c.    any military personnel or equipment intended to be introduced by it into Antarctica subject to the conditions prescribed in paragraph 2 of Article 1 of the present Treaty.

## Article VIII

In order to facilitate the exercise of their functions under the present Treaty, and without prejudice to the respective positions of the Contracting Parties relating to jurisdiction over all other persons in Antarctica, observers designated under paragraph 1 of Article VII and scientific personnel exchanged under sub-paragraph 1(b) of Article III of the Treaty, and members of the staffs accompanying any such persons, shall be subject only to the jurisdiction of the Contracting Party of which they are nationals in respect of all acts or omissions occurring while they are in Antarctica for the purpose of exercising their functions.

Without prejudice to the provisions of paragraph 1 of this Article, and pending the adoption of measures in pursuance of subparagraph 1(e) of Article IX, the Contracting Parties concerned in any case of dispute with regard to the exercise of jurisdiction in Antarctica shall immediately consult together with a view to reaching a mutually acceptable solution.

## Article IX

Representatives of the Contracting Parties named in the preamble to the present Treaty shall meet at the City of Canberra within two months after the date of entry into force of the Treaty, and thereafter at suitable intervals and places, for the purpose of exchanging information, consulting together on matters of common interest pertaining to Antarctica, and formulating and considering, and recommending to their Governments, measures in furtherance of the principles and objectives of the Treaty, including measures regarding:

a. use of Antarctica for peaceful purposes only;
b. facilitation of scientific research in Antarctica;
c. facilitation of international scientific cooperation in Antarctica;
d. facilitation of the exercise of the rights of inspection provided for in Article VII of the Treaty;
e. questions relating to the exercise of jurisdiction in Antarctica;
f. preservation and conservation of living resources in Antarctica.

Each Contracting Party which has become a party to the present Treaty by accession under Article XIII shall be entitled to appoint representatives to participate in the meetings referred to in paragraph 1 of the present Article, during such times as that Contracting Party demonstrates its interest in Antarctica by conducting substantial research activity there, such as the establishment of a scientific station or the despatch of a scientific expedition.

Reports from the observers referred to in Article VII of the present Treaty shall be transmitted to the representatives of the Contracting Parties participating in the meetings referred to in paragraph 1 of the present Article.

The measures referred to in paragraph 1 of this Article shall become effective when approved by all the Contracting Parties whose representatives were entitled to participate in the meetings held to consider those measures.

Any or all of the rights established in the present Treaty may be exercised as from the date of entry into force of the Treaty whether or not any measures facilitating the exercise of such rights have been proposed, considered or approved as provided in this Article.

### Article X

Each of the Contracting Parties undertakes to exert appropriate efforts, consistent with the Charter of the United Nations, to the end that no one engages in any activity in Antarctica contrary to the principles or purposes of the present Treaty.

### Article XI

If any dispute arises between two or more of the Contracting Parties concerning the interpretation or application of the present Treaty, those Contracting Parties shall consult among themselves with a view to having the dispute resolved by negotiation, inquiry, mediation, conciliation, arbitration, judicial settlement or other peaceful means of their own choice.

Any dispute of this character not so resolved shall, with the consent, in each case, of all parties to the dispute, be referred to the International Court of Justice for settlement; but failure to reach agreement on reference to the International Court shall not absolve parties to the dispute from the responsibility of continuing to seek to resolve it by any of the various peaceful means referred to in paragraph I of this Article.

### Article XII

I.   a.   The present Treaty may be modified or amended at any time by unanimous agreement of the Contracting Parties whose representatives are entitled to participate in the meetings provided for under Article IX. Any such modification or amendment shall enter into force when the depositary Government has received notice from all such Contracting Parties that they have ratified it.

    b.   Such modification or amendment shall thereafter enter into force as to any other Contracting Party when notice of ratification by it has been received by the depositary Government. Any such Contracting Party from which no notice of ratification is received within a period of two years from the date of entry into force of the modification or amendment in accordance with the provision of subparagraph I (a) of this Article shall be deemed to have withdrawn from the present Treaty on the date of the expiration of such period.

2.   a.   If after the expiration of thirty years from the date of entry into force of the present Treaty, any of the Contracting Parties whose representatives are entitled to participate in the meetings provided for under Article IX so requests by a communication addressed to the depositary Government, a Conference of all the Contracting Parties shall be held as soon as practicable to review the operation of the Treaty.

    b.   Any modification or amendment to the present Treaty which is approved at such a Conference by a majority of the Contracting Parties there represented, including a majority of those whose representatives are entitled to participate in the meetings provided for under Article IX, shall be communicated by the depositary Government to all Contracting Parties immediately after the termination of the Conference and shall enter into force in accordance with the provisions of paragraph I of the present Article.

c.  If any such modification or amendment has not entered into force in accordance with the provisions of subparagraph I (a) of this Article within a period of two years after the date of its communication to all the Contracting Parties, any Contracting Party may at any time after the expiration of that period give notice to the depositary Government of its withdrawal from the present Treaty; and such withdrawal shall take effect two years after the receipt of the notice by the depositary Government.

## Article XIII

The present Treaty shall be subject to ratification by the signatory States. It shall be open for accession by any State which is a Member of the United Nations, or by any other State which may be invited to accede to the Treaty with the consent of all the Contracting Parties whose representatives are entitled to participate in the meetings provided for under Article IX of the Treaty.

Ratification of or accession to the present Treaty shall be effected by each State in accordance with its constitutional processes.

Instruments of ratification and instruments of accession shall be deposited with the Government of the United States of America, hereby designated as the depositary Government.

The depositary Government shall inform all signatory and acceding States of the date of each deposit of an instrument of ratification or accession, and the date of entry into force of the Treaty and of any modification or amendment thereto.

Upon the deposit of instruments of ratification by all the signatory States, the present Treaty shall enter into force for those States and for States which have deposited instruments of accession. Thereafter the Treaty shall enter into force for any acceding State upon the deposit of its instruments of accession.

The present Treaty shall be registered by the depositary Government pursuant to Article 102 of the Charter of the United Nations.

## Article XIV

The present Treaty, done in the English, French, Russian and Spanish languages, each version being equally authentic, shall be deposited in the archives of the Government of the United States of America, which shall transmit duly certified copies thereof to the Governments of the signatory and acceding States.

Treaty, and prescribes also, though in none-too-clear terms, how nations other than the original 12 may qualify to join in—by conducting 'substantial scientific activity' in Antarctica.

Article 10 enjoins contracting parties not to engage in activities that run contrary to the purposes of the Treaty, and Article 11 provides for settlement of disputes by standard procedures. Article 12 allows first for the Treaty to be modified or amended at any time by unanimous agreement of all parties, and second for it to be reviewed thirty years after coming into force, any proposed modifications to be approved by majority vote rather than unanimously.

Article 13 specifies that the Treaty is open for accession by any State that may be invited to join with the consent of all the Contracting Parties: each state shall ratify the Treaty in accordance with its own constitutional processes, and the United States is nominated as the depositary Government. Article 14 specifies the four languages in which the Treaty will be deposited.

## Antarctic Treaty achievement

The Treaty thus began as a statement of intent by 12 nations to maintain indefinitely a status quo that, for the 2 or 3 years up to and including the IGY, had proved fruitful and rewarding. It did not solve Antarctica's political problems: some it ignored and others it sidestepped. However, the Treaty effectively kept the continent free from military activities (other than logistic support for exploration), and from nuclear testing and dumping. It internationalized Antarctica to the degree that scientists of any Treaty nation were free to work anywhere without reference to sovereignty, and provided a forum in which further discussions and developments could take place.

## Development of the Treaty System

Brilliant the Treaty may have been as a political measure, but it was in no sense a blueprint for managing a continent. In the years since 1961 the Treaty powers have gradually assumed management responsibilities, spinning from the original document a system of governance that has come to be called the Antarctic Treaty System.

Two levels of membership are defined. Consultative parties qualify by pursuing scientific research in Antarctica, and have full rights to discussion and voting. Acceding parties agree to be bound by the Treaty and its measures, but are not active in research and have no rights of discussion or voting. Poland was first to accede to the Treaty, followed later in the1960s by Czechoslovakia, Denmark and the Netherlands. The 1970s saw the accession of Romania, the German Democratic Republic, Brazil, Bulgaria and the German Federal Republic, and Poland's admission to consultative status.

During the 1980s no fewer than 18 countries acceded. Tropical Papua New Guinea rather improbably found itself a member when it achieved independence from Australia. Several other countries with no previous interests in Antarctica thought it wise to join when discussions on mineral development began (Convention on the Regulation of Antarctic Mineral Resource Activities (CRAMRA), p. 262). During the same decade 11 acceded countries set up research operations that qualified them for consultative status. Currently (late 1999) there are 26 consultative parties and 17 acceding parties.

How does the Treaty work? It has no secretariat—not even a fax machine or filing cabinet—largely because the delegates have never been able to agree in which country to site it. Do you find that reassuring, in an organization that seeks to manage a continent? Well, at least it keeps the budget low. The Treaty creates no law of its own. Delegates of consultative parties meet, discuss issues, and agree unanimously on 'measures' and 'resolutions' that they pass to their respective governments for ratification.

Measures are mandatory, and have to be taken into each government's national legislation. Resolutions are advisory, for governments to follow but not necessarily to cover by legislation. Visitors to Antarctica remain under laws and regulations of their own countries, created by their own legislatures to be consistent with Treaty recommendations. This leads to slight differences in rights: I am told that a Briton may smoke while visiting the penguins, but an American may not.

Feeling the need, in the early 1960s, to make a positive move on behalf of the Treaty, the consultative parties discussed conservation issues, on which they could readily agree. The Agreed Measures for the Conservation of Antarctic Flora and Fauna, promulgated in 1964, concerned ways in which the continent could best be protected for purposes of scientific research. More ambitiously in 1972 they elaborated a Convention for the Conservation of Antarctic Seals, setting up guidelines for member states in case seal hunting should start again.

Hunting did not start, and that Convention was never tested. However, 10 years later in 1982 came the Convention on the Conservation of Antarctic Marine Living Resources (CCAMLR). This was a more elaborate attempt to monitor and regulate commercial fisheries for fin fish and krill, which were already well established in the Southern Ocean. To provide a better understanding of the ecological background, the northern boundary of CCAMLR extended beyond the Treaty boundary at 60°S latitude, to cover the whole of the Southern Ocean.

## The minerals issue

Deliberations of Treaty meetings were for a long time held in virtual secrecy, not surprisingly attracting little public attention. Secrecy did, however, attract the hostility both of conservation groups and of the United Nations General Assembly, the former concerned with environmental protection, the latter concerned to share more equitably whatever resources Antarctica might have to offer. When in the 1980s it became known that the consultative parties were discussing ways in which mineral exploitation in Antarctica might be managed, protests came from all sides. Here was a clique of nations that seemed to be proposing, with no reference to other countries or international bodies, quietly to carve up the mineral resources of a continent among themselves.

Hammered out laboriously through 7 years of special consultative meetings, the 1988 Convention on the Regulation of Antarctic Mineral Resource Activities (CRAMRA) was a complex document, eight times as long as the Antarctic Treaty itself. Though it proposed to allow only exploitation activities that met strict environmental monitoring requirements, from the outset the Convention was savaged both by conservation organizations and by non-Treaty powers.

Conservationists opposed it broadly on the grounds that, however well intentioned, it could not protect the environment adequately: anyway, mineral exploitation was unnecessary in Antarctica, and should be banned rather than regulated. Many scientists experienced in Antarctic research programmes found themselves in agreement, regarding CRAMRA as fundamentally flawed, over-complicated and virtually unworkable.

The environmentalists' strongest arguments were that the few minerals of value available in Antarctica could be mined elsewhere, and that a convention that seemed to encourage possibilities of mining in the world's last great wilderness ran contrary to the spirit of the times. Two claimant nations, France and Australia, yielded to environmentalist pressures and declined to ratify. Other nations demurred, CRAMRA foundered, and the whole question of minerals development in Antarctica was quietly dropped. Activities relating to mineral resources, other than scientific research, are now specifically prohibited: Treaty members are effectively barred from mining or drilling for oil and gas for at least 50 years.

Since the furore over CRAMRA, Treaty delegates have found it expedient to take the public more into their confidence, and invite the participation of non-governmental organizations and agencies in their deliberations.

Delegates to the 16th Consultative Meeting in 1991, the 30th anniversary meeting, saw no reason to review Treaty operations as allowed under Article XII(2)a. They noted that the Treaty had '. . . united countries active in Antarctica in a uniquely successful agreement for the peaceful use of a continent', and that research and cooperation between the Treaty parties had '. . . signalled to the world that nations can work together for their mutual benefit and for the benefit of international peace and cooperation . . . to preserve a major part of this planet, for the benefit of all mankind, as a zone of peace, where the environment is protected and science is pre-eminent'.

## The 1991 Protocol

Science is indeed pre-eminent in Antarctica, but is the environment adequately protected? Long before CRAMRA, it had become apparent that the Treaty System lacked a coherent package of environmental protection measures, with results that are all too obvious to those who have seen the accumulated rubbish of the last half-century. When CRAMRA died, special Treaty consultative meetings in 1990 and 1991 salvaged from its ashes a lengthy and complex series of measures, the Protocol on Environmental Protection to the Antarctic Treaty (Box 11.2), designed to meet this need and expected to placate the conservationists.

Where many of the earlier environmental measures arising within the Treaty system seem concerned with safeguarding scientific research first and the Antarctic

## Box 11.2  *The Protocol on Environmental Protection*

*This is a long document, much longer than the Treaty, which can be summarized as follows. Treaty parties commit themselves to '. . . the comprehensive protection of the Antarctic environment and its dependent and associated ecosystems'. To this end, all future activities in the Treaty area must be planned and conducted in ways that limit adverse impacts on the environment, avoiding adverse effects on climate or weather patterns, air or water quality, significant changes in atmospheric, terrestrial, glacial or marine environments, or detrimental changes in distribution, abundance or productivity of flora or fauna.*

*Future activities in Antarctica must not increase the jeopardy of endangered or threatened species, nor hazard areas of biological, scientific, historic, aesthetic or wilderness significance. Activities must be planned and conducted on the basis of information sufficient to allow prior assessments of, and informed judgements about, their possible environmental impacts. They must provide for regular and effective monitoring to ensure that no adverse changes are occurring, accord priority to scientific research, preserve the value of Antarctica as an area for the conduct of research, and be modified, suspended or cancelled if they prove detrimental.*

*Parties are required to cooperate in planning and conducting Antarctic activities, and share information arising from them. All activities relating to mineral resources, other than scientific research, are specifically prohibited.*

*The Protocol provides for the establishment of a Committee for Environmental Protection, to advise and make recommendations on its own effectiveness, and also for a system of inspection. Parties are required to provide prompt and effective responses to emergencies arising from their activities, including those that endanger the environment. They agree to make rules and set procedures covering liability for damage arising from their activities, and to report annually on steps they have taken to implement the Protocol.*

*The Protocol may be modified or amended at any time, and reviewed on request by one of the parties after 50 years. Five annexes cover procedures for environmental impact assessment, conservation of Antarctic fauna and flora, waste disposal and management, prevention of marine pollution, and area protection and management.*

environment only second, the Protocol gives undisputed priority to environmental protection. Though designed particularly to deal with activities of national expeditions, it has at least the potential for being applied with equal rigour and impartiality to all who visit Antarctica, for whatever purpose.

Critics have been quick to identify shortcomings—broadly, that the Protocol reinforces the Treaty's scientific elitism, and concerns itself with minutiae but fails to set standards or provide for monitoring, the practicalities of inspection or enforcement of standards. Scientists and administrators are concerned at the effort and expense that will be required from national expeditions to meet the very rigorous requirements of the Protocol. Those whose first interest was the welfare of the continent itself were more concerned that several key notions took 5 or more years to rectify the Protocol and establish the all-important Committee for Environmental Protection. It is far from clear how key protective measures will be applied.

Yet during those same 6 years numbers of tourists visiting the continent doubled, and there is nothing to stop them doubling again during the next 5 years, and the next ... So how does the Protocol address tourism?

## Tourism under the Treaty

Tourism and the Treaty have grown up together, though not entirely in a spirit of harmony. Antarctica's first seaborne tourists arrived in January 1958, when the Treaty was under negotiation. Scheduled cruises began in 1966, 5 years after the first Treaty consultative meeting. During the early years of tourism, successive Antarctic Treaty Consultative meetings expressed unease at its advent, concerned mainly that tourists might interfere with scientific activities. However, numbers of tourists remained low (Box 11.3), and the consultative parties had more pressing matters to deal with.

A recommendation from the meeting of 1975 to designate 'Areas of Special Tourist Interest', where tourists and their effects could be monitored, unfortunately came to nothing. No such areas were ever defined, and opportunities for research were lost. During the later period of growth, when numbers of tourists began to exceed numbers of scientists and support staff in Antarctica, successive Treaty meetings expressed mounting concern. The US National Science Foundation set up an operation to collect statistics of passenger numbers and landings, but nothing else was done by the national expeditions to investigate, monitor or control this new and clearly burgeoning industry.

## Self-regulation

Such controls as there were came from the tourist industry itself. Lars-Eric Lindblad, the Swedish-American entrepreneur who pioneered Antarctic cruising during the 1960s and 1970s, encouraged very high standards of environmental awareness among his staff and passengers, an awareness that spread as the industry grew. In 1991 Lindblad was one of the founder members of the International Association of Antarctica Tour Operators (IAATO), and a prime mover in establishing the Guidelines for Visitors and Guidelines for Tour Operators, which all IAATO members are pledged to observe.

If you found your cruise interesting and disciplined, with good prior information and guidelines, an experienced cruise leader, competent Zodiac drivers, and a staff of well-qualified and well-informed naturalists who accompanied you ashore, helped you understand the wildlife, and made sure that everyone observed the guidelines—if you enjoyed all that, then bless the memory of the man who invented the 'Lindblad pattern' of adventure cruising, and set high standards for cruising in Antarctica waters.

## Box 11.3  A growing industry

*Numbers of ships, cruises and passengers involved in tourism grew only slowly through the 1970s and 1980s, when Antarctic cruising was expensive and fairly exclusive. Passenger numbers per year hovered mainly between 1000 and 2000, carried in two or three ships of 80–120 passengers. Then more operators became involved, bringing in both smaller and much bigger ships: some cruises were shortened and cheapened, cruising was advertised more widely, and more people were prepared to take a chance on Antarctica for a holiday of a lifetime. From the late 1980s the industry began to grow rapidly.*

Numbers of passengers and sites visited, visits of ships to sites, and passengers landed, during the period of rapid growth of tourism, 1989–96. Based on data compiled by the US National Science Foundation.

| Year | Passengers | Sites | Ship visits | Passengers landing |
|------|-----------|-------|-------------|--------------------|
| 1989–90 | 3000 | 33 | 164 | 10 300 |
| 1990–91 | 4500 | 51 | 191 | 22 158 |
| 1991–92 | 6250 | 46 | 356 | 24 000 |
| 1992–93 | 7000 | 60 | 365 | 28 327 |
| 1993–94 | 7800 | 77 | 514 | 52,189 |
| 1994–95 | 8100 | 109 | 750 | 57 042 |
| 1995–96 | 9200 | 107 | 846 | 63 782 |
| 1996–97 | 7320 | 117 | 855 | 58 419 |
| 1997–98 | 9473 | — | — | — |
| 1998–99 | 9934 | — | — | — |

*This table shows that, during seven successive summers from 1990 to 1996, numbers of passengers landing in Antarctica and numbers of sites visited increased threefold while ship visits to sites increased fivefold and numbers of passengers landing increased sixfold. Numbers dropped away slightly in 1996–97, but have since continued to increase: there were 9473 passengers in 1997–98, 9934 in 1998–99, and well over 10 000 are projected for the summer ending in 2000.*

*Overall figures remain small compared with those of tourist venues elsewhere in the world, but rapidly increasing passenger numbers and related activities indicate a lively and ebullient industry. Some of the most popular landings now receive visits several times daily at high season, and a few are starting to show signs of physical wear. If numbers continue to increase, several of the landing sites will stand urgently in need of management.*

## Research on tourism

Research on shipborne tourism too came in the form of private enterprise, with logistic support from the industry. Project Antarctic Conservation (PAC), a research team from the Ecology and Management Group of the Scott Polar Research Institute, University of Cambridge, UK, was first in the field, in 1991 starting a 6-year programme of field research that extended to 9 years, and is still running. PAC operated stations at three popular landing sites—Half Moon Island (in cooperation with Argentine researchers) and Hannah Point in the South Shetland Islands, and Cuverville Island on the Danco Coast, Antarctic Peninsula. Researchers also travelled aboard the tour ships, studying the industry at close quarters and visiting many landing sites. The work was supported initially by the World Wildlife Fund, and later by a private charity the Jephcott Trust, with logistic help from British and Argentine national expeditions and the industry and contract work for the UK Foreign and Commonwealth Office.

PAC has documented the growth and development of shipborne tourism, enquired into the motivations and expectations of Antarctic tourists, and studied methods used by tour operators in the field. It has established a database of all known landing sites (currently over 200), and begun to map, make environmental assessments and draw up management plans for the most popular and vulnerable sites. The team has studied tourist impacts on vegetation and wildlife, especially penguins, using a specially developed technique of monitoring the heartbeat of incubating birds. It has tested the relevance of current legislation to the growing industry, and tried to predict future impacts and developments should tourism continue to expand.

Over 20 researchers have been involved, in a multinational team from Britain, Argentina, Australia, France, India, New Zealand, Poland and the United States. Some of our results have already been published: others are currently being written up for publication (Box 11.4). Other groups also are now working on aspects of Antarctic tourism, focussing especially on disturbance to wildlife and ecological assessments of landing sites, which represent the main points of impact of the industry. Between us we are assembling a mound of useful, practical information, which in one way or another will be put to good use in protecting Antarctica.

## Regulation under the Protocol

The Protocol was clearly designed to keep national expeditions in order. Not surprisingly it presents difficulties when applied to an industry that is shipborne rather than land based, not directly under the control of any one national government, does not seek to set up stations, and confines its activities mainly to landings in remote places about which the delegates have little or no information.

Tourism exposes a weakness that entered the Treaty System when sovereignty was devalued. Almost any sovereign government, faced with developing tourism, would quickly find means of pulling together land-management legislation, enabling it to set up national parks, recreational reserves and other protective

## Box 11.4  PAC: What have we found?

Project Antarctic Conservation, based in the Scott Polar Research Institute, University of Cambridge, has been examining polar shipborne tourism at both ends of the world, comparing what is happening in Antarctica with similar developments in Svalbard and other Arctic areas.

So what have we found? We have found an industry that is on the whole well run, with a sound record of environmental concern promoted by its middle management, the field staff, and encouraged by its professional association, the International Association of Antarctica Tour Operators (IAATO). Fortunately it pays the industry to care for the environment: they would lose the support of many clients if they did not.

We have studied many good operators in the field, and some less good. Operators that economize on experienced field staff—boat handlers, guides and Zodiac drivers—need to be monitored carefully. We have urged IAATO to ensure that standards of the best operators are maintained throughout the industry. Self-monitoring within the industry will in our view continue to be Antarctica's main safeguard against environmental damage from tourism, and the industry's main safeguard against cumbersome legislation.

We find the official IAATO guidelines widely accepted by clients as sensible, and in general well followed. However, we are concerned that there is no permanent system of inspection or monitoring, ashore or afloat, to ensure that guidelines continue to be observed, and there are no workable sanctions that can be applied against serious offenders.

Monitoring heartrates of incubating penguins has so far shown us that, on the whole, penguins give each other far more hassle than we give them. Even frequent visits from well-ordered tourist parties do not appear to affect colony size, breeding behaviour, breeding success or levels of skua predation. Visitors who use common sense and observe the guidelines need have no fears of harming penguin stocks. Others need to be kept under whatever strict control is available.

Other species of birds are clearly more sensitive while nesting. Skuas are demonstrative but not readily put off breeding. Giant petrels are easily disturbed early in incubation and brooding, less so in-between, and often accommodate to regular visits: however, it is generally safest to keep away from them. Dominican gulls and Antarctic terns usually do not tolerate the presence of humans, and their breeding colonies should at all costs be avoided.

We have assembled data on more than 200 landing sites and studied in detail some 50 of those that are most frequently visited. In some we are starting to see signs of wear, or natural changes that indicate a need for fewer visits. We are concerned that the Treaty cannot at present manage such sites directly, as they would be managed under sovereign governments.

We see little effort by authorities ashore to educate or inform tourists, which seems to us a seriously missed opportunity. We are currently working toward providing an information and education centre at the Polish research station Henryk Arctowski, King George Island, where visitors will be able to learn more of scientific activities and living in Antarctica, and we shall learn more of visitors.

Current levels of tourism do not seem to us a cause for concern, so long as tour operators maintain high standards of behaviour towards the environment. Should numbers of ships and passengers continue to increase at current rates, should new forms of tourism arise with harsher environmental impacts, should standards in the industry decline—then present measures of protection seem likely to prove inadequate, and lead to serious environmental problems. We work towards the provision of more effective measures under the Protocol.

categories, to limit numbers of visits and visitors—a range of measures to achieve the right balance between recreational use and environmental protection. Governments responsible for Southern Ocean islands outside the Treaty area have such powers, and generally make effective use of them. The Treaty cannot: it has given itself no authority to set up and manage recreational areas (the claimant nations would almost certainly object if it did), and so cannot protect landing sites directly in ways that would be commonplace elsewhere.

This is why tour operators remain free to land you practically anywhere in the Antarctic region where landing is physically possible. Exceptions are the few completely no-go SSSIs and SPAs reserved for scientists, and the immediate environs of research stations. There are no gates or fences, no entrances and exits, no designated recreational areas, no parks, no bulletin boards, and no helpful corps of rangers to monitor behaviour or tell us what is going on. Some passengers welcome this: it helps them to feel that they are entering wilderness, which they have come a long way to see. Others worry that wilderness cannot continue to be used indefinitely in this way, and wonder who, if anyone, can blow the whistle.

As the Treaty cannot manage land *per se*, it seeks instead to manage activities. Annex V of the Protocol, dealing specifically with issues of area protection and management, requires all who propose to do anything in Antarctica, whether scientific or commercial, to file to their governments statements of what they intend to do. From these statements, judgements can be made on possible environmental impacts. If the activities are judged to have 'less than a minor or transitory impact', they are allowed to proceed. If judged to have more than transitory impacts, environmental assessments are required.

However, there is at present no central authority to provide consensus on standards: each government regulates the activities of its own nationals according to its own standards. There are no definitions of the very subjective terms used, and there are great practical difficulties in providing for cumulative impacts, which may result, for example, from many landings in succession.

Though the Protocol provides new categories of protected areas—Antarctic Specially Protected Area (ASPAs) and Antarctic Specially Managed Area (ASMAs)—neither of these can be applied unconditionally to the management of tourist landing sites: ASPAs cannot be entered without permit, and ASMAs, designed more for station areas than for remote sites, seem to require people on the spot who are actively managing them. When the Protocol was being drawn up, landing was what tour operators had already been doing for a quarter of a century. Was there nobody around who could point this out? Or that everywhere else in the world where wilderness is intruded by man, management planning is a prime requirement?

These problems will no doubt disappear as the Protocol is brought more into use and its effectiveness tested. Perhaps it will achieve all that its designers, with the best possible intentions, built into its structure. However, danger for the future may lie in the cumbersome machinery of the Treaty System—its inability to generate simple, relevant legislation, and the occasional voids in understanding between those who work in Antarctica and the multinational diplomats, representing many nations and a wide variety of national interests, that seek to manage the continent through annual meetings.

## Antarctica—a World Park?

Several interested bodies, lacking faith in the Treaty System, have proposed that the whole of Antarctica be given the status of a park—an 'international park' or 'world park', or as some would prefer, an 'international wildlife reserve'. These concepts have a certain appeal. So magnificent an area as Antarctica merits special consideration: to designate it as something unique in world conservation would be entirely appropriate.

Proponents are at a disadvantage in that there are no precedents. There are plenty of large-scale national parks elsewhere in the world, and indeed some that cross international boundaries. However, there is no large tract of land already under international management, apart from Antarctica itself, that is already subject to one kind of experiment in government, and is unlikely to be released readily for another.

'Park' is a term subject to many conflicting interpretations. Would there be recreational facilities with information centres and camping areas? Or only refuges, reserves and sanctuaries for wildlife and scientists? Would ordinary mortals without a PhD be allowed in? Whatever its form, who would maintain the park? Who would work out its purposes and objectives, and manage it? Who would be the park keepers? Above all, who would fund it, and how much would it cost?

Draft proposals for such a park make it clear that, with goodwill and energy, it would be perfectly possible for Antarctica to become one. Under the Protocol the area is already a 'nature reserve, devoted to peace and science'. If there were general agreement that this was the solution, it would not be difficult to upgrade it, consult with such agencies as the International Union for the Conservation of Nature and Natural Resources (which has had some very sensible things to say about Antarctic management), appoint the necessary management boards, and run the continent like a large national park, but under an international body.

Which body would that be? I hope not the United Nations: perhaps a group based on the Treaty powers (better to have them in than out), but with experienced managers in authority, and diplomats, lawyers and scientists in advisory roles. I do not know if this would prove better or worse than the present regime: much would depend on the policies to be adopted, and I have yet to see a fully professional management plan for a world park drawn up. But then, I haven't seen a management plan for Antarctica from the present regime either.

Is the change likely to happen? My guess is no: not in any foreseeable future. I see much support at the level of 'Antarctica-a-World-Park' splashed across T-shirts, but very little at the level of hard thought and planning that would be required for the concept to work. 'Antarctica-a-World-Park' should not have to take its turn with 'Save-the-Whale' and 'Protect-the-Rain-Forest'. I honour proponents who raise the issue, but hope they will not succeed prematurely. Antarctica would be ill-served by losing its present system of governance before finding an alternative that is clearly better.

For a park system to work credibly would require massive funding over a long period. National funding for Antarctic research seems currently to be declining, as governments see less and less reason to invest in a frozen continent. An expensive new management scheme for Antarctica would have little appeal at present to any hard-pressed international agency. It would have no appeal at all to Treaty powers, so long as the low-cost Antarctic Treaty System (remember, not even a filing cabinet) provides a cheaper alternative.

However, I could be wrong in my guess. We are dealing with forces similar to those that in 1991 caught the Treaty at a disadvantage, and swept away CRAMRA.

## Keeping in touch

The goodwill that many travellers feel for Antarctica usually remains with them all the way home, and occasionally lasts longer. I'll guarantee a whiff of nostalgia when you open your suitcase and send your windproofs to the cleaners. The whiff will probably return when you get them back, for the smell of penguins can be subdued but never entirely suppressed. There will be another burst of memories as you sort through your photographs, and yet another when you show your videos to whomever you can persuade to watch.

Many travellers regard their Antarctic cruise as a turning point in their lives. They want to keep in touch, possibly to return, certainly to learn more about the place and its problems, perhaps to contribute in some way to its protection. Of these, a proportion retain their interest for many years or for ever. The Antarctic bug—the one the shipboard naturalists didn't warn them about—has claimed many victims.

For armchair travellers to make a start there is an enormous literature of books, magazine articles, and scientific and non-scientific journals. Every public library, every university and college library is bound to have something on Antarctica. Some of the books listed here as 'Further reading' at the end of each chapter may get you started.

If you surf the Internet, try addresses http://www.icair.iac.org.nz, a New Zealand data and information base, and http://www.nerc-bas.ac.uk, a British one. Libraries have access to a massive Internet catalogue of Antarctic references, and others are available on CD/ROM.

If you want to keep up to date with what is going on in Antarctica, join the New Zealand Antarctic Society and subscribe to their splendid quarterly journal *Antarctic*. You do not need to be a New Zealander—just express an interest in Antarctica and pay your dues, and they'll be glad of your support. Within New Zealand enquire to the National Secretary, PO box 404, Christchurch; from overseas enquire to PO Box 2110, Wellington, New Zealand.

Heritage trusts? The New Zealand Heritage Trust, International Antarctic Centre, Orchard Road, Christchurch, New Zealand, has a fine record for looking after the Ross Dependency historic huts. The British equivalent, newer and with reputation still to be made, is the UK Antarctic Heritage Trust, Blackdown Beacon, Fernden Lane, Nr Haslemere, Surrey GU27 3BS. Both would welcome your support. The combined New Zealand/UK Antarctic Heritage Trusts' web page address is http://www.heritage-antarctica-org

Environmental pressure groups? Try the Antarctica and Southern Ocean Coalition (ASOC), 424 C Street NE, Washington, DC 20002, USA, or Private Bag 92/507, Wellesley Street, Auckland, New Zealand, and join them if you like their policies or want to improve them. Greenpeace International and World Wild

Life Fund International run Antarctic campaigns: get in touch with their local offices and see if you support what they want for Antarctica. Try, too, the political parties that make up your own government. If you are a citizen of a Treaty nation, they should have views on controversial Antarctic issues: see what they have to say.

Whether or not you keep in touch, keep your memories alive and warm. Antarctica really was, and is, a wonderful place. It needs friends—folk who will cherish it for its own sake, not just for the living, the knowledge or the prestige that they gain from it. If you enjoyed Antarctica, tell your friends about it. If they are the right kinds of people, don't be afraid to get them to visit Antarctica too.

## Further reading

Auburn, F. M. 1982. *Antarctic Law and Politics.* London, Hurst.

Barnes, J. N. 1982. *Lets Save Antarctica!* Victoria, Greenhouse Publications.

Beck, P. 1986. *The International Politics of Antarctica.* London, Croome Helm.

Chaturvedi, S. 1995. *The Polar Regions: A Political Geography.* London, John Wiley.

Hall, C. M. and Johnston, M. E. (editors). 1995. *Polar Tourism: Tourism in the Arctic and Antarctic Regions.* London, John Wiley.

Jørgensen-Dahl, A. and Østreng, W. 1991. *The Antarctic Treaty System in World Politics.* Basingstoke, Macmillan.

Suter, K. 1991. *Antarctica: Private Property or Public Heritage?* London, Zed Books.

Triggs, G. D. 1987. *The Antarctic Treaty Regime.* Cambridge, Cambridge University Press.

**Figure 11.1** *Farewell to Antarctica.*

# Index

References to pictures are in **bold**